BIBLE VERSUS ARCHAEOLOGY

Are archaeological discoveries consistent with the Bible?

King Menkaure – was he the Pharaoh of the Exodus?

By

Daniel Moshe Levy

Rubin Mass Publishers, Jerusalem

Translated from the Hebrew by: **Adam Moshe Levy**
Edited by: **Yehonathan Tommer**
Maps: **Joel Steinberg**

Original book in Hebrew:

Mikra Mul Archeologia (Rubin Mass Publishers, Jerusalem, 2011)

First edition, July 2020

ISBN 978-965-09-0355-8

Ebook edition: ISBN 978-965-09-0356-5

Rubin Mass Ltd., Publishers and booksellers

POBox 990, Jerusalem 9100901, Israel

rmass@barak.net.il www.rubinmass.net www.rubinmass.co.il

Tel +972-2-6277863 Fax +972-2-6277864

Printed in Israel

Contents

Preface

The Exodus from Egypt is one of the most important events in the Bible.

Today we also know the names of the kings of ancient Egypt and the major events which occurred during their lifetimes.

Scholars have suggested that the Exodus from Egypt took place in the New Kingdom Period in Egypt (18th-20th dynasties).

Who was the pharaoh when the Exodus from Egypt occurred? His identity is not known. Yet what all the names, like Rameses II and Merneptah, have in common is that there is no resemblance between what we know about them and what is written about the pharaoh of the Exodus in the Bible.

One school of thought led by Velikovsky and his disciples dates the Exodus from Egypt to between the 12th and 14th dynasties. But here, too, one cannot point to a recognizable personality that suitably fits the pharaoh of the Exodus from Egypt.

In our research, we investigated the 4th dynasty, a more ancient period which contains few records, but sufficient to conclude without any doubt that King Men-Ka-Ure, from this dynasty, was the pharaoh mentioned at the time of the Exodus.

This subject is only part of the larger puzzle in the relationship between archaeology and the Scriptures. Scholars, who accept the academic timeline, find a correlation between the two disciplines to be difficult. However, when we change over to our suggested timeline, the results fit the Scriptures like hand in glove. Many examples of this will be given later; identifying the pharaoh of the Exodus from Egypt provides us merely with an overall headline for them.

Earlier scholars already criticized the accepted timeline. The purpose of this book, most of whose findings were published in Hebrew entitled '*The Bible and Archaeology*', is to show the correct timeline that emerges from the archaeological findings. We hope the reader will be convinced by the considerable evidence we present to show that this is indeed the true timeline.

To enable an unbroken reading of the book we have transferred some chapters to the appendices at the back of the book and we shortened a number of quotations.

My thanks and well-wishes go to the many people who helped in the preparation of this book.

Daniel Moshe Levy

Archaeological remains in the Biblical city of Gezer

Introduction: Comparing Archaeology with the Bible

The archaeological garden on the bottom of The Temple Mount

This book examines the identity of the Egyptian King at the time of the Exodus from Egypt. The subject is part of a much wider project which involves a comparison of what is written in the Bible with what is scientifically known about antiquity. Let's start by saying a few words about the development of research of the ancient world and the resulting difficulties that have arisen.

In 1798 Napoleon Bonaparte landed with his army on the coast of Egypt and conquered the entire country. The French conquest lasted only a short time and was considered a failure at the time. However, today we know that this episode was of immense importance to the history of culture, because during the French presence research began into ancient Egyptian inscriptions which resulted in the deciphering of Egyptian hieroglyphics by the French scholar Jean-Francois Champollion (1822) using the Rosette stone. This introduced the science of **Egyptology**.

The Rosette stone, inscribed in
hieroglyphtic, demotic, and Greek.

Hieroglyphic Inscription

A generation later, in 1837, the British Orientalist Henry Creswicke Rawlinson succeeded in deciphering the Akkadian Cuneiform script used by the Assyrians and Babylonians followed by excavations which began in the ancient cities of Assyria (and later in Babylon.)

The excavations revealed many inscriptions, among them those from the Kings mentioned in the Bible: Sennacherib and Nebuchadnezzar. The study of the Akkadian inscriptions is known as the science of **Assyriology**.

In the Land of Israel, there are almost no ancient inscriptions. However, towards the end of the nineteenth century, the British scholar Flinders Petrie invented a technique that allows us to learn about past life by examining the otherwise 'silent' remains (pottery, graves and the like).

This method, which developed and grew more sophisticated, is known as the science of **Archaeology**.

Egyptologists, Assyriologists and Archaeologists allow us direct access to life in the past. What happens if we ask them "have you found any evidence in your studies of events described in the Bible"?

The truth is, as long as we are discussing the period from the middle of the First Temple era in Jerusalem onwards, the answer is generaliy positive. However, if we go back further to the Exodus from Egypt, Joshua's conquest of the Land, or the time in which Kings David and Solomon ruled, the parallels are weak, if non-existent.

Let us begin with the Exodus from Egypt, which, according to the conventional view, apparently occurred during the 18th or 19th pharaonic dynasties. Many Egyptian relics and documents from this period have been found. What do they tell us about the Exodus from Egypt?

One scholar of ancient Egypt writes: "In Egyptian writings there is no mention of Joseph, or of the Children of Israel dwelling in Egypt, nor of Moses and the Exodus from Egypt."[1]

Another scholar writes: "There is not enough evidence from Egyptian sources to corroborate the story of the Exodus."[2]

The Bible relates how after the Exodus the Children of Israel wandered for 40 years in the Sinai Desert. The search for traces of such nomadic wanderings has ended without results. One writer who took part in many archaeological surveys in the Sinai states: "Residential sites from the period of the 18th-20th dynasties were not detected, despite dozens of surveys."[3]

After wandering in the desert, the Children of Israel entered Canaan (the Land of Israel) led by Joshua. The Bible states that the first city conquered by Joshua was *Jericho*, followed by *Ai*; Joshua then conquered the entire south of the country within days. (Joshua 10:42). What can be found in the archaeological records?

The archaeologist Zertal writes about findings in Israel dating to the 18th and 19th dynasties: "Excavations have revealed that no city existed in Jericho in Joshua's time. The situation is similar at Ai ... the overall picture completely contradicts the biblical story of a united campaign of conquest."[4]

Furthermore, it is known from Egyptian documents that the country at this time was under Egyptian rule, yet there is no trace of this in the Books of Joshua and Judges. As Zertal writes: "Another issue between the biblical literature and the archaeological findings is the absence of Egypt from any mention at all in the stories of occupation of the Land of israel."[5]

[Zertal himself uncovered an altar on Mount Ebal and speculates that this was the altar built by Joshua. On the other hand, he writes: "If this is correct, it is only one

---

[1] J. Wilson, The History of the People of Israel, Vol 1, Jerusalem 1965, P. 192.(Hebrew)
[2] A. Malamat, The Exodus from Egypt – Egyptian Analogies, Eretz Israel 25 (1966) P. 231.(Hebrew)
[3] B. Zass, Sinai between the 4th and 1st centuries BCE, in: Z. Meshel & I. Finkelstein (eds.) Sinai in Antiquitiy, Tel Aviv 1980, p. 46. (Hebrew)
[4] A. Zertal, New Light on the Israeilite Settlement, in: I. Zaharoni (ed.), Derekh Eretz - On Pottery, Stone and Man, 1996, pp. 160-161. (Hebrew)
[5] A. Zertal, The "Ainun Pottery" – History, Meaning, Future, Judea and Samaria in Research Studies 12, Ariel 2003 , p. 10. (Hebrew)

piece of archaeological evidence pointing to the authenticity of **parts** of the biblical story."[6]]

Several hundred years after Joshua, at the time of the 21st dynasty in Egypt, King Solomon reigned in Jerusalem. The Scriptures describe him as one of the richest men in existence: "King Solomon was richer than any other king" (Kings I, 10:23). However, excavations in Jerusalem have turned up only very meager remains from this period.[7]

The entrance to the antiquity quarter of Jerusalem

The Bible also tells us about the sheer number of horses kept by Solomon (Chronicles II 1:14). Where did Solomon house thousands of his horses? "There is no clear answer to this and, except for small stables for individual horses no other stables have been discovered elsewhere." [8]

---

[6] A. Zertal, New Light on the Israelite Settlement, in: I. Zaharoni (editor) Derekh Eretz – On Pottery, Stone and Man, 1996, p. 167. (Hebrew)
[7] A. Kloner, Survey of Jerusalem – The Southern Sector, Jerusalem 2000, p. 11; I. Finkelstein, The Beginning of the State in Israel and Judea, Eretz Israel 26 1999, p.132-141; H. Geva, Innovations in Archaelogical Research in Jerusalem during the 1990s, Qadmoniot 122 (2002), pp. 72-73. (Hebrew)
[8] Y. Aharoni, The Archaeology of the Land of Israel, Jerusalem 1978, pp. 196-197. (Hebrew)

The Book of Kings recounts how in the early reign of King Solomon, the King of Egypt conquered the city of Gezer (Kings I 9:16). Nothing is known about this occupation from Egyptian documents: "This event is puzzling, as Egyptian sources do not mention any military campaign during the 21st dynasty." [9]

Taking these and other cases into account there is, apparently, a definite contradiction between the narrative in the Bible about these periods and archaeological finds. Consequently, some scholars argue that the Bible is not true.

On the other hand, other scholars argue that the events depicted in the Bible took place in a period earlier than is generally thought and that the findings from these periods provide evidence for the truth of the biblical stories.

We will adopt this latter approach and for a starting point take an Egyptian text that helps to date the period of Joseph in Egypt to the 3rd pharaonic dynasty.

Accordingly, the Exodus took place during the 4th dynasty, Joshua conquered the land (of Canaan) during the 5th dynasty and Solomon ruled during the 12th pharaonic dynasty.

Using this system, we will reveal many archaeological findings that accurately parallel those in the Bible.

---

[9] W. G. Dever, Gezer – A Crossroad in ancient Israel, Tel Aviv 1998, p. 22. (Hebrew)

Section 1: From Joseph to Solomon

Chapter 1: Joseph in the Egyptian Records

Seven Years of Famine - The Architect of the Pyramids - A Powerful Ruler - An Amazing Genius - Son of the Ox - Standing up to tests – The Vanished Tomb - A Tradition that ties Joseph to Imhotep

Seven Years of Famine

On the island of Sehel in the south of Egypt an inscription engraved on a rock describes how at the time of King Djoser during the 3rd dynasty, a famine occurred that lasted for seven years. The King then asked for the advice of the viceroy, Imhotep, second in command to the King.

It also tells that he set aside (dedicated) an extensive swathe of land for the priests.[10]

The seven years of famine remind us, of course, of the story the Torah tells about Joseph: "and the seven years of famine began, just as Joseph had said". (Genesis 41:54)

Also setting aside land for the priests resembles what was written about Joseph in his time: "Only the land he did not buy was the land that belonged to the priests... because the king gave them an allowance to live on." (ibid 47:22) Therefore let us check what else we know about Imhotep, Viceroy to the King.

The Architect of the Pyramids

It was customary during the ancient dynasties in Egypt to build a one-level building above the king's tomb. At the time of King Djoser, during the 3rd dynasty, architectural achievements were upgraded. Based on plans by Imhotep, a 46-meter multi-level high step pyramid was erected above the grave, and a temple city was built around it, surrounded by a wall. The architectural standard of the pyramid and the city built around it was of an un-proportionally higher level than anything accepted as standard until then.

In subsequent generations, kings also built their burial monuments based on this model. These pyramids adorn Egypt to this day.

Being so, Imhotep was the man who introduced the concept of pyramids to the world.

---

[10] J. Wilson, the Tradition of Seven Lean Years in Egypt, in: J. B. Pritchard (ed.) ANET, Princeton 1969, pp. 31-32; A. Eggebrecht, Das alte Ägypten, München 1984, p. 48.

The Step-Pyramid in Saqqara

A Powerful Ruler

Imhotep bore the following titles: 'First for the King', 'Supervisor of the Great Palace', 'Keeper of the Seals of Lower Egypt', 'Priest of Heliopolis' and others.[11]

These titles are similar to those which the Scriptures tell us were attributed to Joseph. Pharaoh said to him:"I will put you in charge of my country, and all my people will obey your orders. Your authority will be second only to mine... The king removed from his finger a ring engraved with the royal seal and put it on Joseph's finger...and he gave him a wife, the daughter of Potiphera, a priest in the city of Heliopolis." (ibid 41: 45)

An Amazing Genius

Imhotep is considered the greatest of Egyptian sages "revered by later generations of Egyptians as the traditional wise man."[12] With the passage of time, he became the Deity of Healing and Knowledge. He was also the patron of the scribes. Before they began their work, they would pour out libations in his honor.

The people saw him as a redeemer, a power of salvation, and believed he could solve their problems in a dream. They would sleep in his temple in the hope that

---

[11] D. Wildung, Lexikon der Ägeptologie, Wiesbaden 1980, III, pp. 145-147; D. Silverman, Ancient Egypt, London 1997, p. 178; I. Shaw & R. Nicholson, Dictionary of Ancient Egypt, London 1996, pp. 140-141.
[12] L. Cottrel, The Lost Pharaohs, London 1956, p. 59.

he would appear to them in a dream and give the supplicant assistance. His cult was centered in the city of Saqqara, situated beside the pyramid he had built. Today, that temple is called in Arabic 'Joseph's prison'.

Before metamorphosing into an independent Deity in his own right, Imhotep was identified with Shmun, the God of Wisdom. Shmun is described as 'proficient in foreign languages' and 'Lord of the Foreign Lands'.[13] His cult was centered in the city named after him: Shmun (today el-Ashmunein) sited on the 'Bahr Yusuf' canal (known as Joseph's Canal).

The Scriptures tell us how Pharaoh addresses Joseph in amazement: "You have greater wisdom and insight than anyone else." (ibid, 39) It is therefore understandable why the Egyptians saw him as the wisest of men.

During the seven years of famine the Canaanites came to be at the mercy of Joseph. As the Scriptures tell us: "The famine was so severe that there was no food anywhere, and the people of Egypt and Canaan became weak with hunger... When all the money in Egypt and Canaan was spent." (ibid 47:13-15) This suits his title as 'Lord of the Foreign Lands' of the deity with which Imhotep is identified.

Even the title: 'proficient of Foreign Languages' jibes with the Israelite tradition that Joseph knew seventy languages (Babylonian Talmud, Sota, 36b). The fact that the cult's center of Imhotep sits on a canal called explicitly after Joseph's name strengthens the identification between them even more.

Son of the Ox

Imhotep was the most sacred personality ever in Egypt.[14]

Besides being identified with the God 'Shmun' and a God in his own right, he was included in the worship of another god in the image of an ox called Ptah, worshipped in a cult of the Serapis. Imhotep was known also as the son of Ptah. This reminds us of a title that the Scriptures give Joseph: "Joseph has the horns of a wild ox". (Deuteronomy 33:17)

Standing up to Tests

The cult of Imhotep and 'Shmun' spread to other peoples. The Greeks identified Imhotep with the Deity of Medicine – Asclepius – and Shmum with Hermes, the Deity of Wisdom.

The Egyptian Deity also reached the Phoenicians who called him 'Eschmun'. As in Egypt, the Phoenicians believed that they would find a cure for their ailments

---

[13] R. Giveon, The Stones of Sinai speak, Jerusalem 1983, p.124. (Hebrew)
[14] M. Lurker, The Gods and Symbols of Ancient Egypt, London 1995, p. 45.

in the temple, for which they had to prepare and practice celibacy for three days.[15]

They had a legend explaining how Imhotep changed from a man to a deity: "Eschmun was initially a handsome lad. The Mother of the gods fell in love with him, and Eschmun ran away from her and died. The goddess brought him back to life and made him a deity."[16]

These words, of course, remind us of what was written about Joseph: "Joseph was well-built and good looking, and after a while his master's wife began to desire Joseph and asked him to go to bed with her. He refused... one day she caught him but he escaped." (Genesis 39:6-12)

The Vanished Tomb

The tombs of admired personalities usually became after their death pilgrimage sites for the masses but this was not the case with Imhotep, whose burial place is unknown.

Modern research has made great, though unsuccessful, efforts to locate the grave.[17] It is amazing that the builder of the pyramids himself did not leave a grave, a fact mentioned in an Egyptian song written thousands of years ago:

"As for those who built house, their place is no more. Behold what hath become of them. I have heard the words of Imhotep and Harzozef whose utterances are of much reputation. Yet how are the places thereof? Their walls are in ruin, their places are no more, as if they had never been." [18]

Where did the grave of Imhotep disappear to?

Identifying Joseph with Imhotep solves the mystery; because Joseph requested that his bones be sent up to the Land of Canaan and that the brothers should not bury him in Egypt. (Genesis 50:25)

The Children of Israel fulfilled his request and buried him in Shechem (Nablus): "The body of Joseph, which the people of Israel had brought from Egypt, was buried at Shechem". (Joshua 24: 32)

We have found the grave of Imhotep, which indeed serves as a pilgrimage center. Not in Egypt, but in the Land of Israel.

A Tradition that ties Joseph to Imhotep

The Israelite sages already noted that Imhotep was Joseph, acclaiming that the cult of Serapis we mentioned "Serapis is Joseph". (Babylonian Talmud Avodah Zara

---

[15] Z. Herman, Carthage - The Sea Power, p. 130. (Hebrew)
[16] Y. M. Grintz, Hebrew Encyclopedia, Vol. 7, p. 431. (Hebrew)
[17] D. Wildung, Lexikon der Ägeptologie, Wiesbaden 1980, III, pp. 145-147; I. Shaw & R. Nicholson, Dictionary of Ancient Egypt, London 1996, pp. 140-141.
[18] J. H. Breasted, A History of Egypt, New York 1951, p. 206.

43A) In addition, the name of the temple of Imhotep at Saqqaras known by the locals as 'Joseph's prison', connects the two.

The lexicon of Egyptology expresses surprise at this: "The reason that the temple of Asclepius is called 'Joseph's prison' is not known."[19] However, according to what we have explained here, the matter is perfectly understandable.

Summary: Joseph lived during the period of the 3rd dynasty in Egypt. He was known to Egyptians as Imhotep famed for his wisdom and was the viceroy to King Djoser.

(For further see Appendix 1)

---

[19] D. Wildung, Ibid.

Chapter 2: Slavery and the Exodus from Egypt

When did the Bondage in Egypt take place? - The Hymn of the Cannibal - Who was the Pharaoh of the Enslavement? - Who was the 'Evil Pharaoh'? - Who is the 'Pharaoh of the Exodus from Egypt'? - Testimony about a heavy disaster - Remembering the Exodus from Egypt in Later Generations

When did the Bondage in Egypt take place?

The population of the world is divided into a number of races distinguished from each other by their bodily features. The branch of science that deals with this is called *Anthropology*.

Anthropologists discovered that the Egyptian people belong to the family known as the Mediterranean race, distinguished by long skulls.

However, in antiquity another race lived in Egypt, descendants of a Northern race (Armenoids) distinguished by a thick skull.

This people were already known to early scholars: "The first was the finding by Petrie and Quibell of 3000 graves of a people who were quite different from the Egyptians... At first he thought he had discovered a new race of foreigners who invaded Egypt at some unknown date, keeping themselves apart from the indigenous inhabitants and so preserving their primitive customs."[20]

The earthenware utensils used by these people, who were referred to as the 'people of Gerzian culture' are similar to utensils unearthed in the Land of Israel.

For example, they include vessels with a 'shelf-handle' used in the Land of Israel which first "appeared in Egypt with the start of Gerzian culture."[21] From here the scholars deduced their origins: "Archaeological findings show that these people came from (or via) the Land of Israel."[22]

The Egyptian language absorbed many Hebrew words borrowed from these immigrants, and Egypt owes its development and economic success to them.[23]

---

[20] L. Cottrel, The Lost Pharaohs, London 1956, pp. 45, 47.

[21] M. Dothan, The Stratigraphy and Chronology of the Land of Israel in the late Chalcolithic, Doctorate, Jerusalem 1959 p. 94. (Hebrew)

[22] Y. M. Grintz, Studies in Early Biblical Ethnology and History, 1969, p. 28-29. (Hebrew)

[23] A. Gardiner, Egypt of the Pharaohs, Oxford 1964, p. 386; R. Engelbach, Mechanical and Technical Processes, by: S. R. K. Glanville (ed.), The Legacy of Egypt, Oxford 1943, p.125.

However, as time passed they declined in their greatness and became desperately poor, marked by the utensils placed at the heads of the deceased in their graves:

"In the earliest burials these jars were filled with a scented vegetable fat. As time went on, the amount of scented fat was reduced and the remainder of the jar sealed with mud until finally, at the very end of time, only mud filled the jar. Although we might most easily explain this in terms of the gradual debasement."[24]

By the beginning of the 5th dynasty, this people ceased to exist, and the guess is that they had presumably assimilated. It can reasonably be suggested that this people are the Children of Israel who, when they came to Egypt were close to the Royal family, and later on became slaves.

The reason that all traces of them vanished in the 5th dynasty is not because they assimilated, but because they left Egypt before the 5th dynasty began. From this we can conclude that the Exodus from Egypt took place at the end of the 4th dynasty which is the period of slavery in Egypt.

(For further see Appendix 2)

The Hymn of the Cannibal

'Uni' (Unas) was a king in the 5th dynasty.

The walls of his pyramid are engraved with an inscription called the Hymn of the Cannibal, in which Uni scoffs at the gods: "He is that eateth their magic and swalloweth their lordliness".[25]

A line in this poem is attributed to a deity who does not belong in the Egyptian pantheon, but was responsible for the slaying of the firstborn. "It is the king who will be judged with Him-whose-name-is-hidden on that day of slaying the first-born."[26]

If so, the firstborn were slaughtered on a certain day by a deity unknown to the Egyptians. This appears to be an Egyptian parallel to the story of "The plague of the firstborn" mentioned in the Book of Exodus (12:29).

The Hymn of the Cannibal was written during the 5th dynasty. If the Exodus from Egypt only took place during 18th or 19th dynasties, as it is customary to say, how was it already known in the 5th dynasty?

---

[24] M. A. Hoffman, Egypt before the Pharaohs, New York 1979, p. 117.
[25] A. Erman, Literature of the Ancient Egypt, London 1927, p. 6.
[26] M.Gilula, The smiting of the first-born – an Egyptian myth?, TA 4 (1977), pp. 95.

Some scholars predate the Exodus to the 12th to 14th dynastoies (Velikovsky and those following his methodology). However, in their view the inscription from the days of the 5th dynasty, is also not understood.

The fact that the Egyptians knew of the story about the slaughter of the firstborn in the 5th dynasty proves that the Exodus from Egypt occurred beforehand in the final days of the fourth dynasty.

The causeway of Uni in Saqqara

Who was the Pharaoh of Enslavement?

The building of pyramids began during the 3rd dynasty which as we said was the period in which Joseph lived,

Construction continued apace during the 4th dynasty and differs from its predecessors in two ways:

1. The pyramids were much bigger.

2. The pyramids changed their form, from stepped ⬜ to straight △ .

The founder of the 4th dynasty, known as King Sneferu, first built step pyramids. Afterwards he covered them over and changed them to be straight, and built successive pyramids. The construction of these huge pyramids was a vast project, the likes of which were not achieved again after the fall of the 4th dynasty.

Where was the vast manpower for this monumental work obtained? Some scholars explain that the Egyptian people volunteered to build the pyramids as a religious obligation, though it is hard to believe that religious fervor could sustain many years of backbreaking labor. Other scholars concluded that a limited labor force was required for the task. However, it is a fact that for the remaining history of ancient Egypt, no building even approached the dimensions of the pyramids of the 4th dynasty.

Moreover, as the 4th dynasty coincided with the period of slavery in Egypt, the pyramids were most likely constructed by the Children of Israel as the source of cheap labor.

As the founder of the 4th dynasty, King Sneferu, who was the first to build giant pyramids, appears to have been the 'Pharaoh in power during the last days of Israelite enslavement

(For further see Appendix 3)

Who was the 'Evil Pharaoh?'

The Book of Exodus recounts how after the Egyptians enslaved the Children of Israel into doing back-breaking work, an even more difficult period followed with the king's commandment to kill all of the male children: "Take every new-born Hebrew boy and throw him into the Nile." (Exodus 1:2)

The Israelite tradition explains that Pharaoh did this because the astrologers told him: "The Savior of Israel has been conceived in his mother's womb."

According to this tradition, Moses was subsequently born and "The whole house was filled with light". Moses was in mortal danger, but was saved by the daughter of Pharaoh. Her handmaidens sought to persuade her to carry out her father's decree, but an angel came and killed the handmaidens and Moses was saved. (Midrash Shmot Raba 1, 18-23)

Can we find out who that Pharaoh was? For this purpose, let us examine what is known about the generation after King Sneferu.

The Grea Pyramid of Khufo

After Sneferu's death, his throne was inherited by his son Khufo (Cheops), who built the largest of all the pyramids (145 meters high). In the Egyptian tradition he is considered a cruel king, and when the Greek historian Herodotus visited Egypt, the Egyptians told him that Hufo was so cruel that he did not even show mercy to his own daughter.

The following fable, written during the 12th dynasty, tells how a soothsayer predicted the eventual fate of King Khufo's family.

A magician told Khufo that a pregnant woman is carrying three children in her womb who are destined to takeover rule from his family. The king "was very annoyed" when he heard this, and the magician consoled him saying that this would not happen during his rule, but only when his grandson came to power. After the birth of the children who were destined to be future kings of the 5th dynasty their uniqueness was already visible in their gold-like limbs '. A slave-girl, who wanted to inform the king about the birth of the children, was eaten by a crocodile and so the children were saved.[27]

This Egyptian fable about Khufo has much in common with the Israelite tradition about pharaoh who commanded that all the children be killed, and it is hard to imagine that the two stories are similar simply by coincidence. It follows therefore, that cruel king Khufo is the Pharaoh who commanded that the children be killed.

Ivory figure of Khufo. This diminutive ivory statuette is the only known figure of Khufo.

Summary: King Khufo is the 'Evil pharaoh' who commanded the killing of the children, and his own daughter saved Moses.

---

[27] Y. M. Grintz, From the Ancient Egyptian Literature, Jerusalem 1975, p.78-88. (Hebrew)

Who was the 'Pharaoh of the Exodus from Egypt'?

After the death of Khufo (Cheops), his son Khafre (Chephren) succeeded him to the throne. He also built giant pyramids, like the subsequent monarch, King Menkaure (Micerynus).

Statue of Khafre

Menkaure died disastrous death: "Evidence that Menkaure met an untimely death is to be seen in all the buildings of his piramyd complex."[28]

---

[28] I. E. Edwards, The Pyramids of Egypt, 1972, p. 116.

When Menkaure died, he was succeeded by his younger brother Shepseska and not Menkaure's eldest son, Huenra: "Menkaures eldest son did not succeed him, presumably because he predeceased his father."[29]

A temple honoring Menkaure was built beside his tomb, according to the accepted custom. Contrary to these temples, which were adorned with tablets depicting the victories of the king over the enemies of Egypt, the tablets in the temple built in honor of Menkaure are missing.

"Due to historical accident," wrote Hawass, "there are no reliefs in Menkaure`s temple... Shepseskaf decorated Menkaure's pyramid complex with statues instead of reliefs." [30]

Menkaure's successor did not build pyramids. He made do with a modest tomb and also abolished faith in the Deity 'Ra'.[31]

After the death of Shepseskaf a new family seized power, bringing to an end the 4th dynasty which built the great pyramids.

In light of what we have learned, it is apparent that King Menkaure, the last of the pyramid builders, was the Pharaoh during whose time the Exodus from Egypt took place.

His firstborn son did not inherit the throne, because he died in the plague that killed the firstborn. Nor was his temple decorated with victory tablets for these would have been a ridiculous joke in the view of the terrible defeat that he suffered.

The Exodus of the slaves from Egypt explains why from that time on no gigantic pyramids were built.

The abolition of the God Ra at that time brings to life the verse "I will punish all the gods of Egypt." (Exodus 12:12)

In a later Egyptian fable it is told that Menkaure received a prophetic message about his death, and when he heard it he grew angry and "cursed the Lord".[32]

The fable continues that he received a second message and realized that his fate was sealed, yet despite this he tried to attack the honor of God.

The Scriptures teach that when the words of the Lord were delivered to him the Pharaoh of the Exodus from Egypt responded with scorn, "And Pharaoh said: who is the Lord? why should I listen to him?" (Exodus 5:2) And even though he was

---

[29] P. A. Clayton, Chronicle of the Pharaohs, London 1994, p. 58.
[30] Hawass, The Programs of the Royal Funerary Complexes of the Fourth Dynasty, in: D. O'Connor and D. P. Silverman (eds.) Ancient Egyptian kingship, Leiden 1996, p. 235.
[31] I. E. S. Edwards, The Pyramids of Egypt, London 1955, p. 133.
[32] The Writings of Herodotus, Vol 2, 133.

warned that he would be punished if he didn't retract when he saw that disaster had come, he continued to stiffen his neck until the bitter end.

The Egyptian tale about how Menkaure remained stubborn against God is the same as that told in the Scriptures about the Exodus from Egypt.

Summary: 'The Pharaoh of the Exodus' is King Menkaure.[33]

King Menkaure

---

[33] We should note that the bitter end of drowning in the sea befell even the empty sarcophagus of Menkaure that was found in his pyramid: It was loaded onto a ship to take it to the British museum but the ship sank in the Mediteranean Sea (M. R. Bunson, Encyclopedia of Ancient Egypt, NY 2002, p. 237).

Testimonies about a Heavy Disaster

Two inscriptions record a difficult era in Egypt: 'The prophecy of Nefer-Rohu' which opens with the words "Up, my heart, and bewail this land whence thou art sprung... things to be dreaded" etc. [34] And a scroll of lamentations that is attributed to a sage named Ip-wer.[35]

These inscriptions, researched by I. Velikovsky, indicate a similarity between the story in the papyrus scroll and the stories in the Torah about the plagues in Egypt. [36]

They prove that these testimonies are about the fall of the 4th dynasty[37], and we can learn from them that in those days Egypt was hit by a number of disasters:

A) Enemies living in the land.

B) Natural disasters.

C) Mass deaths.

D) Defeat on the battlefield.

A) Enemies living in the Land

The translator of the "Admonitions of Ip-wer" writes in the introduction to his work: "Mention is twice made of the "enemies of the land" ... the scion order is reversed, so that the slaves now usurp the place of their former masters".[38]

On papyrus it is written: "Forsooth, gold and lapis lazuli, silver and malachite, are fastened on the necks of female slaves." "A few lawles men, have ventured to despoil the land of the kingship."[39]

From other statements, it is possible to understand that the enemies were not local Egyptians, but from Asia.

"A foreign tribe from abroad has come to Egypt." (Ip-wer)[40] "Asiatics shall descend into Egypt." (Nefer-Rohu)

These were shepherds, who came to Egypt with their herds, as the final words of the testimony of Nefe-Rohu testify: "... so as not to allow the Asiatics to go down

---

[34] A. Gardiner, JEA, London 1914, pp. 100-106.
Some read 'Neferti' instead of Nefer-Rohu.
[35] A. Gardiner, The Admonitions of an Egyptian Sage, Hildesheim, 1969.
[36] I. Velikovsky, Ages in Chaos, New York 1952, p. 22-47.
[37] See Appendix 4.
[38] A. Gardiner, The Admonitions of an Egyptian Sage, p. 9-10.
[39] ibid pp. 31, 61.
[40] ibid p. 30.

into Egypt, that they may beg for water after (their) wonted wise, so as to give their cattle to drink."

The rebellion was not only against the upper strata of society but even against the king: "are done, that have never happened for long time past: the king has been taken away by poor men... men have ventured to rebel against the Uraeus."[41] ('Uraeus' – the crown of the king)

Even the Deities of Egypt were affected: "(He who was ignorant of) his god, (now) offers to him with the incense of another, not known..."[42] (Ip-wer). "Re removes himself from men... The nome of Heliopolis will not be the land of birth of any god." (Nefer-Rohu. Heliopolis was the cult center of *Re*, the Deity of Egypt.)

To point criticism in the direction of the King was unthinkable in the Egyptian texts but in these testimonies we find even these words: "Confusion is what dost put throughout the land... it is because thou hast acted so as to bring these things about. Thou hast spoken falsehood."[43]

However, the king is not the principle guilty party, there is one man who is seen as the central cause of the sufferings. Thus spoke Ip-wer: "Is there a herdsmen that loves death? Then would'st thou commanded to make reply: it is because one man loves and another hates(?)."[44]

The 'hate man' is the 'poor man' who is mentioned a number of times:

"The poor man has come to the estate of the divine Ennead (the palace). Fear of the terror he inspires, the poor man begs... He is seized, laden with his possessions... Is the poor man vigilant? The day downs upon him without his dreading it. Men flee... tents are what they make like the dwellers of the hills."

"Destroyed is the performance of that for which they are sent by servants in the missions of their lords, without their being afraid of them... The storehouse of the king is the common property of everyone, and the entire palace is without its revenues."[45]

The slaves that rebel and plunder the property of the Egyptians and their jewelry are the Children of Israel, as the Scriptures write: "Every Israelite woman will go to her Egyptian neighbors and will ask for clothing and for gold and silver jewelry. The Israelite will put these things on their sons and daughters and carry away the wealth of the Egyptian." (Exodus 3:22)

---

[41] ibid p. 54, 53.
[42] ibid p. 62.
[43] ibid p. 85.
[44] Ibid.
[45] ibid pp. 50, 71, 72.

They came to Egypt because of their animals as it is written: "We have come to live in this country because in the land of Canaan there is no pasture for our flocks". (Genesis 47: 4)

Portrait of Menkaure – the Pharaoh of the Exodus

The poor man who disperses terror and is ostracized, but in the end they look for him at night, is Moses, as it is written: "He (Pharaoh) said to Moses: Get out of my sight. Don't let me ever see you again". (Exodus 10:28) "That same night the king sent for Moses". (ibid 12:31)

When this happened they indeed began to flee: "And the Egyptians urged the people to hurry and leave the country". (Exodus 12:33)

The Scriptures say as the Egyptian papyrus says.

The population was hit by diseases: "(men's) hearts are violent. Plague is throughout the land" [46]

B) Natural Disasters

Ip-wer describes how the Nile, the source of all life in Egypt, has become unfit to drink: "The river is blood, and men drink of it. Men shrink from (tasting?) human beings, and thirst after water." [47]

The fields of wheat were also hit: "That has perished, which yesterday was seen. The land is left over to its weariness like the cutting of flax" "No fruit nor herbs are found for the birds." "All is ruin." [48]

Everything is covered in darkness: "The land is not light. " [49]

These are the words of Ip-wer. Nefe-Rohu describes it thus: "Perished are those good things, the ponds of those who slit fish, teeming with fish and fowl... The earth is fallen into misery... The beasts of the desert shall drink from the rivers of Egypt... The sun is veiled... None can live, when the sun is veiled by clouds."

These sentences bring to mind what is written in the Torah about the blows that hit Egypt: blood, wild animals, plague, hail, locusts and darkness.

C) Mass deaths

"None there is who weepeth because of death" (Nefe-Rohu). "Men are few. He who places his brother in the ground is everywhere." "The childrens of princes are cats out in the streets" [50] (Ip-wer).

The descriptions of course parallel those of the plague of the firstborn.

D) Defeat on the battlefield

The Egyptians set out to make war on their enemies, however that was when the forces of nature intervened: "Happened that never had happened. Men shall take weapons of warfare; the land lives in uproar." (Nefe-Rohu)

Ip-wer tells us of the reason for war: "Then we protect ourselves (?). Multiplied warriors to repel the people of the Bow." [51]

In the history of the world there is only one known case where a whole army set out to make war in order to return a nation 'that bows' and that was at the Exodus

---

[46] ibid p. 25.
[47] ibid p. 27.
[48] ibid pp. 44, 45, 69.
[49] ibid p. 70.
[50] ibid pp. 30, 51.
[51] ibid p. 91.

from Egypt, when the Egyptians went out to bring back the Children of Israel who went to make sacrifices to the Lord and did not return.

Ip-wer continues to tell how celestial forces intervened and separated between the Egyptians and their enemies: "Lack of people... the west to diminish... so long as (?) the gods in the midst there of endure ."[52]

The Book of Exodus also tells how a heavenly force stood between the people of Israel and the Egyptians. As it is written:

"The angel of God, who had been in front of the army of Israel, moved and went to the rear. The pillar of cloud also moved until it was between the Egyptians and the Israelite... and so the armies could not come near each over all night." (Exodus 14:19-20) "The Lord put darkness between you and the Egyptians." (Joshua 24:7)

Ip-wer continues to tell how despite the intervention of heavenly forces, the Egyptian soldiers did not cease to move forward, to advance towards their enemies: "A fighter goes forth, that [he?] may destroy the wrongs that they have brought about."

This is in line with Scripture that tells how despite the hiding of the Israelites, the Egyptians continued to pursue them at night: "The Egyptians pursued them and went after them" (ibid 14:23).

According to the words of Ip-wer, the enemies numbered more than a million people, and when day came the Egyptians were grasped with fear and trembling from the heavenly forces that were accompanying them:

"Today fear... more than a million of people. Not seen... between heaven and earth fears on account of everyone." [53] However, there was already no way back: "The road is dragged." [54]

The Israelite people, when they left Egypt, indeed numbered more than a million people: "There were about 600,000 men, not counting women and children" (ibid 12:37).

When daylight began to appear, the Egyptians were shocked by the pillars of fire and cloud that was below them on the ground and their top reached the heavens: "Just before dawn the Lord looked down from the pillar of fire and cloud at the Egyptian army and threw them into a panic." (ibid, 14:24)

---

[52] ibid p. 78.
See further appendix 5.
[53] ibid. p. 83.
Ip-wer also tells what was accompanying the enemies. It was fire: "The fire has mounted up on high. Its burning goes forth against the enemies of the land" (ibid p. 52).
[54] ibid p. 85.

The horsemen at the head of the Egyptians could no longer escape: "He made the wheels of their chariots get stuck, so that they moved with great difficulty." (Exodus 14:25)

Ip-wer tells how the event ended in disaster, and in connection with this he mentions a flood and a staff that causes wind:

"... People send a servant (?) to poor men. He walks upon the road until he sees the flood... He is belabored (?) with blows of the stick, and wrongfully slain. Would that thou mightest taste some of these miseries!" "Egypt has come to pour out water. He who poured water on the ground. He has captured the strong man in misery." [55]

The miraculous staff from the words of Ip-wer is also mentioned in the story of the exodus from Egypt. It is the staff with which Moses brought up a mighty wind: as it is written:

"The Lord said to Moses:... lift up your walking stick and hold it out over the sea... Moses held out his hand over the sea, and the Lord drove the sea back with a strong east wind." (ibid 14:15-21)

When morning came and the Egyptians tried to flee, Moses returned the waters to their courses and the Egyptians saw how their division of chariots was destroyed:

"The Egyptians said: 'Let's get out of here!... So Moses held out his hand over the sea... The water returned and covered the chariots." (Exodus 14:25-28)

According to Ip-wer, all of the pursuers were destroyed: "They like Asiatics... They have come to an end for themselves. There are none found to stand and [protect] themselves." [56] Exactly the same thing is written in the Torah about the chariots of Pharaoh: "Not one of them was left" (Exodus 14:28).

The event shook the entire world: "All foreign tribes are full of its fear", as it is written in the Torah "The nations have heard, and they tremble with fear" (Exodus 15:15).

(For further see Appendices 4, 5, 6, 7, 8, 9)

---

[55] ibid pp. 85, 55.
[56] Ibid, p. 91.

Comparison of Egyptian text written on papyrus with verses in the Torah

Verse	Papyrus
"There will be loud crying all over Egypt such as there has never been before." (Exodus 11:6)	"Up, my heart, and bewail this land whence thou art sprung… things to be dreaded."
"Every Israelite woman will go to her Egyptian neighbors and will ask for clothing and for gold and silver jewelry. The Israelite will put these things on their sons and daughters and carry away the wealth of the Egyptian." (Exodus 3, 22) "In this way the Israelites carried away the wealth of the Egyptian" (ibid 12:36).	"Forsooth, gold and lapis lazuli, silver and malachite, are fastened on the necks of female slaves .A few lawless men, have ventured to despoil the land of the kingship."
"The Israelite had many children and became so numerous and strong that Egypt was filled with them." (Exodus 1:7)	"A foreign tribe from abroad has come to Egypt." "Asiatics shall descend into Egypt."
"Who is the Lord? why should I listen to him? I do not know the Lord" (Exodus 5:2) "The magicians said to the king: God has done this." (ibid 8:19) "I will punish all the gods of Egypt." (ibid 12:12) "When I defeat them, the Egyptian will know that I am the Lord." (ibid 14:18)	"(He who was ignorant of) his god, (now) offers to him with the incense of another, not known…" "Re removes himself from men… The Nome of Heliopolis will not be the land of birth of any god"
"Then the Lord said to Moses: Go and see the king… He (Pharaoh) said to Moses: Get out of my sight, Don't let me ever see you again." (Exodus 10:1-28)	"The poor man has come to the estate of the divine Ennead (the palace) … Fear of the terror he inspires, the poor man begs… He is seized, laden with his possessions…Is the poor man

"That same night the king sent for Moses." (ibid 12:31)	vigilant? The day downs upon him without his dreading it."
"All the water was turned into blood. The fish in the river died, and it smelled so bad that the Egyptians could not drink from it." (Exodus 7:20-21)	'The river is blood, and men drink of it. Men shrink fron (tasting?) human beings, and thirst after water.' "Perished are those good things, the ponds of those who slit fish, teeming with fish and fowl."
"All over Egypt the hail struck down... It beat down all the plants in the fields... The flax and the barley were ruined." The locusts came over the whole country... They ate everything that the hail had left." (Exodos 9:25-31. 10:13-15)	"That has perished, which yesterday was seen. The land is left over to its weariness like the cutting of flax" "No fruit nor herbs are found for the birds... All is ruin The earth is fallen into miser"
"There was total darkness throughout Egypt for three days" (Exodus 10,22)	"The land is not light! The sun is veiled... None can live, when the sun is veiled by clouds "
"At midnight the Lord killed all the first-born sons in Egypt... There was loud crying throughout Egypt, because there was not home in which there was not a dead son." (Exodus 12:29-30)	"None there is who wept because of death". "Men are few. He who places his brother in the ground is everywhere" "The children of princes are cats out in the streets"
"Moses and Aaron replied: Allow us to travel three days into the desert to offer sacrifices to the Lord. When the king of Egypt was told that the people had escaped... and he pursued the Israelites, who were leaving triumphantly." (Exodus 5:3, 14:5-8)	"Then we protect ourselves (?). Multiplide warriors to repel the people of the Bow."
"There were about 600,000 men, not counting women and children." (ibid 12:37)	"More than a million of people. Not seen."
"The angel of God, who had been in front of the army of Israel, moved and went to the rear. The pillar of	"So long as (?) the gods in the midst thereof endure."

cloud also moved until it was between the Egyptians and the Israelite... and so the armies could not come near each over all night." (Exodus 14:19-20) "The Lord put darkness between you and the Egyptians." (Joshua 24,7)	
"The Egyptians pursued them and went after them." (ibid 14-23)	"A fighter goes forth, that [he?] may destroy the wrongs that they have brought about."
"The Lord looked down from the pillar of fire and cloud at the Egyptian army and threw them into a panic." (ibid 14:24)	"Today fear... between heaven and earth fears on account of everyone"
"The Lord said to Moses: ... lift up your walking stick and hold it out over the sea... Moses held out his hand over the sea, and the Lord drove the sea back with a strong east wind." (ibid 14:15-21).	"Blows of the stick"
"He made the wheels of their chariots get stuck, so that they moved with great difficulty." (Exodus 14:25)	"The road is dragged."
"So Moses held out his hand over the sea... The water returned and covered the chariots." (Exodus 14:27-28)	"People send a servant (?) to poor men. He walks upon the road until he sees the flood..." "Egypt has come to pour out water. He who poured water on the ground. He has captured the strong man in misery."
"Not one of them was left". (Exodus 14:28)	"They like Asiatics... They have come to an end for themselves. There are none found to stand and [protect] themselves."
"The nations have heard, and they tremble with fear" (Exodus 15:15).	"All foreign tribes are full of its fear"

Memory of the Exodus from Egypt in Later Generations

During the Hellenistic period the Egyptians knew very little about their past, though they preserved a dark memory of its angry days.

So the Egyptian historian Manetho Timaeus, writes: "I don't know why God whipped up a hostile storm, and unexpectedly some people of obscure descent from eastern parts had the audacity to invade the land and easily capture it by force without a battle."

He tells with some exaggeration of the disaster that these Eastern peoples caused Egypt and ends by saying: "They left Egypt and crossed the desert into Syria. They built a city in the region now called Judea and called it Hierosolyma." [57]

Another inscription from the same period tells of a king who met his death in a war against these Asians. This happened after a storm caused a blackout that prevented people from seeing each other. [58]

This is how we understand the plague of darkness, during which "The Egyptians could not see each other" (Exodus 10:23).

A description follows of the disaster that occurred at a site called 'Pi-Haroti' which is also mentioned in the Torah ('Pi-Hahiroth') as the site of Pharaoh's downfall. (ibid 14:9) (This discovery is also noted by Velikovsky.)

(For further see: Appendix 9)

Summary: The findings that point to the infiltration of Egypt by peoples from the East and their disappearance at the end of the 4th dynasty complement the period of slavery in Egypt. The Israelites built the great pyramids, and the Exodus from Egypt took place at the end of the 4th dynasty.

---

[57] Josephus Flavius – Against Apion, 1, 14, translated by J. Barclay, Leiden-Boston 2007, p. 52, 59.
[58] G. Gayon, Les Travaux de Chou les tribulations de Geb d`apres leNaos 2248 d`Ismailia, KEMI Revue de philoligie et d`archeologie egyptiennes et coptes, VI (1936), 1-42.

King Menkaure

Chapter 3: The Desert Generation

A People surviving in the desert – Survival without water and food Resources –Temporary dwellings – Mount Sinai - Answers to Questions - 'The Graves of Craving' – Hor Haggidgad – The End of Settlememt – Arad – The cities of Og, King of Bashan

A People surviving in the desert

Surveys and excavations in the Sinai desert, and the southern Negev show that at one time during the Old Kingdom in Egypt, a large population lived in the desert. Even then it was an extremely dry area, as botanists testify:

"Vegetation in the early Bronze Age was similar to what we see today in this region... so that we can conclude that the local climate has not changed." [59]

What brought people to live in such a dry region? Some have tried to connect settlement to copper mining in the area, but the settlements were far from the copper mines. Others tend to give political reasons: "Without a geopolitical incentive it is hard to understand the growth of settlements in the Negev and Sinai during the Early Bronze Age." [60]

What were those geopolitical reasons? There's no knowing. For all we know that is "a wide spread of settlements for which at the moment we have no historical explanation." [61]

On the other hand, the Beersheba and Arava valleys which are more suited to settlement remained uninhabited during this period.[62] "Despite the existence of water resources, no sites have been discovered from this period."[63]

---

[59] N. Liphschitz & Y. Waisel, A Climate History of the Sinai Peninsula in Light of Dendrochronological Studies, in: G. Gvirtzman et al (eds.) Sinai, Tel Aviv 1987, pp. 520-521. (Hebrew)
    Research into the rocks came to the same conclusion [A. Danin, The Biogenic Weathering of Limestones and Rocks by Lichens and Cyanobacteria as a tool for the Research of the Climate, Cathedra 28, 1983. (Hebrew)]
[60] M. Heiman, Nomads and settlers in the Negev mountains in the ancient bronze age, in: S. Ahituv (ed.) Studies in the archaeology of Nomads in the Negev and Sinai, Beer Sheba 1998, p. 104. (Hebrew)
[61] Y. Beit-Aryeh, Southern Sinai in the Early Bronze Age, in: G. Gvirtzman et al (eds.) Sinai, Tel Aviv 1987, p. 623. (Hebrew)
[62] Y. Aharoni, The Archaeology of the Land of Israel, Tel Aviv 1978, p. 80 (Hebrew); R. Cohen, The New Encyclopedia of Archaeological Excavations in The Holy Land, Jerusalem 1993, p. 1123.
[63] M. Heiman, Shepherds and Farmers in the area of Kadesh Barnea, Sdeh Boker 1989, p. 26. (Hebrew)

The findings "display difficulties that are impossible to ignore and require an explanation." [64] Yet scholars haven't been able to answer why people chose to live in the desert.

Survival without Water and Food Resources

Archaeologists who investigated the remnants of settlement in the Negev Mountains have not found an answer to how people were able to survive in settlements located in completely arid desert areas far from water resources.[65]

Their food resources also remain a mystery. Many grindstones were discovered which apparently show that they had grain to grind. Therfore, some scholars have assumed that people were employed in agriculture. [66] However other scholars claim the opposite as findings show that few scythe blades were found to indicate widespread farming activities. [67]

A few small items were found to suggest trading and imports, though only on a very small scale. "It is impossible to point to a commercial system that could provide a means of existence worthy of its name." [68]

Furthermore, almost no evidence exists of the grain people ate "despite the discovery of domestic grinding stones." [69]

Research, therefore, has not found an answer to the question what people survived on.

Temporary Dwellings

Excavated sites uncovered the remains of living rooms containing branches indicating "the existence of wood in the rooms used for roofing." [70]

At most archaeological sites earthenware shards of utensils used in antiquity can be found. However, no earthenware remains have been found in any of these

---

[64] B. Zass, Sinai between the 4th and 1st centuries BCE, in: Z. Meshel & I. Finkelstein(eds.), Sinai in Antiquity, Tel Aviv 1980, p. 46-47. (Hebrew)

[65] M. Heiman, Nomads and settlers in the Negev Mountains during the Ancient Bronze Age, in: S. Ahituv (ed.) Studies in the archaeology of Nomads in the Negev and Sinai, Beer Sheva 1998, p. 109. (Hebrew)

[66] I. Finkelstein, the Socio-Demographic structure of the Intermediate Bronze Age, Eretz Israel 20 (1989) p. 79. (Hebrew)

[67] M. Heiman, Nomads and settlers in the Negev mountains in the Early Bronze Age, in :S. Ahituv (ed.) Studies in the Archaeology of Nomads in the Negev and Sinai, Beer Shea 1998, p. 109. (Hebrew)

[68] ibid, p. 113.

[69] W. G. Dever, The New Encyclopedia of Archaeological Excavations in the Holy Land, Jerusalem 1993, p. 159.

[70] Y. Beit Aryeh, Settlements from the Ancient Bronze Age in the south of Sinai, in: Z. Meshel & I. Finkelstein (eds.) Sinai in Antiquity, Tel Aviv 1980, p. 3007. (Hebrew) ; also W. G. Dever, ibid.

desert sites. This indicates that the place was abandoned soon after it was erected, before the first pot had been broken.

Why did these nomadic desert dwellers build dwellings when they had no intention of remaining in them? "An answer hasn't yet been given to this phenomenon which repeats itself in many places in the Negev and Sinai." [71]

To answer these questions, let us present a main area of settlement in the region of Santa Katerina in the southern Sinai desert.

Mount Sinai

Excavations at Jabbal Mussa, which is usually identified with Mount Sinai, have unearthed "a large settlement... containing a very large number of sheep and goats bones, as well as many shells, which suggests a connection to the Red Sea... not even one complete pot has been found which proves that the inhabitants of the site left in peaceful circumstances." [72]

Mount Sinai (Jabbal Mussa)

A large number of graves, called 'Nawamis' by the Bedouin remain around Jabbal Mussa of passing desert nomads. These 'Nawamis' demonstrate that their builders were not desert inhabitants, but people who came from an inhabited land. "One of the striking things about these Nawamis is the quality of the

---

[71] Hadashot Archaeologist (Archaeological News) 74-75, p. 38-39. (Hebrew)
[72] R. Giveon, The Stones of Sinai speak p. 54-55. (Hebrew)

construction. The construction is of a very sophisticated nature, that requires wisdom and it testifies to a developed building tradition." [73]

We can deduce the origins of these buildings from their openings. Nawamis face west without exception, identical to the Egyptian custom of always placing a doorway in buildings facing west of their graves. [74]

Similarly, a portion of the remnants of all the pottery found in this site are vessels that are recognizable from the Gerzian culture in Egypt. [75]

Furthermore, "the uniformity of these Nawamis across the whole Sinai desert impressively testifies to a tradition common to all members of the society. Yet we still find certain differences... each graveyard served as a burial plot for a different social group, something like a tribe." [76]

If that is so, these remains by Mount Sinai perfectly match what is told in the Bible about the Children of Israel who reached Mount Sinai from Egypt via the Red Sea, after several generations of working in the building industry.

The building tradition was developed from one common tradition, but separated into tribes. They had goats and sheep in extremely large numbers, as the verse states: "many sheep, goats, and cattle also went with them" (Exodus 12:38), similar to the remains found in the excavations.

They dwelt beside Mount Sinai for a year (Numbers 10:11). After that, they left peaceably.

A number of published studies reached the conclusion that these remnants in the deserts of the southern Negev and Sinai are those of the Children of Israel. [77]

Answers to Questions

Scriptural accounts can answer all the questions we have raised above.

The Children of Israel did not live in the desert of their own free will, but because they were not permitted to leave it (Numbers 14:29), and so we do not find any remains of settlement from those days, either in the Arava Valley or in the Beersheba Valley, even though they were much more suitable for habitation.

---

[73] A. Goren, The Nawamis in Southern Sinai, in: S. Ahituv (ed.) Studies in the archaeology of Nomads in the Negev and Sinai, Beer Sheva 1998, p. 68-69. (Hebrew)
[74] A. Goren, ibid, p. 74.
[75] Mumford and Parcak, Pharonic Ventures into South Sinai, The Journal of Egyptian Archaeology 89 (2003), p. 85.
[76] Y. Tsafrir, Monks and Monasthern in Southern Sinai, Qadmoniot 9 (1970), p. 9. (Hebrew)
[77] Y. Etzion, The lost Bible, Jerusalem 1992, p. 75 (Hebrew) ; E. Anati, Har Karkom: A Holy Mountain in the Paran Desert (Israel), BCSP 22, 1985, pp. 129-131 ; D. Alon, New Light on the Exodus from Egypt, Jerusalem 1999, p. 13 onwards. (Hebrew)

The Children of Israel at that time ate *Manna* after "grinding it or pounding it into flour". (Numbers 11:8)

This wondrous manna was not grain, neither was it an agricultural produce or something purchased. Instead it descended every day from the heavens. It left behind no remains, as it would melt in the heat of the sun (Exodus 16:21), and therefore we do not find any trace of it.

The Israelites also ventured into completely dry areas, where they found water to drink from rocks that were split open (ibid 20:11). They dwelt in huts (Leviticus 23:43) which, according to tradition, were a building whose ceiling was made of branches, similar to those buildings which the scholars discovered.

They could not know how long they would wait at each station, because they were dependent on the cloud that accompanied them.

"The people broke camp at the command of the Lord, and at his command they set up camp. As long as the cloud stayed over the tent, they stayed in the same camp... Sometimes the cloud remained only from evening until morning, and they moved on as soon as the cloud lifted." (Numbers 9:18-21)

Because of their lack of advance knowledge for how long they would remain in each stop they might build themselves a dwelling and be forced to resume their journey even before they settled in. This explains why no earthenware was found in these dwelling.

'The Graves of Craving'

After they camped by Mount Sinai, the Children of Israel relocated to the south of the Negev desert. Remnants from this journey also remain.

The first stop after Mount Sinai was a place called 'Kibroth Hattaavaa' ('The Graves of Craving'), where a flood of birds to eat was showered on them. The people fell on the birds and many of them died through overeating. This is the source of the name 'The Graves of Craving': "because there they buried the people who had craved meat" (Numbers 11:34).

The second stop was 'Hazeroth', where Miriam the prophetess was plagued with leprosy, and all the people waited for her there for seven days. (Numbers 11:35-12:16)

Where were these stops? The location of Hazeroth is well known and today the place is called 'Hudra', (about 50 km north of Jabbal Mussa), whereas the location of 'The Graves of Craving' is not known.

However archaeological findings can show us where they were located, since many gravestones known as Nawamis have been found in the area around Mount Sinai, as well as at 'Hatzeroth'.

Gravestones like these have also been found in 'Tbeik' [78] on the road from Jabbal Mussa (Mount Sinai) to Hudra (Hazeroth).

No remains of graves have been found anywhere else along the biblical route that show any long period of stay even though archaeologists do not deny "the impressive number of their stopping places." [79]

In light of this we can almost certainly determine that 'Tbeik' is to be identified as 'Kibroth Hattaavah' - 'The Graves of Craving'.

Hor Haggidgad

After 'The Graves of Craving' and 'Hazeroth' the Children of Israel continued northwards to a place called 'Kadesh Barnea', which is identified as 'Ein Kadis' close to today's border between Israel and Egypt.

From 'Kadesh Barnea' the people refused to continue to the land of Canaan and they received an order to return southwards back in the direction of the Red Sea. (Numbers 14:25)

Between Kadesh Barnea and the eastern Red Sea there are many mountainous ridges known as 'Mount Seir' (Jabbal A-Saira, in the northeast of Sinai), and those who left Egypt were forced to spend the rest of their days wandering among them. (Deuteronomy 2:1)

The Scriptures list the names of these places where the Children of Israel camped. A number of these places are not recognizable today, however one of them can be reasonably identified as "Hor Haggidgad". (Numbers 33:36) "Hor Haggigad" ('Jabbal Adid') lies on the way from Kadesh Barnea to Eilat. [80]

Archaeological surveys carried out in the areas around Kadesh Barnea were not disappointing and indicated significant settlement. [81] from Kadesh Barnea southwards: "The route passes by numerous sites from the Early Bronze Age," [82] and is clearly visible in aerial photographs.

---

[78] O. Bar-Yosef et al, Nawamis and Habitation Sites near Gebel Gunna, IEJ 36 (1986), pp 121-135.

[79] A. Goren, The Nawamis in Southern Sinai, in: S. Ahituv (ed.) Studies in the Archaeology of
Nomads in the Negev and Sinai, Beer Sheva 1998, p. 80. (Hebrew)

[80] I. Press, Encyclopedia of Palestine, Jerusalem 1946, p. 145. (Hebrew)

[81] R. Cohen, Kadesh Barnea, in: G. Gvirtzman et al (eds.) Sinai, Tel Aviv 1987, p. 663. (Hebrew) Also M. Heiman, Nomads and Settlers in the Negev mountains in the ancient Bronze Age, in: S. Ahituv (ed.) Studies in the Archaeology of Nomads in the Negev and Sinai,   Beer   Sheva   1998,
p. 108. (Hebrew)

[82] E. Anati, Hadashot Arkheologiot - Excavations and Surveys in Israel 113 (2001), p. 118. (Hebrew)

Likewise, in the area close to the Red Sea, "the southern tip of the Negev is characterized by an unusual number of ancient sites. We know today of 1600 sites, even though less than 5% of the area has been surveyed." [83]

A rich number of findings were found in this group of sites particularly around the much publicized 'Jabbal Adid' today known as Mount Karkom. [84]

We learn here that 'Hor Haggidgad', about which the Scriptures say almost nothing, the generation of the desert spent a significant part of their lives.

The End of Settlement

The findings show that the southern desert was inhabited during the Old Kingdom of Egypt, though settlement here did not last very long, as a scholar of this area writes:

"It seems that settlement was very short- lived and lasted only a few decades... The wealth of findings shows a physically developed culture, but also indicate its sudden abandonment... Was this a willing or necessary abandonment because of an intended move further to the north?" [85]

The Scriptures give a positive answer. After nearly 40 years wandering around Mount Seir, they were instructed to travel to the land of Canaan: "Then the Lord told me that we had spent enough time wandering about in those hills and that we should go north." (Deuteronomy 2:2)

The Children of Israel left the desert at this point and began the journey to the settled Land of Israel and from here on we will accompany them on this journey.

Arad

The Scriptures tell us that when the Children of Israel were on the way to the land of Canaan the king of the city of Arad came out to meet them. They fought a war with him and they destroyed his city and all the other cities under his jurisdiction. (Numbers 21:2-3)

This story is considered Scriptural evidence of its existence, even though no remains have been found of the city of Arad and surrounding areas at the time of

---

[83] U. Avner, Ancient Sites in the Eilat Region, in: Y. Aviram et al, (eds.) Eilat - Studies in the Archaeology, History and Geography of Eilat and the Aravah, Jerusalem 1995, p. 398. (Hebrew)
[84] E. Anati, Har Karkom: A Holy Mountain in the Paran Desert (Israel), BCSP 22, 1985, pp. 129-131.
[85] R. Cohen, The Ancient Settlement of the Central Negev - Vol 1, The Israel Antiquities Authority, Jerusalem 1999, p . 298. (Hebrew)

the 18th and 19th dynasties, which is the accepted time of the Israelite Desert Generation. [86]

Arad's Wall

However, after we have seen that the correct period of the Desert Generation is not during the 18th and 19th dynasties, but in the period of the Old Kingdom, we can check what the archaeologists write about that early era:

"A large, walled city... the city was surrounded by small settlements. These rural communities were undoubtedly dependent to some degree or other on the big city of Arad." [87]

In this case, archaeological findings confirm the Scriptural text exactly and can even resolve a contradiction in the Scriptures themselves.

In the Book of Numbers (21:3) it states that in the last days of Moses they fought the king of Arad and defeated him. However, in the Book of Joshua (12:14) the King of Arad is mentioned among the kings whose cities were attacked by Joshua. When was Arad attacked, in the time of Moses or of Joshua?

---

[86] N. Na'aman & I. Finkelstein, From Nomadism to Monarchy, Jerusalem 1990, p. 9 (Hebrew); I. Finkelstein & N. Silverman, The Beginnings of Israel, Tel Aviv 2003, p. 77 (Hebrew); Z. Hertzog, The Arad Fortresses, in: R. Amiran et all (eds.) Arad, Tel Aviv 1997, p. 137. (Hebrew)
[87] R. Amiran and O. Ilan, The New Encyclopedia of Archaeological Excavations in the Holy Land, Jerusalem 1993, pp. 76, 80.

This problem has confounded generations of commentators to which several weak answers have been given; however, archaeology itself gives a clear answer.

The excavations in Arad showed that the city awas destroyed in the time of the Old Kingdom, and was rebuilt a short time later. About the second layer the archaeologists say: "Despite the destruction it seems that this layer continued from the first and there was no chronological gap between them, or a change of population." [88]

Both layers of the excavations of Arad revealed that both conquests mentioned in the Scriptures took place: the first in the time of Moses and the second in the time of Joshua.

So archaeology gives us the answer to the double conquest: settlement was renewed immediately after the first conquest and a second conquest was necessary for its recapture. The Scriptures write exactly as things happened and do not require any explanation.

(For further see Appendix 10)

Remains of houses in Arad from Moses's period

The Cities of Og, King of Bashan

After the victory over Arad the Children of Israel continued their journey to the Land of Israel. They bypassed the lands of Edom and Moab and conquered the lands "of the kings of the Amorites" east of the Jordan River. The northern part of

---

[88] Ibid.

"the lands of the Amorites" is the land of Og, King of Bashan, of whom the Scriptures tell us ruled 60 cities "fortified with high walls" (Deuteronomy 3: 5).

Surveys made in the Golan (which is part of the Kingdom of Bashan) found that from that time "huge compounds surrounded by stone walls reached significant heights... On the defensive side walls were built to an extreme height", [89] which exactly confirms the words written in the Scriptures about "high walls".

Research of the remains shows that the cities in this area were destroyed as a result of an enemy attack: "The dense cities, their size, their mighty fortificationspoint to a great culture that flourished at the time in the Golan, which collapsed after an enemy siege." [90]

In light of the above we can infer that the Children of Israel were the enemy who conquered the cities of the kingdom of Bashan, and these 'sites' exist to this day in the Golan Heights.

After the victory over Og it was time for Moses to depart from this world. Leadership of the people of Israel now passed from Moses to his student Joshua and planning began for the conquest of the land of Canaan west of the Jordan River, which will be discussed in the next chapter.

Summary: the Children of Israel wandered in the desert during the period of the Old Kingdom in Egypt, and the remains of their wandering were found in the Sinai and the Negev deserts.

---

[89] C. Epstein and S. Gutman, The Golan, in: M. Kochavi (ed.), Judea Samaria and the Golan, Jerusalem 1972, p. 244. (Hebrew)

[90] M. Kochavi, The Land of Geshur: History of Region in the Biblical Period, Eretz Israel 25 (1996), p. 195. (Hebrew) See further: M. Livneh, Golan - 20 years and 2000 more, Jerusalem 1989, p. 75-77 (Hebrew) ; Y. Paz, Urbanization in the Golan, in: D. Amit & R. Kleter (eds.) cities and urbanization in the Land of Israel and its neighbors in Ancient Times, Jerusalem 2002, p. 9. (Hebrew)

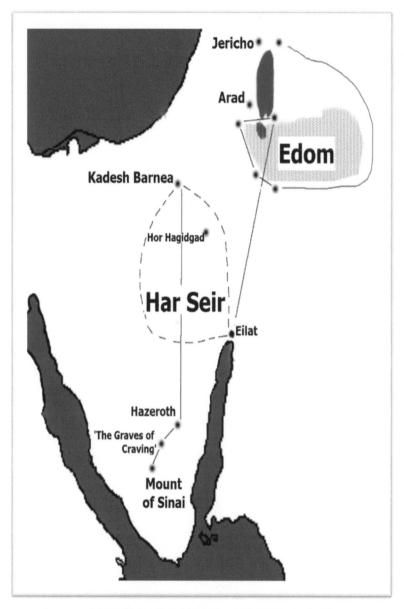

Journeys of the Children of Israel from Mount Sinai to the land of Canaan.

In the second year after they left Egypt they travelled from Mount of Sinai to Kadesh Barnea. For the next 38 years they wandered in the area between Kadesh Barnea and Eilat. In the 40th year they left Eilat until they reached the site opposite Jericho.

Chapter 4: Joshua's Conquests

An Atmosphere of Fear – The Collapse of the Walls of Jericho – The Sacking of Arad and Jericho – The Nomadic Invaders from the desert – Secondary Burials - Ai – The Disengagement of the Land of Israel from Egypt – The Episode of the Blessings and the Curses – Why was the Mountain Desolate? – The Palace of Piram King of Jarmuth – Archaeological remains solve conflicting stories about the conquest of Hebron - A Solution to the Mystery of Madon

An Atmosphere of Fear

During the period of the 1st to the 5th dynasties (known as the Early Bronze Age) cities were established in the Land of Israel for the first time. That is why this period is known as the 'Urban Phase'.

Towards the end of this period, the inhabitants diverted many of their resources to preparations for war. The walls during this period are extremely thick, much more than all the walls known to us from the fortifications of the land in later periods.

A Thick wall from the EBA

The walls teach us that the people lived in fear, as one scholar of this period writes: "It is hard to find a logical reason for the thickness of the walls, since the means

of attack at the disposal of potential enemies did not require them to be so thick."
[91]

One scholar concluded from this behavior that "the people were afraid". [92]
Another fact teaches us about the widespread fear throughout the land; dispersed
settlements were abandoned and people moved into fortified cities. [93]

It seems that the rural settlers had reason to fear, because in fact the dwellings of
the 'Urban Phase' were destroyed during the 5th dynasty in Egypt. Why?

One scholar of this period writes: "The causes that brought about the swift
destruction of the cities in the land of Israel during this period have not been fully
explained. Some depended upon a cumulative effect... Others think that it was
the infiltration of migrant tribes across the boundaries, or military campaigns by
Egyptian kings of the 5th dynasty."

Afterwards "there came about in the land a new area of inhabitancy that was
completely different from the remnants of the city phase preceding them. This
culture came from the east bank of the Jordan River and from southern Syria."
[94]

After we have seen (in chapter 2) that the Exodus from Egypt occurred at the end
of the 4th dynasty, it is clear that that the conquest of Joshua took place during the
5th dynasty and, as we said before the evidence provided above for the conquest
by Joshua is identical with the Scriptural account.

The Scriptures also speak of fear, as the woman Rahab says to the spies: "Your
terror is fallen upon us, and all the inhabitants of the land faint because of you...
Our hearts did melt". (Joshua 2:9-11) Likewise, it tells about "cities well fortified".
(Numbers 13:28)

The Children of Israel emerged from the deserts and under the leadership of Moses
initially conquered the land of Sichon and Og, which was on the eastern bank of
the Jordan River and Southern Syria, and they absorbed the physical culture, as it

---

[91] A. Ben-Tor, The Early Bronze Age in Eretz-Israel, Qadmoniot 16, 1971, p. 111. (Hebrew)
[92] J. Callaway, The New Encyclopedia of Archaeological Excavations in the Holy Land,
Jerusalem 1993, p. 44.
[93] A. Ofer, The New Encyclopedia of Archaeological Excavations in the Holy Land,
Jerusalem 1993, p. 815; Z. Gal, Tel Rekhesh and Tel Qarney Hittin, Eretz Israel 15 (1981),
p. 221 (Hebrew); M. Broshi & R. Gophna, The Settlements and Population of Eretz-Israel
in the Early Bronze Age II-III, Eretz Israel 17 (1984), p. 156 (Hebrew); R. Grinberg, The
settlements of the Hula Valley in the Urban Phase of the Early Bronze Age, Eretz Israel
21 (1991), p. 130 (Hebrew); A. Be Tor , Trade in the Land of Israel during the Early
Bronze Age, in: B. Z. Kedar et al (eds.) Commerce in Palestine through the Ages,
Jerusalem 1990, p. 15. (Hebrew)
[94] Gopha, The History of Eretz Israel – Vol. 1, Jerusalem 1982, p. 119-120. (Hebrew)
Some researchers hold that the destruction of cities in the land of Israel was at the end
of the 6th dynasty, but most of them date it to the 5th dynasty.

is written: "The people of Israel captured all the Amoritic cities, and settled in them." (Numbers 21:25)

When Moses died and Joshua inherited the leadership they crossed the Jordan and conquered most of the cities in the Land of Israel wiped out its population (Joshua 11:14) and, on the ruins of the Canaanite cities built their own settlements.

The Collapse of the Walls of Jericho

The Scriptures tell us that the first city Joshua conquered was Jericho (ibid, chapter 6).

In the introduction above we quoted an archaeologist who said that "no city existed in Jericho in Joshua's time". This would be correct if Joshua's conquest had taken place during the 18th and 19th dynasties. However now that we have shown that Joshua's conquest occurred during the 5th dynasty (at the end of the Early Bronze Age), let's examine this in the words of the British archaeologist Kathleen Kenyon, who excavated the site, and uncovered a thriving city from the days of the 5th dynasty which was damaged by a natural disaster:

"The excavations revealed several instances of collapse in the walls which strongly suggests an earthquake. The face of the wall collapsed outward in a tip of intact bricks and there are no signs to suggest that the collapse resulted from attempts to breach the walls or undermine them by an enemy." [95]

The findings show that after the collapse, people living there tried to use whatever materials were at their disposal to rebuild the walls, which suggests they were in a state of despair, when their enemies arrived. "At a time when the town wall had been razed to the ground, news of imminent danger caused the inhabitants to rapidly rebuild their defenses. Before the task was completed, they were overwhelmed. The disaster was total, for this ended the Early Bronze Age of Jericho." [96]

In the book "The Lost Bible" the author points to the parallel between the archaeological findings and the Scriptural description of Joshua's conquest of Jericho by.[97]

This is what the Scriptures say: "Joshua ordered the people to shout... they gave a loud shout, and the walls collapsed. Then the army went straight up the hill into the city and captured it." (Joshua 6:16-19)

---

[95] K. M. Kenyon, Digging up Jericho, London 1957, p. 176.
[96] Ibid, p, 189.
[97] Y. Etzion, The Lost Bible, Jerusalem 1992, p 61-65. (Hebrew)

The Scriptures tell us that before this city was conquered, the walls fell down by themselves, and Kenyon also found that the walls of the city were destroyed on their own, perhaps by an earthquake, before the city was conquered and destroyed.

Kenyon therefore found the walls that fell un front of Joshua, and additional signs which corroborate the words of the Scriptures, as explained above.

The Sacking of Arad and Jericho

During the conquest of the land the Children of Israel took all the spoils for themselves, though in the first two cities they consecrated all the spoils, that is to say they burned all the booty that was fit to be burned.

The first city was Arad. "Then the Israelites made a vow to the Lord: If you will let us conquer these people, we will unconditionally dedicate them and their cities to you and will destroyed them. The Lord heard them and helped them conquer the Canaanites. So the Israelites completely destroyed them and their cities." (Numbers 21:2-3)

After Arad they did the same at Jericho: "Joshua said… The city and everything in it must be totally destroyed as an offering to the Lord… Then they set fire to the city and burned it to the ground along with everything in it." (Joshua 6:16-24)

Burnt layers were also found in other places, though in Arad and Jericho the fires were especially intense. In Arad: "thick layers of charcoal were found throughout the site." [98] In Jericho: "the normally mud coloured bricks burnt to a bright red throughout, clear evidence of the strength of the fire." [99]

The remains of the cities destroyed by the Children of Israel exist to this day. In Jericho, Joshua also prohibited the rebuilding of the city: "Anyone who tries to rebuild the city of Jericho will be under the Lord's curse". (Joshua 6: 26)

Indeed, the excavations of Jericho revealed that the conquerors declined to build on the mound of the destroyed city, but only outside its bounds As Kenyon writes:

"They must have lived in tents or very flimsy structures… Though they lived on the 'tel', they were not really interested in its town. … Houses have been revealed only on the slopes of the hill." [100]

---

[98] R. Amiran and O. Ilan, The New Encyclopedia of Archaeological Excavations in the Holy Land, Jerusalem 1993, p. 76.
[99] K. M. Kenyon, Digging up Jericho, London 1957, p. 189.
[100] Ibid. p.192.
(This tells us that the prohibition to build the city applied only to the mound and but not its surroundings.)

The findings in Jericho which show that the conquerors completely burned the city down and did not rebuild it match exactly the story of the conquest of Joshua.

The Nomadic Invaders from the desert

Kenyon wrote a book about her excavations in Jericho and she gave the name "Nomadic Invaders" to the chapter that deals with the conquest of the city during the 5th dynasty. This is because the remains left by the conquerors prove that they came from the desert. But from which desert?

In Kenyon's opinion these were the deserts of Northern Syria. Other scholars say that they came from the Eurasian plains.

However, we can point to deserts that are closer where remains identical to those of the conquerors of Jericho were found. These are the deserts of Sinai and the Negev. [101]

Consequently, archaeologists of the southern district suggest that these people came from the Sinai and the Negev. "The New Ethnic invaders were not the Amorites or from the northeast , but from the Sinai." [102]

Secondary Burials

The new conquerors lived in the area and also dug themselves graves used mainly for secondary burials. That is to say, the bones of those who died elsewhere were brought for burial here. Graves like these were also found in other places in the Land. [103]

We find differences in burial customs: "The newcomers had a nomadic way of life when they arrived, which can best be explained as evidence of a number of a tribal groups, coming together in the same migration period as a loose tribal confederation." [104]

---

[101] E. Eisenberg, Nahal Rephaim - A Bronze Age Village in Southwestern Jerusalem, Qadmoniot 103-104 (1994), p. 95. (Hebrew)

[102] R. Cohen, Middle Bronze Age Settlements in the Negev Mountains, in: S. Ahituv (ed.) Studies in the Archaeology of the Nomads in the Negev and Sinai, Beer Sheva 1998, p. 129. (Hebrew)

[103] It is customary to say that these graveyards were used for many years by nomadic people, who would travel away from their place and on their return come back with their dead.
However a thorough investigation of a large graveyard on the mountain of Hebron revealed that all of the graves were dug during one summer:
"The tombs must have been dug, and the shafts were then filled in during a single summer season, between the rains. (W. G. Dever, The New Encyclopedia of Archaeological Excavations in the Holy Land, Jerusalem 1993, p. 666.)
That is to say, the reburial was a big project that was carried out only once.

[104] K. M. Kenyon, Digging up Jericho, London 1957, p. 207.

The graves further inland teach "that as the tribesmen penetrated into Palestine, the clear outlines of the nomadic system tended to blurr." [105] That is to say Jericho was their first stop in the land.

Their religion was different from all other peoples of antiquity, because we find hardly any idols among them. "As opposed to the many idols found in Syria we do not know of any one similar findings in the land, except for two idols on Mount Yeruham." [106]

The conquerors from the desert whose remains were found by Kenyon are of course the Children of Israel and the Scriptures tell us that their first stop in the land was in Jericho. (ibid 4:19)

The reason for secondary burial is obvious because the Scriptures stress the great importance of burying in the Land of Israel and therefore Jacob and Joseph requested that their bones be brought for burial in the Holy Land(Genesis 47:29-31; ibid 50:25).

This is why in the first year of their settlement in the Land the new inhabitants dug graves for the dead they brought with them.

It is forbidden in the Ten Commandments for the people of Israel to make idols and in the first generation of their arrival in the Land they still observed this prohibition. (Judges 2:7)

This is why almost no idols are found among the possessions of these conquerors from the desert.

Summary: Jericho was conquered by "Nomadic Invaders" comprising a number of desert tribes who did not serve idols and came together to the Land of Israel bringing their dead with them for reburial in the Land.

These are the exact characteristics specified in the Scriptures describing the Children of Israel at the time of Joshua.

Ai

After the conquest of Jericho, Joshua conquered the city of Ai (Joshua 7:2-8) Where was Ai?

---

[105] Ibid.

[106] M. Kochavi, The Middle Bronze Age 1 in the Land of Israel, Qadmoniot 6 (1969) p. 43. Afterwards images were fund at two more sites, Jebel Qaakir and Nahal Rephaim (R. Gophna, The Archaeology of Ancient Israel in the Biblical Period, Unit 5, Tel Aviv 1989, p. 122 (Hebrew); E. Eisenberg, Nahal Rephaim - A Bronze Age Village in Southwestern Jerusalem, Qadmoniot 103-104 (1994), p. 85-88. (Hebrew)

According to the Scriptures Ai is located east of Bethel (Joshua ibid; Genesis 12:8) and according to this reference, Ai is identified with a large hill known as 'A-Tel' located east of Bethel.

An excavation took place on this site in the 30's of the last century, financed by Baron de Rothschild, which aimed to discover traces of the route of the conquest narrated in the Bible.

The digging of Ai

The project turned out to be a great disappointment: No city dating to the 18th - 20th dynasties (the Late Bronze Age) was found, which is the accepted period of Joshua's conquest. An additional excavation during the 1960's yielded similar results.

These excavations led Scriptural archaeologists to give only a measure of credibility (if at all) to the Book of Joshua. In order to bridge between the Scriptures and archaeological findings, efforts were made to find the city of Ai elsewhere. [107] However, these attempts at alternative sites also failed to find remains of any city from the designated period.

---

[107] Y. M. Grintz, Studies in Early Biblical Ethnology and History, 1969, p. 278-289; Y. Ben Nun, Come to Ai, in: Z. H. Erlich & Y. Eshel (eds.) Judea and Samaria Research Studies – Vol. 2 (1992), p. 43-64. (Hebrew)

Now that we have concluded that the conquest of Joshua was not by the 18th-20th dynasties, rather earlier, by the 5th dynasty, we can go back and again examine the findings at the excavated site.

Apparently the remains of a large city dating to the time of the ancient dynasties was uncovered. This city continued to exist until it was conquered and destroyed. When did this happen?

So writes the excavator: "Violent destruction overtook the city **during the 5th dynasty**. No definite identification of the aggressor has been made... It was never rebuilt because the "dark age" descended upon the land with the appearance of **nomadic invaders** from the desert." [108]

In light of what we have said 'til now it is clear that the anonymous destroyers of Ai were the Children of Israel and they were the "nomadic invaders from the desert". Also the fact that Ai was not rebuilt anew is told in the Scriptures: "Joshua burned Ai and left it in ruins. It is still like that today." (Joshua 8:28)

Summary: The findings at Ai also show that the conquest of Joshua occurred during the 5th dynasty.

Sacred Pottery from Ai

---

[108] J. Callaway, The New Encyclopedia of Archaeological Excavations in the Holy Land, Jerusalem 1993, p. 44.

Now that we have concluded that the conquest of Joshua was not by the 18th-20th dynasties, rather earlier, by the 5th dynasty, we can go back and again examine the findings at the excavated site.

Apparently the remains of a large city dating to the time of the ancient dynasties was uncovered. This city continued to exist until it was conquered and destroyed. When did this happen?

So writes the excavator: "Violent destruction overtook the city **during the 5th dynasty**. No definite identification of the aggressor has been made... It was never rebuilt because the "dark age" descended upon the land with the appearance of **nomadic invaders** from the desert." [108]

In light of what we have said 'til now it is clear that the anonymous destroyers of Ai were the Children of Israel and they were the "nomadic invaders from the desert". Also the fact that Ai was not rebuilt anew is told in the Scriptures: "Joshua burned Ai and left it in ruins. It is still like that today." (Joshua 8:28)

Summary: The findings at Ai also show that the conquest of Joshua occurred during the 5th dynasty.

Sacred Pottery from Ai

---

[108] J. Callaway, The New Encyclopedia of Archaeological Excavations in the Holy Land, Jerusalem 1993, p. 44.

The findings in Jericho which show that the conquerors completely burned the city down and did not rebuild it match exactly the story of the conquest of Joshua.

The Nomadic Invaders from the desert

Kenyon wrote a book about her excavations in Jericho and she gave the name "Nomadic Invaders" to the chapter that deals with the conquest of the city during the 5th dynasty. This is because the remains left by the conquerors prove that they came from the desert. But from which desert?

In Kenyon's opinion these were the deserts of Northern Syria. Other scholars say that they came from the Eurasian plains.

However, we can point to deserts that are closer where remains identical to those of the conquerors of Jericho were found. These are the deserts of Sinai and the Negev. [101]

Consequently, archaeologists of the southern district suggest that these people came from the Sinai and the Negev. "The New Ethnic invaders were not the Amorites or from the northeast , but from the Sinai." [102]

Secondary Burials

The new conquerors lived in the area and also dug themselves graves used mainly for secondary burials. That is to say, the bones of those who died elsewhere were brought for burial here. Graves like these were also found in other places in the Land. [103]

We find differences in burial customs: "The newcomers had a nomadic way of life when they arrived, which can best be explained as evidence of a number of a tribal groups, coming together in the same migration period as a loose tribal confederation." [104]

---

[101] E. Eisenberg, Nahal Rephaim - A Bronze Age Village in Southwestern Jerusalem, Qadmoniot 103-104 (1994), p. 95. (Hebrew)

[102] R. Cohen, Middle Bronze Age Settlements in the Negev Mountains, in: S. Ahituv (ed.) Studies in the Archaeology of the Nomads in the Negev and Sinai, Beer Sheva 1998, p. 129. (Hebrew)

[103] It is customary to say that these graveyards were used for many years by nomadic people, who would travel away from their place and on their return come back with their dead.

However a thorough investigation of a large graveyard on the mountain of Hebron revealed that all of the graves were dug during one summer:

"The tombs must have been dug, and the shafts were then filled in during a single summer season, between the rains. (W. G. Dever, The New Encyclopedia of Archaeological Excavations in the Holy Land, Jerusalem 1993, p. 666.)

That is to say, the reburial was a big project that was carried out only once.

[104] K. M. Kenyon, Digging up Jericho, London 1957, p. 207.

The graves further inland teach "that as the tribesmen penetrated into Palestine, the clear outlines of the nomadic system tended to blurr." [105] That is to say Jericho was their first stop in the land.

Their religion was different from all other peoples of antiquity, because we find hardly any idols among them. "As opposed to the many idols found in Syria we do not know of any one similar findings in the land, except for two idols on Mount Yeruham." [106]

The conquerors from the desert whose remains were found by Kenyon are of course the Children of Israel and the Scriptures tell us that their first stop in the land was in Jericho. (ibid 4:19)

The reason for secondary burial is obvious because the Scriptures stress the great importance of burying in the Land of Israel and therefore Jacob and Joseph requested that their bones be brought for burial in the Holy Land(Genesis 47:29-31; ibid 50:25).

This is why in the first year of their settlement in the Land the new inhabitants dug graves for the dead they brought with them.

It is forbidden in the Ten Commandments for the people of Israel to make idols and in the first generation of their arrival in the Land they still observed this prohibition. (Judges 2:7)

This is why almost no idols are found among the possessions of these conquerors from the desert.

Summary: Jericho was conquered by "Nomadic Invaders" comprising a number of desert tribes who did not serve idols and came together to the Land of Israel bringing their dead with them for reburial in the Land.

These are the exact characteristics specified in the Scriptures describing the Children of Israel at the time of Joshua.

Ai

After the conquest of Jericho, Joshua conquered the city of Ai (Joshua 7:2-8) Where was Ai?

---

[105] Ibid.
[106] M. Kochavi, The Middle Bronze Age 1 in the Land of Israel, Qadmoniot 6 (1969) p. 43. Afterwards images were fund at two more sites, Jebel Qaakir and Nahal Rephaim (R. Gophna, The Archaeology of Ancient Israel in the Biblical Period, Unit 5, Tel Aviv 1989, p. 122 (Hebrew); E. Eisenberg, Nahal Rephaim - A Bronze Age Village in Southwestern Jerusalem, Qadmoniot 103-104 (1994), p. 85-88. (Hebrew)

According to the Scriptures Ai is located east of Bethel (Joshua ibid; Genesis and according to this reference, Ai is identified with a large hill known as '. located east of Bethel.

An excavation took place on this site in the 30's of the last century, financ Baron de Rothschild, which aimed to discover traces of the route of the con narrated in the Bible.

The digging of Ai

The project turned out to be a great disappointment: No city dating to the 20th dynasties (the Late Bronze Age) was found, which is the accepted peri Joshua's conquest. An additional excavation during the 1960's yielded si results.

These excavations led Scriptural archaeologists to give only a measur credibility (if at all) to the Book of Joshua. In order to bridge between Scriptures and archaeological findings, efforts were made to find the city c elsewhere. [107] However, these attempts at alternative sites also failed to remains of any city from the designated period.

---

[107] Y. M. Grintz, Studies in Early Biblical Ethnology and History, 1969, p. 278-289; Y. Nun, Come to Ai, in: Z. H. Erlich & Y. Eshel (eds.) Judea and Samaria Research Stu – Vol. 2 (1992), p. 43-64. (Hebrew)

The Disengagement of the Land of Israel from Egypt

The excavations at Ai taught us about the process the city underwent during the Early Bronze Age. Initially it was under Egyptian influence and later freed itself of it: "The overwhelming fact is that Egypt lost whatever influence it had." [109]

This process of disengagement from Egypt occurred countrywide as a scholar of the period writes: "The severance of the Egyptian connection was absolute. Not a single Egyptian object has been discovered in the Land of Israel during this period." [110]

What were the initial reasons for Egyptian influence, and how was it lost afterwards? This is what the Scriptures reveal: during the time of Joseph the land of Canaan came to be dependent on Egypt as is written: "And famine reigned over all the Land…The people of Egypt and Canaan became weak with hunger. As they bought grain, Joseph collected all the money and took it to the palace. All the money in Egypt and Canaan was spent." (Genesis 47:13-14).

This dependence ended during the time of Moses when Egypt was crushed by the plagues and its army was destroyed. This was the cause for Egypt's loss of control over Canaan (and therefore Egypt was not mentioned in the story of the conquest of Joshua).

The legend of the Exodus from Egypt explains the absence of Egypt from archaeological findings in the Land of Israel during the 5th dynasty.

The Episode of the Blessings and the Curses

The Scriptures go on to tell us how, after the conquest of Ai, Joshua assembled the people between Mount Gerizim and Mount Ebal (the place of the city Shechem) and he read out to them the blessings and the curses in the Book of Deuteronomy. (Ibid 8:30-34)

This story is difficult to understand, because the distance from Ai to the mountains of Gerizim and Ebal is especially far and that area had not been conquered by Joshua. So how did Joshua lead the entire nation there?

This problem gave birth to different attempts to explain the Scriptures in a non-literal way. [111]

To understand what is written let's turn for assistance to the findings of Professor Finkelstein who conducted a survey of the area between Ai northwards and found

---

[109] Ibid.

[110] A. Ben-Tor, Trade in the Land of Israel during the Early Bronze Age, in: B. Z. Kedar et al (eds.) Commerce in Palestine throughout the ages, Jerusalem 1990, p. 15. (Hebrew)

[111] Z. H. Ehrlich, The Conquest of the Land – Spatial Aspect, in: Z. H. Ehrlich and Y. Eshel (eds.), Judea and Samaria Research Studies – Vol. 2 (1992), pp. 11-22. (Hebrew)

that this area was then sparsely populated: "Forty sites from this period were examined, only one of which was fortified - Ai." [112]

That is, on the way from Jericho to Mount Gerizim and Mount Ebal there was only one obstacle which they had to overcome and that was the city of Ai.

Now we understand how after the conquest of Ai the Children of Israel could go all the way to Mount Gerizim and Mount Ebal with no-one obstructing them.

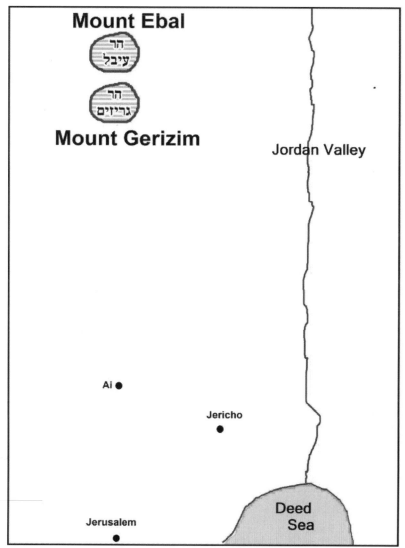

Ai and the Mountains of Gerizim and Ebal

---

[112] I. Finkelstein, The Southern Samarian Hills Survey, The New Encyclopedia of Archaeological Excavations in the Holy Land, Jerusalem 1993, p. 1313.

Why was the Mountain Desolate?

As we have said, the area between Ai and Shechem was completely uninhabited during that period and even further north from here the mountain was desolate. Why?

An examination of the earthenware vessels of that period indicates differences between the north and south of the Land, [113] and from here the idea that the land was also politically divided between northern and southern Canaan.

Some have tried in this way to explain the lack of settlement on the mountain:

"At the center of the mountain ridge is a clear area where there are no urban dwellings ... which may be explained for social and political reasons stemming from the fact that this was a buffer area between the two centers of rule in northern Canaan and southern Canaan." [114]

The Book of Joshua teaches that the Land was also divided between two alliances: an alliance of the southern Kings led by the King of Jerusalem, and of the northern Kings led by the King of Hatzor. (Joshua 10:3-5. Ibid, 11:1-5)

However, it is still not clear why this unsettled area was confined only to the center of the mountain and did not include the lower areas as well.

Subsequent chapters (Joshua 15:1-19:51) in which the land was parceled out to the tribes will reveal that the division between the north and south does not explain the absence of settlements in the center of the mountain.

The real reason appears in the dialogue between Joshua and the Children of the tribe of Menashe who told him that they didn't want the hill country to which Joshua replied: "the hill country will be yours. Even though it is a forest, you will clear it." (Joshua 17:16-18) The mountain in those days was wooded and therefore it was not possible to settle it.

The Palace of Piram, King of Jarmuth

After the conquest of Ai, the Canaanite city known as Gibeon surrendered to the Children of Israel. The King of Jerusalem, who was shocked by the betrayal of the Gibeonites appealed to his friends to join him in a war against the Gibeonites: "Adoni-Zedek, the King of Jerusalem, sent the following message to Hoham the King of Hebron and to Piram the King of Jarmuth and to Japhia the King of Lachish and to Debir the King of a Eglon saying: Come and help me attack Gibeon". (Joshua 10: 3-4)

---

[113] R. Amiran, The Ancient Pottery of Eretz Israel, Jerusalem 1963, p. 55. (Hebrew)
[114] N. Getchov, Wider Exchanges in the city settlements of the land of Israel during the period of the Early Bronze Age, in: D. Amit and R. Kleter (Eds.), Cities and Urbanization in the Land of Israel and its Neighbours in the Ancient Days, 2003, p. 10. (Hebrew)

The Gibeonites, who saw the armies approaching, called to Joshua who made war against the Canaanites and defeated them.

From this story we learn that Jarmuth was one of the greatest cities in the land during those days.

Tel Jarmuth

Jarmuth is identified with the place called Khirbet Yarmuch, close to Ramat Bet Shemesh. [115] What did the excavations there reveal about the conquest of Joshua?

Academic research which dated the conquest of Joshua to the end of the Late Bronze Age did not find any remains in the area. [116] On the contrary, remains from the Early Bronze Age – the actual time of the conquest of Joshua – indicate that a very large city (160 dunams) once stood here "protected by a fortification system of exceptional size and complexity." [117]

Subsequent excavations in Jarmuth revealed that in this period "a very impressive complex of remarkable monumental buildings, like a palace, stood here." [118]

---

[115] Z. Kalai, Biblical Encyclopedia, Vol 3, 1965, p. 866. (Hebrew)
[116] P. De Miroschedji, The New Encylopedia of Archaeological Excavations in the Holy Land, Jerusalem 1993, p. 661.
[117] P. De Miroschedji, The New Encyclopedia of Archaeological Excavations in the Holy Land, Jerusalem 1993, p. 662.
[118] P. De Miroschedji, Excavations and Surveys in Israel Vol 14 (1994), p. 107.

These have shown that this palace belonged to Piram the Canaanite King of Jarmuth who fought against Joshua.

Remains of Piram's Palace

Archaeological remains solve conflicting stories about the conquest of Hebron

After finding remains of the city of Jarmuth from the time of Joshua, let us search for Hebron, one of the allied cities in a covenant with Jarmuth.

The Book of Joshua mentions the conquest of Hebron twice: the first time it is written that Joshua 'and the entire nation of Israel' destroyed it in the war against the Kings of the South when he invaded the Land. (Joshua 10: 36-37) On the second occasion it is written that Caleb conquered it several years later. (Ibid 14:12, 15:14)

So who conquered Hebron, Joshua or Caleb? The apparent contradiction between the stories brought a moderate scholar like Kaufman to say that "it is possible some blurring has fallen into the tradition of the conquest of Hebron." [119]

Could archaeology answer this question? A city was found at the excavations there in recent years dating from the end of the Early Bronze Age whose inhabitancy was clearly renewed after the first conquest.

---

[119] Y. Kaufman, The Book of Joshua, page 36. (Hebrew)

This is what the excavator writes: "This city was destroyed by a fierce fire and its inhabitancy was renewed shortly afterwards... Both strata are characteristically similar so we cannot show any differences between them." [120]

The first strata at the site indicates that the city was destroyed during the conquest of Joshua; the second by Caleb. Archaeology provides an answer to the double conquest of Arad (see the previous chapter), as well as of Hebron; inhabitancy was renewed immediately after the first conquest which required a reconquest.

Remains of Canaanite house in Hebron from Joshua's Qoncuest Period

A Solution to the Mystery of Madon

After Joshua defeated the five kings of the South, he turned to the alliance of the four Kings of the North. In this war, which also ended in an Israelite victory, we learn about the supremacy of the city of 'Madon'.

The Scriptures state: "King Jabin of Hatzor sent word to King Jobab of Madon, to the Kings of Shimron and Achshaph, and to the Kings in the hill country in the North... to fight against Israel". (Joshua 11:1-5)

Madon is mentioned as the first city invited to join the war and the only city whose monarch is mentioned by name. In the list of 31 cities attacked by Joshua

---

[120] E. Eisenberg, Hebron during the Third Century BCE, in: D. Amit and R. Kleter (eds.), Cities and Urbanization in the Land of Israel and its Neighbours in Antiquity, p. 8 (Hebrew); also in: E. Eisenberg and A. Nagorski, Hadashot Arkheologiot - Excavations and Surveys in Israel 114, 2002 p. 91.

the King of Madon is referred to as first among the kings of the North even before the King of Hatzor. (ibid, 12:9-24)

This indicates that the city of Madon was apparently the largest of all the cities in northern Israel. Yet, despite its importance, it is strange that we do not know where Madon was located. [121]

On the other hand, a very large *tel* exists in Galilee which has not been identified from the Scriptures. This is the tel of 'Beth Yerah' (Khirbet Kerak) on the banks of the Sea of Galilee close to the settlement of Kinneret, where the largest city (about 200 dunams) in Israel was located during the Early Bronze Age. The city was destroyed in the 5th dynasty and remained in ruins until the Second Temple era.

Since the conquest of Joshua is dated to between the 18th -20th dynasties when Beth Yerah was desolate, no-one thought of identifying it as 'Madon'. But because the conquest of Joshua occurred during the 5th dynasty, a connection can be made between the unidentified tel of Beth Yerah and the great biblical city Madon.

(For further see Appendix 11)

Summary: Joshua and the Children of Israel entered the Land during the 5th dynasty in Egypt. The hill of Beth Yerah at the Sea of Galilee which was the biggest settlement in the Land of Israel during the Early Bronze Age is the Scriptural big city of Madon that Joshua fought against and defeated.

---

[121] In Karnei Hittin near Tiberias there is a Tel, by the Arabic name of Tel Midin, where some want to site Madon. However this Tel cannot be the Madon of Joshua, because it is too small and does not fit the great importance given to Madon in the Book of Joshua. See: Gal, Tel Rechesh and Tel Karnei Hittin, Eretz Israel 15, 1981, p. 220 (Hebrew); idem, The New Encyclopedia of Archaeological Excavations in the Holy Land, Jerusalem 1993, p. 1428. (Hebrew)

Chapter 5: The Period of the Judges

The Great Stone in Shechem – the remnants of the Canaanites – Abimelech and the people of Shechem

The period when the Children of Israel penetrated Canaan is called **EBA III** (Early Bronze Age III). The people of the EBA III were displaced to make way for the people of the **Midetererne Bronze Age** – the Children of Israel at the days of Joshua's qoncuest – about them discussed in the previous chapter.

The next period is called the **MBA IIa** (Middle Bronze Age IIa) which was a period after Joshua's qoncuest discussed below.

The Great Stone in Shechem

Excavations in Shechem uncovered a temple dating from the beginning of the Middle Bronze Age IIa which served continuously as a place of worship for succeeding generations. A huge stone placed on a prepared base was found in the temple. [122]

---

[122] Campbell, The New Encyclopedia of Archaeological Excavations in the Holy Land, Jerusalem 1993, p. 1352.

What is the significance of this stone? The answer say the Scriptures lies in an event that took place in Shechem after the conquest of the Land. "Joshua gathered all the tribes of Israel together at Shechem... The people then said to Joshua; we will serve the Lord our God. We will obey his commands. So Joshua made a covenant with the people that day ... Then he took a large stone and set it up underneath the oak tree in the Lord's sanctuary. He said to all the people: This stone will be our witness". (Joshua 24:1, 24-27)

It can be deduced that the great stone found at the excavations of Shechem is the stone that Joshua set up. (This is a discovery mentioned in the book 'The Lost Bible'. [123])

This stone returned to its place, so visitors can see the same stone that bears witness that the Children of Israel swore to serve the Lord God alone.

Remnants of the Canaanites

At the end of the EBA III, most Canaanite inhabitants of the Land of Israel had disappeared. However, in a number of settlements (Hatzor, Beth Shean, Megiddo and others) Canaanite culture continued for a longer period known as 'the Early Bronze Age IV'.

This culture was confined essentially to the north of the Land, as is mentioned by Professor Ben-tor: "it seems that the cities of the North held out for a longer time more than those in the south of the Land of Israel." [124]

Why did the Canaanite culture persist in these settlements after it had ceased in the rest of the Land?

The Scriptures tell that Joshua did not complete the conquest of all the land from the Canaanites (Joshua 13:1). There were places that were not conquered at all, like the land of the Lebanon and there were places that even though they were conquered, Canaanite enclaves remained. Most of these enclaves were in the north of the Land like Beth Shean and Megiddo. (Judges 1:27)

During the period of the Judges after Joshua the Canaanites held out and actually outnumbered the Children of Israel, until they were vanquished during the time of Deborah and Barack. (ibid 4:24)

The Canaanite capital was at Hatzor. It was the first city to be attacked by Joshua (Joshua 11:10); however, the Canaanites returned to it. "Jabin, the King of Canaan," dwelt in this city until its final destruction by Barak (Judges 14:2).

---

[123] Y. Etzion, The Lost Bible, Jerusalem 1992, p. 97. (Hebrew)
[124] A. Ben-Tor, The Archaeology of Ancient Israel in the Biblical Period, Tel Aviv 1989, unit 4, page 66 (Hebrew) For the findings in Hatzor see: A. Ben-Tor, The New Encyclopedia of Archaeological Excavations in the Holy Land, Jerusalem 1993, p. 605.

Remnants of the Early Bronze Age IV were found in Hatzor, Megiddo and Beth Shean which marks the period of the Judges, after the conquest of Joshua until the time of Deborah.

Abimelech and the people of Shechem

After Deborah was Gideon, the Judge came to power to free Israel and after he died, Abimelech, his son, ruled over the people. But this was only after he murdered all his brothers with the help of the people of Shechem, with the exception of Yotam who escaped Abimelech's sword.

Yotam then stood on the mountain of Shechem and scoffed at his brother, the King, the murderer and his friends, and cried: "May fire blaze out from Abimelech and burn up the men of Shechem" (Judges 9:20).

Less than three years later Yotam's curse came to pass. Abimelech quarreled with the citizens of Shechem, and the wrangling led to a war between Abimelech and Shechem. The inhabitants of Shechem escaped to the stronghold of the temple 'Baal of the Covenant', where Joshua made his covenant to serve the Lord, and Abimelech burned down the town with all its inhabitants.

What do the archaeological finds in this place tell us about the period of the Judges (MBA IIa)?

As in other cities no city walls were found from this period. However, around the temple signs of fortifications and of destruction that occurred in the middle of this period were found two strata from the Middle Bronze Age IIa divided by one layer of destruction. [125]

Who destroyed the temple of Shechem? Scholars say maybe that the Egyptian army destroyed the structure. However, the Scriptures reveal that it was Abimelech, that in the end he killed the people of Shechem who helped him to kill all his brothers.

Summary: The period of the Judges was the archaeological period called 'Middle Bronze IIa'.

---

[125] A. Kampinsky, The Land of Israel and Syria in the last stages of the MB IIB period, doctorate, Jerusalem 1974, p. 67.

Chapter 6: The Period of David and Solomon

When did David and Solomon live? – Burials at home? – Inhabitants of the land – A wall from heavy stones – An Unexplained Bank – Why David did not conquer Gezer? - Who was Solomon's father-in-law? – How did the gates of Solomon look? – The Chariot Cities – The people of the Land of Israel in Egyptian pictures – David's Warriors are admired by the Egyptians – The Takeover of the Land of Israel by the King of Egypt – The Execrations Text

When did David and Solomon live?

From what has been said up until now, Joseph lived during the 3rd dynasty in Egypt and the Exodus from Egypt took place during the 4th dynasty. Joshua's conquest of the Land occurred during the 5th dynasty, and not during the 18th or 19th dynasties as is popularly assumed.

It is also clear that we should not look for clues to the time when David and Solomon lived in findings from the 21st dynasty, but from a much earlier period: the 12th dynasty.

Solomon's period has been identified with a spectacular increase in population, and great wealth. Of this prosperity the Scriptures write: "The people of Judah and Israel were as numerous as the grains of sand on the seashore, they ate and drank and were happy." (Kings I, 4:20)

Economically: "All of Solomon's drinking cups were gold, and all the utensils were of pure gold. No silver was used, since it was not considered valuable in Solomon's day. He had a fleet of ocean-going ships... Every three years his fleet would return, bringing gold, silver, ivory." (ibid 10:21-23) "During his reign silver was as common in Jerusalem as stone." (ibid, 27)

Archaeological research shows this to be the situation in the Land of Israel during the 12th dynasty, otherwise known as the Middle Bronze Age IIb[126], marked by a population explosion when, "at this time a dense system of settlements" had been established throughout the land. [127] The wave of

---

[126] See Appendix 12: 'During which dynasty was the period Middle Bronze Age IIb?'
[127] N. Na'aman, The History of the Land of Israel – Vol. 1, Jerusalem 1982, p. 166. (Hebrew)

unprecedented settlement also reached the central mountain area which was sparsely settled. [128]

The findings also indicate that this was "one of the few periods of prosperity and economic boom ... The wealth derived from their trade, which flowed through the Land of Israel." [129]

These figures show that the period of David and Solomon should be dated to the 12th dynasty in Egypt. What else do we know about the Land of Israel during this time?

Antiquity graves in Jerusalem's cemetery

Burials at home?

The excavations show that during the time of the 12th dynasty people were buried in cellars and under the floors of domestic dwellings.[130]

The Scriptures also explain the type of burial at the time of David.

It is told of the prophet Samuel (who anointed King David) "They buried him at his home in Ramah" (Samuel I, 25:1), and we hear about Joab, the commander of the army of David that "he was buried in his home in the open country". (Kings I, 2:34)

---

[128] Y. Magen and I. Finkelstein, Archaeological Survey of the Hill Country of Benjamin, Jerusalem 1993, p. 24. (Hebrew); I. Finkelstein, The Archaeology of Israelite Settlement, Jerusalem 1988, p. 339.
[129] Y. Aharoni, The Archaeology of the Land of Israel, Tel Aviv 1978, p. 97. (Hebrew)
[130]A. Kampinsky, The Archaeology of Ancient Israel in the Biblical Period, units 4, 1989, p. 25-53; Y. Aharoni, The Archaeology of the Land of Israel, Tel Aviv 1978, p. 92. (Hebrew)

Burial inside houses seems very strange in modern times, and the commentator "Daat Mikra" explains that the word "house" does not mean 'his house', rather it means 'his grave'.

However, archaeological findings show that the verses are to be understood literally. People who died in Davidic times were buried in the house where they lived during their lifetime.

Inhabitants of the Land

Hardly any evidence remains of the period under discussion in the Land of Israel, though external records listing the names of the inhabitants of the Land teach us the composition of the population.

"Records from the period leave no doubt that the local population belonged to the same ethnic culture and that its language was strikingly close to that of ancient Hebrew." [131] Yet certain differences arose symbolized in the earthenware vessels from the northern and southern parts of the Land, "marking perhaps different political groups." [132]

This also matches well with the beginning of the period of the Kingdom of Israel.

The people of Israel (who spoke Hebrew) were united in the days of David and Solomon, but afterwards they split into two kingdoms: The Kingdom of Judah in the south and the Kingdom of Israel in the north.

A wall from heavy stones

During the same period under discussion many cities were built in the Land of Israel. [133] Three of them were encircled by a wall made of particularly large stones. "The method of building using gigantic stones is called Cyclopean and known only from Shechem, Jerusalem and Hebron." [134]

Why only these cities?

The Scriptures say the following about the period of David and Solomon: David began his kingdom in Hebron and from there he transferred to Jerusalem where his son Solomon also reigned. In the following generation, Rehoboam the son of Solomon wanted to rule from Shechem, as it is written: "Rehoboam went to

Shechem, were all the people of northern Israel gathered to make him king," (Kings1, 12:1) but he was forced to flee.

---

[131] B. Mazar, Canaan and Israel, Jerusalem 1974, p. 13. (Hebrew)
[132] A. Kampinsky, The Land of Israel in the Last Stages of the MB IIB period, Doctorate, Jerusalem 1974, p. 117-118. (Hebrew)
[133] B. Mazar, Canaan and Israel, Jerusalem 1974, p. 76. (Hebrew)
[134] E. Eisenberg, Jerusalem and its Environs in the Middle Bronze II, in: A. Faust and E. Baruch (eds.) New Studies on Jerusalem – Proceeding of the Seventh Conference, Ramat Gan 2001, p. 9. (Hebrew)

The remains of the 'Cyclopean Wall' in Hebron

The capital cities of the House of David were therefore Hebron, Jerusalem and Shechem.

The Royal household preferred using large stones in its constructions. This is what the Scriptures tell us about the buildings that King Solomon built.

Of the holy Temple it is written: "At King Solomon's command they cut fine large stones", and of the King's palace it is written: "The foundations were made of large stones, some of them twelve feet long and over fifteen feet long". (Kings I, 5:17; ibid 7:10) Now we understand why Hebron, Jerusalem, and Shechem, being the royal cities of the House of David, merited cyclopean walls.

An unexpected mound of earth

An army aiming to conquer a walled city would pile up mounds of earth that would allow them to climb up over the walls and invade the city.

This is how Jerusalem was conquered "The Babylonians have built siege mounds around the City to capture it." (Jeremiah 32:24) and many other cities were conquered in the same way.

In cities from the area we are dealing with, a strange mound of earth was added close to every wall. The classic example of this phenomenon was revealed at Tel Dan in the north, where a broad mound was uncovered that completely covered the city walls. In other places the mound was big enough to significantly reduce the protection given by the wall. This was quite amazing, in the words of a scholar of sieges in antiquity: "a detailed study of the mounds of earth used in sieges brings us to wonder about the purpose of these mounds. Because of them, attackers found a hardened filling all ready for them." [135]

The riddle is considered to be an unsolved problem: "Why were these mounds of earth built? The answer has not yet been given, and may never be." [136]

Dating them to an event that took place toward the end of King David's reign can give us the answer. A man by the name of Sheva, son of Bichri, rebelled against the king and hid away in a city called 'Abel Beth Maacha' in the Upper Galilee. King David's army built a siege fortification: "They built ramps of earth against the outer wall" (Samuel II, 20:15). In the end a wise woman managed to persuade the townspeople to behead the rebel.

This episode showed that fortified cities could be used as a refuge for rebels, and therefore after they built the rampart against Abel Beth Maachah, they did this also at other cities, to allow the King's army to enter when it was needed.

In the beginning they built at Dan, the nearest city to Abel Beth Maachah where the work was carried out thoroughly. Afterwards they continued to other cities.

Also the inner doors of the walls during that period were built in a way that they could not be locked from inside the city, teaches that the authorities suspected an internal enemy, as a scholar of the gates writes. "The gates surprisingly were not designated in any way to protect the city from an external enemy... We can estimate the purpose of the fortresses's gate was to give protection also against the danger of an uprising inside the city." [137]

The rebellion of Sheva, son of Bichri, is the key to understanding the phenomenon of the earthen mounds. David and Solomon, in their time had more to worry about an internal enemy than external enemies, so the authorities reduced the protection that the walls gave.

---

[135] I. Efal, Siege and its Ancient Near Eastern Manifestations, Jerusalem 1996, p. 83, illumination 158. (Hebrew)

[136] A. Biran, The Middle Bronze II Ramparts in Tel Dan, Eretz Israel 21, 1990, p. 64. (Hebrew).
Some want to explain that this mound was intended to prevent the attackers coming closer to the wall (Yadin). However the mounds were built at a low angle and climbing up them was easy. So writes the excavator of Shiloh: "in some of the steeper places this mound makes an easier, more gentle slope than the angle of the surface before it was poured" (I. Finkelstein, Shiloh – the Holy Centre to the Tribes of Israel, in: I. Zaharoni (ed.), Derekh Eretz - On Pottery, Stone and Man, 1996, p. 176).
Another explanation is that they were intended to support the wall (Hertzog), according to this "we should say that the positive purpose of these mounds was so great until it was built despite the knowledge that enemies would use them." (I. Efal, ibid)

[137] Hertzog, Biblical Encyclopedia, Vol. 8, p. 238-39.

Why David did not conquer Gezer?

David conquered the entire Land of Israel, except for one enclave: the city of Gezer, which was captured only by his son Solomon, and then also by a foreign army.

The Scriptures tell us "T6he King of Egypt attacked Gezer and captured it, killing its inhabitants and setting fire to the city. Then he gave it as a wedding gift to his daughter when she married Solomon". (Kings I, 9:15)

Why David did not conquer Gezer?

The grave of Pharaoh's daughter in East Jerusalem

Here, once again, we are helped by archaeological excavations at the site which revealed that during this period Gezer was particularly strong, and the tower or fortress was "the largest single-phase defense work known in the country." [138] This fact apparently deterred David from attacking.

From this period the excavators found "a meter or more of burned bricks in every field investigated." These are the leftover signs of the fire that Pharaoh lit.

Who was Solomon's father-in-law?

It was fashionable among Egyptian kings of the 12th dynasty to be called by the names of Senwosret and Amenemhet. Can we identify which of them was Solomon's father-in-law who conquered Gezer?

It seems we can, because many scarabs (seals\talismans) bearing the name of Senwosret I were found at Tel Gezer. There are also other objects that hint at the Egyptian presence at this site. For instance, a jug imprinted with a royal seal "testifiying that it was stamped during the life of the king in the name of his administration." [139]

Many scarabs were also found in the Land of Israel, from Senwosret II, the son of Senwosret I, though not even one was found in Gezer. [140] His father clearly did not bequeath the place to him. Senwosret I was apparently Solomon's father-in-law.

Senwosret I – Solomon's Father in law

---

[138] W. G. Dever, The New Encyclopedia of Archaeological Excavations in the Holy Land, Jerusalem 1993, p. 501.
[139] R. Giveon, Footsteps of Pharaoh in Canaan, Tel Aviv 1984, p. 26. (Hebrew)
[140] ibid. p. 28-29.

How did the Gates of Solomon appear?

We mentioned above the fortified tower, built by the Canaanites to protect Gezer. Later the city had a gate built with three extrusions on each side, facing each other to support the ceiling.

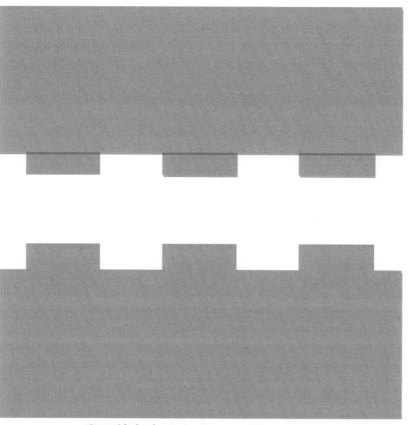

Gate with the three extrusions, viewed from above

Other gates with these extrusions were built at Megiddo, Hatzor and other places in the Land of Israel and Syria.

Many explanations have been given to the purpose of these extrusions; yet there is no answer to "why all these gates had exactly three pairs of extrusions?" [141]

According to what was said until now, this construction was characteristic during the reign of Solomon, who built Hatzor, Megiddo, Gezer, and other unnamed cities in Syria and Lebanon. As it is written "King Solomon used forced labor to build the Temple... He also used it to rebuild the cities of Hatzor, Megiddo, and

---

[141] Z. Hertzog, Biblical Encyclopedia, Vol. 8, p. 238. (Hebrew)

Gezer". (Kings I, 9:15) "He carried out all his plans for building in Jerusalem, in Lebanon, and throughout the territory he ruled over." (Chronicles II, 8:6)

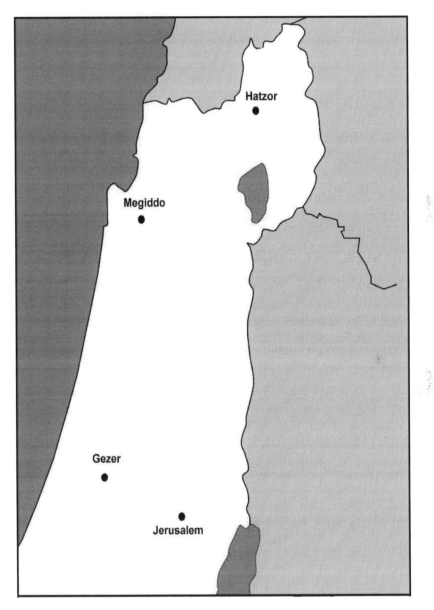

Hatzor, Megiddo, Gezer

The reason for the three extrusions in these places, one opposite one another, was a defining feature of Solomon's time. "The doorway and doorposts had rectangular frames, and were Meheza, one opposite the other three times". (Kings I, 7:5)

What is "*Meheza'*"? Rashi writes it is an extrusion that protrudes from the wall: "The head of one beam meets the other beam three times through the whole ceiling, and I do not know exactly how it is".

'Meheza', according to archaeologists, is an extrusion that sticks out from the gate.

King Solomon's gates had three extrusions on each side, opposite each other. We find this style also in the cities he built. [142]

The Chariot Cities

With the growing use of horses, it became obligatory to increase the size of the gates in order to allow chariots to pass through. [143] In the past gates were narrow, and had cornered openings, the new gates are wide and allow a straight opening.

This engineering development corresponds with Solomon's reign, about which we are told, "gathered together chariots and horsemen: and he had a thousand and four hundred chariots, and twelve thousand horsemen, whom he bestowed in the cities for chariots, and with the king at Jerusalem.built up a force of fourteen hundred chariots and twelve cavalries". (Kings I, 10:26)

"No stables were found anywhere during Solomon's time", archaeologist Y. Aharoni was quoted in the preface of this book. However, having determined that Solomon's era dates to the 12th dynasty, we suddenly find stables.

Aharoni himself writes: "The most impressive of these fortified compounds were set up near the cities... in many cases are empty of buildings... Maybe they were intended for horses and chariots as this was the revolutionary new idea of the period." [144]

These compounds are Solomon's chariot cities.

The People of the Land of Israel in Egyptian images

In the Egyptian world view Pharaoh was the ruler of all humanity, and all other peoples who did not follow his rule were rebels. Therefore, in Egyptian art, lesser peoples were always depicted as humbled and cast down.

An extraordinary situation occurred during the 12th dynasty in the picture on the grave of a prince from the reign of Senwosret II, we see Asiatics who are called 'The children of the land of Shet' carrying weapons and walking erect. This is also boldly shown in pictures of Sinai dated from the same dynasty in which "these Asiatics are walking armed." [145]

---

[142] We will deal with the gates of the six cells, which are mistakenly called 'the Gates of Solomon', in the chapter: 'The Babylonian period'.
[143] S. Yeivin, The Biblical Encyclopedia, Vol. 2, p. 235. (Hebrew)
[144] Y. Aharoni, the Archaeology of the Land of Israel, p. 93, 96. (Hebrew)
[145] R. Giveon, The Stones of Sinai Speak, Jerusalem 1983, p. 141. (Hebrew)

These abnormal pictures were apparently drawn in the days of Solomon, of whom it is said: "And the whole world wanted to come and listen to the wisdom that God had given him". (Kings I, 10:24)

The Egyptians were not able to feel superior to the Israelites; rather the opposite, the Israelites received a lot of respect.

We should add that the Egyptian Kings never gave their daughters to foreigners, and the marriage of Solomon to the daughter of Pharaoh is an event that has no parallel in Egyptian history. [146]

It fits in well with the unusually respectful relations which the Children of Shet (the Children of Israel) enjoyed during the 12th dynasty.

(For further see Appendix 14)

David's Warriors are admired by the Egyptians

In the picture 'The Children of Shet' dated to the time of Solomon people are pictured carrying arms, and are understood to be soldiers. [147] They are pictured with goats, and one person is playing a harp. What is the connection between the soldiers, the goats and the harp?

Maybe the identity of the commander of these soldiers offers a clue. The inscription accompanying the picture gives the name of the commander: "rule of the hill-country, 'Absh', a name well known in Hebrew as Abishai (II Sam., 10:10)." [148]

The inscription tells us further that the number of people was 37. Do we know the Abishai who led 37 warriors?

The Scriptures tell us that David had 37 mighty warriors and the officer commanding these warriors was Abishai. "Abishai was the leader of 'The Famous Thirty'... There were thirty-seven famous soldiers in all." (Samuel II, 23:18-39)

Now we understand the image on the grave of the prince, since David and his army were famous beyond the borders of Israel, as it is written: "David's fame spread everywhere". (Chronicles I, 14:17)

---

[146] A. Malamat, Israel in Biblical Times, Jerusalem 1983, p. 210-211. (Hebrew)
[147] M. Bietak, Avaris the capital of the Hyksos, London 1996 p. 14.
[148] J. H. Breasted, A History of Egypt, New York 1951, p. 188.

The entrance to the prince's grave

Absha, the commander of the 37 warriors

Therefore, the Egyptian prince chose to decorate his grave with the likenesses of David's great warriors and to embellish the picture with symbols from the life of David, which are the harp and the goat. About the harp it is written: "David would get his harp and play it" (Samuel I, 16:23), and about the mountain goats: "David and his men east of Wild Goats Rocks" (ibid 24:2). [149]

The Takeover of the Land of Israel by the King of Egypt

The good relations with Senwosret I and Senwosret II did not last very long. An inscription of an officer who served in the army of Senwosret III tells about the war waged against the king of the Land of Israel named 'Yekhee', who dwelt in Shechem. In the battle between them, Senwosret III was victorious and so the Land of Israel came under Egyptian rule. [150]

As we have said above Senwosret I and the II lived during the time of Solomon. Accordingly, Senwosret III lived in the generation after the reign of Solomon. Egyptian records from this period match that which is told in the Book of Kings.

After the death of Solomon, King Rekhavam (Rehoboam) ruled in Shechem. The people rebelled against him and chose Jeroboam son of Nebat instead, who returned from exile in the court of Shishak, King of Egypt. Rekhavam was forced to flee from Shechem to Jerusalem.

This is what the Scriptures tell us: "Then King Rekhavam sent Adoniram, who was in charge of forced labor, to go to the Israelites, but they stoned him to death. Upon learning of this, Rekhavam hurriedly got into his chariot and escaped to Jerusalem". (Kings1, 12:18)

The Scriptures don't explain how Rekhavam was smuggled out (his army certainly would have defeated these stone throwers), however if Jeroboam, who arrived from the court of Shishak, the king of Egypt, stood at the head of a rebellion, it is logical that the rebels were aided by the Egyptian army. Several years later Shishak also conquered Jerusalem.

---

[149] The picture of people bringing a present to the prince, however is not an authentic depiction, since the present (Blue eye-liner) they are bringing comes from Egypt close to where the picture was painted, (R. Giveon, The Stones of Sinai Speak, p.139).
Painting subjects that are not real is very common in the Egyptian faith: "Egyptian artists tended to mix in non-existent elements into their picture... It was quite natural to find vessels that did not exist in reality... The artist did not feel any pangs of conscience" (S. Wachsman, On Sea-Going Vassels Depicted in Egyptian Art, Qadmoniot 89-90 (1990), p. 8).
So we should similarly relate them also to the picture of Abshai and his men. The Prince wanted to decorate his grave with the picture of famous people, and he designed it according to his will.
[150] The inscription from the officer Khu-Se-bek tells us: "His majesty proceeded with great success in the direction of the palace of the King Yekhee and Shechem fell together with the miserables of Rethenu (Land of Israel)." (Translated by R. Vantura. A slightly different meaning can be found in: Wilson, ANET, p. 230.)

An explanation is given in the inscription by the Egyptian officer: the King 'Yekhee', who dwelt in Shechem, is Rekhavam. Senwosret III, (in Greek Sesonksis or Sesostris [151]) who defeated him is the Shishak from the Scriptures.

Statue of Senwosret III – King Shishak

---

[151] Waddel. Manetho, London 1980, p. 66.
The Greek historian Herodotus tells us that Senosret (Sesosteris) was the greatest conqueror of Egypt. On the other hand the historian Josephus Flavius knew that Shishak was the greatest conqueror of Egypt, and therefore he wrote: "As far as Herodotus made a mistake relating his actions to Sesostris" (Antiquities of the Jews 8, 10, 2). However Herodotus did not make a mistake, because Senosret the third (Sesostris) is Shishak.

The Execration Texts

Writings called **The Execration Texts** have been found in Egypt from the time of Senwosret III, and among them are curses on the enemies of Egypt.

Inscribed figurine smashed at a cursing cermonial

The enemies mentioned include the king of Jerusalem, whose name is given as "Yerekaam". [152] The names of other cities in the Land of Israel are also mentioned, but none of the cities from the interior of the land north of Jerusalem. [153]

Other Execration Texts relate to later generations after Senwosret III, and in them there are curses for 'the upper Shet king' (the northern Shet), and 'the king of the lower Shet' (the southern Shet). [154]

We have shown above that 'The land of Shet' is the land of Israel, and these inscriptions can be explained like this:

'Yerekaam', King of Jerusalem' from the Execration Texts, was Rekhavam. The earlier Execration Texts did not throw a curse on the cities north of Jerusalem, because those were ruled by Jeroboam, who was under the protection of the Egyptian king.

A generation later, Egypt lost control of the Land of Israel. (Chronicles II, 14:11) In the later Execration Texts it is written 'The kings of northern and southern Shet', that is to say the kings of Israel in the north and Judah in the south were also the enemies of Egypt.

Professor Finkelstein pointed to a similarity between the findings of the Middle Bronze IIb period and the beginnings of the kingdom in ancient Israel:

"The fact that historical sources of the Middle Bronze Age mention only two main political bodies in the central hill country hints at another possibility: there were several chiefs, but they were organized under two main political entities: a northern one with Shechem, as its center, and a southern one with Jerusalem, as its center... The breakup of the united Israelite monarchy into two separate states – Shechem (later Samaria) and Jerusalem – was also a reflection of the situation in the 2nd millennium." [155]

Summary: Egyptian findings from the 12th dynasty and the original findings from the Land of Israel in the same period match the period of the first kings of Israel.

---

[152] R. Nir, Jerusalem's generations, Tel Aviv 1984, unit 1, p. 4. (Hebrew)
[153] S. Yeivin, Topographic and Ethnic Notes, Atiqot 2 (1959) p. 156-157.
[154] W. F. Albright, The land of Damescus between 1850 and 1750 b.c., BASOR 83 (1941), p. 34.
[155] Finkelstein, "The sociopolitical organization of the central hill country in the second millennium B.C.E", In: A. Biran and J. Aviram (Eds.) Bilical Archaeology Today, Proceedings of the Second International Congress on Biblical Archaeology, Jerusalem 1990, pp. 122-126.

Summary of Section 1

Scholars accept that the Exodus from Egypt dates to the 18th or 19th dynasties in Egypt and David and Solomon ruled in the 21st dynasty.

Archaeologists show a very weak link between the Scriptural testimony and archaeological records, which have brought a number of investigators to claim that what is mentioned in the Scriptures "never happened".

On the other hand, we have demonstrated that the findings show that the Exodus from Egypt took place during the end of the 4th dynasty, the conquest by Joshua during the 5th dynasty, and period of rule by David and Solomon in the 12th dynasty.

From these periods there is a full correlation between the Scriptures and archaeology. These proofs require a new examination of the accepted chronological structure of the ancient East.

This was the subject of Dr Immanuel Velikovsky's (1895-1980) work. In his book *Ages in Chaos*, he suggested that Egyptian history should be dated slightly later than the timeline accepted by academia.

Later, Y. Etzion followed this path. In his book 'The Lost Bible' Etzion brings evidence from the archaeology of the Land of Israel that the timeline should be shortened even further.

Their alternative dates are also problematic. However, the direction they pointed to, that we should make serious changes in the timeline, is certainly correct, as we will show in the following sections.

A genuine 'Solomon Gate' in Gezer

Section 2: An Impossible Timeline

Scriptures	The Land of Israel (Archaeological Period)	Egypt (Dynasty)	Date (BCE)
	Chalcolithic	Pre-dynastic	3000-4500
	Early Bronze Age	1st -5th dynasties	2400-3000
	Intermediate Bronze Age (Middle Bronze Age I)	5th -6th dynasties	2200-2400
		7th -11th dynasties	2000-2200
Period of the Patriarchs	Middle Bronze Age IIa	12th dynasty	1750-2000
Joseph	Middle Bronze Age IIb	13th -17th dynasties	1550-1750
Slavery in Egypt	Late Bronze age I	18th dynasty	1400-1550
Exodus from Egypt and Generation of the Desert	Late Bronze Age II		1330-1400
		19th dynasty	1200-1330
Conquest of Joshua and settlement	Iron Age I	20th dynasty	1090-1200
David and Solomon	Iron Age I-II	21st dynasty	945-1090
Divided Kingdom of Israel and Judah	Iron Age II	22nd-23rd Dynasties (Lubyan)	720-945
Hezekiah, Menashe		24th-25th dynasties (Ethiopian) Assyrian conquest	663-720
End of First Temple		26th dynasty	586-663
Babylonian exile (up to 538)			525-586
Restoration, Ezra		27th dynasty (Persian)	525-430
	Persian		400-430
		28th-30th dynasties	330-400

Chart of Accepted Timeline (There are disagreements about the exact dates, but in general this is the way things are accepted by almost all scholars.)

Introduction to Section 2 – When did History Begin?

Antiquity can be divided into two major periods: the time before the invention of writing, known as prehistoric, which is undocumented; and the time from the invention of writing and thereafter which is called history.

History, therefore, began with the invention of writing which happened at the beginning of the first dynasty in Egypt. The beginning of the first dynasty is dated the same as the beginning of the historical timeline in Egypt. This date is extremely significant also in relation to the archaeological timeline of the Land of Israel, because the strata are dated by reference to a comparison of earthenware vessels found in Egypt.

When did the first dynasty begin? Champollion said it was year 5867 BCE. After him Mariette pinned it at 5004 BCE; Brugsch brought it down to 4455 BCE; Lepsius said 3892 BCE; Breasted said 3400 BCE and after Breasted it was subsequently further reduced to 3000 years BCE.

The year 3000 BCE is the date that was accepted by all academic communities and is in use already for about 50 years. Differences of opinion around this date move upward or downward in the range of 100 years.

The ancient timeline is fixed according to the date of 3000 BCE for the first dynasty in Egypt. But does it match archaeological findings?

Later on we will prove that this date also is much too early and clashes with evidence in the field that requires forceful answers for however as science goes forward, the difficulties grow.

The obvious conclusion from this is that there should be a subsequent significant shortening of the timeline in order to match it with the findings.

At the end of this section we will begin by building an adjustable timeline, and in the end of this book we will have a completely new timeline.

Chapter 7: Periods without Remnants

Egypt – The Land of Israel - Greece and Turkey – Summary

Egypt

Egyptian history begins approximately 3000 years BCE when King Menes united the kingdoms of North and South Egypt into one state.

Menes founded the first dynasty and from then on until the conquest of Egypt by Alexander the Great (330 BCE) 30 dynasties ruled one after another.

How do we know about the existence of these 30 dynasties? We know it from the writings of the Egyptian priest Manetho (3rd Century BCE) and what happened during this long period we learn from the many inscriptions scattered throughout Egypt.

The Egyptians ascribed great importance to eternity and anyone who could have his name inscribed as a memorial for future generations. In addition, the dry climate preserved the papyri from being destroyed.

Consequently, we are able to study events in the land, from one dynasty to another. Writing was already widespread in Egypt by the 12th dynasty (2000-1750 BCE). We could expect to find inscriptions of all the kings from then on; however, this is not the case.

The next 200 years, between the 13th- 17th dynasties, (1750-1550 BCE) very little of those events has been passed down in inscriptions. [156]

The start of the New Kingdom was marked in 1550 BCE with the succession of the 18th -20th dynasties which left an awesome wealth of records.

The last to leave behind their few remnants of any value was the King Rameses III (1200-1170 BCE) and after his death the sources that are available for scholars decrease significantly. Most of the succeeding monarchs did not leave any inscriptions, and if they did, they deal with insignificant events.

At the end of the 20th dynasty (1170-1090 BCE): "Six feeble Ramessids had succeeded each other, with ever lessening declining power and prestige... while we can find nothing from the reign of Ramses X to record, beyond the rifling of the royal tombs." [157]

Kings in the 21st dynasty (1090-945 BCE): "These kings were not great builders... as they showed little initiative in other directions, the century and a half during

---

[156] J. H. Breasted, A History of Egypt, New York 1951, pp. 212-213.
[157] ibid. pp. 508, 511.

which they maintained themselvesheld power was apparently on alinked to a steady industrial and economic decline." [158]

Statue of Rameses III

"Of the course of events during the long half a century reign of King Amenemapat we can now discern nothing". [159]

Libyan rule during the 22nd -23rd dynasties lasted from 945 to 724 BCE. We have many records, about the first part of this period but almost nothing about the second part.

---

[158] Ibid, p. 524.
[159] Ibid.

"Their city has perished so completely that little or no record of their careers has survived."[160] "Egypt has now been under the divided authority for probably over a century and a half... While these conclusions are not based upon contemporary documents – for such conditions in such an age are rarely even indirectly the subject of record." [161]

After the Libyans, Egypt was conquered by the Nubians (the 25th dynasty 763-720 BCE) which initially began after the 24th dynasty. It consisted of four kings, a father and his son, and two additional Kings with similar names: Shabaka and Shabataka, who both reigned for twelve years.

The father and his son engraved inscriptions that recorded their actions; of the middle two kings we don't have any significant inscriptions: "Shabaka... we possess no native records of his conquest of the country." "Shabataka... His name is rare in Egypt." [162]

 After these Nubians the Assyrians reigned over Egypt for a certain period of time, and when the Egyptians managed to free themselves from the Assyrian yoke, Egypt went back to being independent for almost a hundred and forty years (the 26th dynasty 663 - 525 BCE).

During this extremely long period Egypt prospered, enjoying a time of extreme stability and returned to its status as a major power. Despite this fact we find it extremely difficult to find remains from this period:

"Under the pharaohs of the 26th Dynasty, Egypt once more enjoyed a period of economic stability and cultural flowering. Unfortunately, however, only a few incomplete examples of dated royal sculptures or works can be definitely ascribed to this period."[163]

"The architecture of the time has, alas, perished... We possess a fund of popular Greek tradition regarding the twenty sixth dynasty which, if properly used, throws an invaluable light upon a time when native records and monuments, located as they were in the exposed delta, have almost entirely perished." [164]

The explanation that these inscriptions "were in the exposed delta" is amazing. Could the Egyptians have stopped writing outside the delta?

Summary: The Kings of Egypt wrote many inscriptions to immortalize their actions on which today rests the entire chronology of the ancient world. The

---

[160] Ibid. p. 534.
[161] Ibid. p. 537.
[162] Ibid. pp. 550-554.
[163] R. Schulz and M. Seidel, Egypt – The World of the Pharaohs, Koln 1998, p. 285.
[164] ibid p. 579.
A number of religious inscriptions remain that mention the names of the kings of the 26th dynasty and we will talk about them later in chapter 23.

chronology includes hundreds of names for which only a part have inscriptions that are convincing evidence of a royal personage.

The inscription about the other 'kings', in as much as they exist, is a doubtful proof of their real reign as kings. If we leave only those kings who we are certain were really kings in the timeline, we can reduce the timeline by hundreds of years.

The Land of Israel

Rockefeller Museum – the center of the Israeli Antiquity Authority

Archaeological sites in the Land of Israel are generally found in the hills known as *tels*. These are artificial hills created by the remains of previous ancient buildings, which were built over on the ruins of their previous inhabitants.

Tels are composed of vertical strata, one above the other, where the earliest level lies at the bottom and later strata closer to the surface. A settlement that existed throughout the entire ancient timeline should have remnants be found dating to all periods. Though, in reality, the number of levels is less than the number of periods. This is particularly true of sites holding Egyptian artefacts.

For example, Byblos and Beth Shean were two key Egyptian sites. The port city of Byblos, north of Beirut, was one city that Joshua did not conquer (Joshua 13:5) and its inhabitants helped Solomon build the holy Temple (Kings I, 5:32). Byblos, which appears many times in Egyptian records, was an important Egyptian commercial center with Canaan.

Byblos was methodically excavated and the archaeological chronology of the Land of Israel largely rests on the results of these excavations. Rich findings were uncovered here prior to 1200 BCE:

"The results at Byblos have shown to be a curious source of scholarly debate over the complete absence of stratified levels of the Iron Age, for the period 1200-600 BCE." [165]

Another place that has affected the dating of ancient artefacts especially in the Land of Israel is Beth Shean. Excavations there have revealed a similar phenomenon. One of the upper levels revealed an Egyptian temple with the statues of Rameses III who lived as traditionally accepted, in the 12th century BCE. The level above it dates to the Roman period which began with the 1st century BCE. Between these two strata is a very thin layer which curiously extends almost over a thousand years between Rameses III and the Roman period.

Tel Beth Shean

How have scholars addressed this problem? A Persian level dating to the 4th and 5th centuries BCE, they said, had been "missed altogether".[166] Similar things are said about strata from the Hellenistic period dating to between the 3rd and 2nd centuries BCE.[167]

On the other hand, they reduce the date marking the strata with statues of Rameses III to the 11th century BCE, 100 years after the end of Egyptian rule, and in this way they managed to reduce the number of years between the levels.

What are the statues of an Egyptian king doing in a city that Egypt does not control?

---

[165] N. Jidejian, "Byblos Through the Ages", p. 57.
[166] E. Stern, the Material Culture of the Land of the Bible in the Persian Period, Jerusalem 1973, p. 3. (Hebrew)
[167] E. James, Encyclopedia of Archaeological Excavations in the Holy Land, London 1975, p. 215-219.

"Their location in the courtyard of the city's temples at the time when there no longer was any direct Egyptian presence in Beth-Shean is puzzling. It is possible that these monuments cames to be venerated in local tradition and were preserved from stratum to stratum in a cultic context." [168]

In this way the problem was reduced, because the strata are not supposed to span 1000 years, but only 500 years. However, we are still talking about a far longer period for one stratum. In the words of A. Mazar: "It is extremely difficult to ascertain the nature of this stratum, as the published finds from its various buildings date from a period spanning hundreds of years." [169]

We also see this in findings from Canaanite tels that do not cover the entire timeline, as accepted by conventional research.

Greece and Turkey

During antiquity the Mycenaean kingdom in Crete and the Hittite kingdom in Turkey left many remains behind them. Several of their findings are connected to Egypt, during the period of the "New Kingdom" (18th -20th dynasties) which ended in the 12th century BCE. Consequently, the Mycenaean kingdom in Greece and the Hittite kingdom in Turkey have been dated at the end of the 12th century BCE.

What happened after that? The following is written about Turkey (Asia Minor): "Close to the year 1200 BCE the Hittite Empire collapsed... The Chronicles of Asia Minor for hundreds of years to come are shrouded in darkness." [170]

Similarly, in Greece: "the period after the decline of the Mycenean civilization until the eighth century BCE about which we know almost nothing – is called ... the dark ages of Greece. There are no archaeological testimonies here from the period between the Mycenean palaces and temples that were established throughout the Greek world during the sixth and seventh centuries." [171]

"To know what happened during these years requires knowledge so sparse, that there are some who think nothing really happened". [172]

---

[168] A. Mazar, The New Encyclopedia of Archaeological Excavations in the Holy Land, Jerusalem   1993,   p.   220. This explanation does not fit the findings on the site, in the words of E. Yanai: "The investigators ignore the fact that this sculpture was not the only Egyptian finding. Under the floor were also a number of fragments of Egyptian building items", (E. Yannai, Aspects of the Physical Culture in the Land of Israel during the days of the 20th dynasty in Egypt, Doctorate, Tel Aviv 1996, p. 70.)

[169] A. Mazar. The New Encyclopedia of Archaeological Excavations in the Holy Land, Jerusalem 1993, p. 219.

[170] I. J. Gelb, Biblical Encyclopedia, Vol I, p. 474. (Hebrew)

[171] D. Asheri, Encyclopedia Hebraica, Vol 19, p. 429. (Hebrew)

[172] M. Amit, the Generations of classical Greece, Jerusalem 1984, p. 61-62. (Hebrew)

In Greece and Turkey there are not enough archaeological findings to match the accepted timeline.

Summary: In order to date their findings, archaeologists use a timeline for which the 1st dynasty in Egypt began in 3000 BCE, and the 30th dynasty ended in 330 BCE. An examination of the findings shows that some periods left no remains. To overcome this problem some very difficult forced explanations have been made.

The correct way to act when we find these 'empty spaces' in antiquity is to remove hundreds of these irrelevant centuries from the ancient dates and thus shorten the timeline.

Chapter 8: Reconstructed Periods

In dating periods in ancient history an important place is reserved for checking specific styles of ancient writing. When scholars checked the few Egyptian inscriptions from the 26th dynasty (6th and 7th centuries BCE) an embarrassing fact was revealed. The writings were exactly like the inscriptions from the 19th dynasty (13th to 14th centuries BCE). How could this have happened?

The following explanation is given:

"The nation fell back upon the past and consciously endeavoured to restore and rehabilitate the vanished state of olden times ...In the externals of government everything possible was done to clothe it with the appearance of remote antiquity. The writing of the time was also given an archaic colour on formal and official monuments, and its antique forms must have cost the scribes long and weary study... Thus the past was supreme." [173]

Similarly, findings in Babylon from the 6th century at the time of King Nebuchadnezzar - show the same trend of copying the past: "Nebuchadnezzar also harked back to the past, ordering his scribes to compose a number of his royal inscriptions in the long disused script and language of early Babylonia." [174]

"The archaic trend was in ascendancy during his time." [175]

Summary: to accept the conventional timeline we have to believe that in the sixth and seventh centuries BCE people tried to draw a parallel between their own people and with those of the 14th to 12th centuries.

---

[173] J. H. Breasted, A History of Egypt, New York 1951, pp. 570, 576.
[174] W. F. Albright, From Stone Age to Christianity, Baltimore, 1940, p.242.
[175] H. Tadmor, Biblical Encyclopedia, Vol. 5, p. 105. (Hebrew)

Chapter 9: Kings and their Doubles

Rameses II and Amasis - Nebuchadnezzar I and Nebuchadnezzar II

Ramses II and Amasis

In the previous chapter we discussed the style of writing from the 19th dynasty (14th -13th centuries BCE) which reappears again during the 26th dynasty (the 7th and 6th centuries BCE).

Also when we compare what is told about the great builder of the 19th dynasty, Rameses II, with what is told about the great builder of the 26th dynasty, Amasis ('Ahmose II') we find a similarity:

Rameses II left behind many remains: "Few of the great temples of Egypt have not some chamber, hall, colonnade or pylon which bears his number." [176]

Among the many wonderful statues in Memphis is a huge prostrate statue of Rameses at the entrance to the Temple of 'Ptah'.[177] ('Ptah' – is the name of an Egyptian god).

Of Amasis on the other hand, we have no remains, and about his exploits we know only from the book of the Greek historian Herodotus (5th century BCE). These are his words: "To the other temples of much note Amasis also made magnificent offerings - at Memphis, for instance, he gave the recumbent colossus in front of the temple of Hefaistos, (Hefaistos – the Greek name for Ptah)." [178]

Nothing from all this has remained.

That is to say, there were two Kings who built in all the temples of Egypt and they are Rameses II and Amasis. While the creations of Rameses II have been preserved, all the buildings by Amasis have disappeared without a trace.

At the entrance to the Temple of 'Ptah' in Memphis lie vast stone likenesses of the two kings one next to the other. Herodotus discerned only that of Amasis, whereas today's scholars found only that of Rameses.

---

[176] J. H. Breasted, A History of Egypt, New York 1951, p. 443.
[177] E. Ya'ari, a Guide for tourists in Egypt, p. 165. (Hebrew)
[178] The History of Herodotos, book 2, 176.

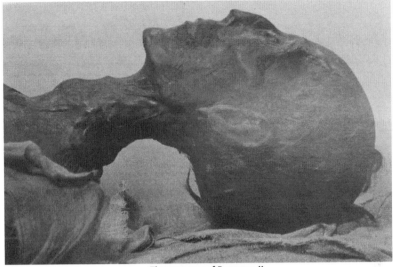

The mummy of Rameses II

Nebuchadnezzar I and Nebuchadnezzar II

Above we showed the case in Egypt; but what about Babylon? Here too is a surprising likeness between the Kings of the two periods.

Nebuchadnezzar I, who lived during the 12th century BCE, was the greatest of all Babylonian kings. He crossed the Euphrates and brought all the lands to the west under Babylon's control. He introduced many reforms and elevated the god Merodach above all the other gods.

Nebuchadnezzar II, who lived during the 6th century, was the greatest of Babylonian conquerors. He ruled over all the lands west of the Euphrates. He also elevated Merodach and implemented all the new ideas introduced by Nebuchadnezzar I, as stated by Professor Tadmor:

"The Babylonian picture of the world came together at the time of Nebuchadnezzar I during the 12th century BCE and strengthened during the time of Nebuchadnezzar II in the 6th century BCE." [179]

Summary: the accepted timeline forces us to believe that they were identical kings who lived separated by hundreds of years. Isn't it more logical to say we are speaking about the same king who was mistakenly mentioned twice?

---

[179] H. Tadmor, The Rise of Cyrud and the historical background to his proclamation, in: H. Tadmor (ed.) the Restoration - The Persian Period, Jerusalem 1983, p. 6. (Hebrew)

Chapter 10: Carbon-14

The archaeological method of dating is apparently derived from the natural sciences, based on calculations by astronomers and the by carbon-14 dating system. In the chapter below we consider the astronomers' calculations, and in this chapter we will deal with Carbon-14.

Carbon-14 is an element found in organic material (plants and animals), which starts to slowly disappear from the moment of death (or the cutting down of the plant). The speed at which it disappears is known so that the amount of carbon-14 in the remains can be used to calculate the time of death of a certain organic finding.

Do these dating checks prove the accuracy of the method? The answer is negative, because the results were later than the accepted dates. In Mesopotamia (Iraq), "during the 4th century BCE civilization was founded and developed... Through radiological dating (Carbon-14) we found that the dates are much later. It is still hard to fix the absolute times according to this method." [180]

In Egypt the situation is similar. So, for example, a check on the grave of King Djoser (from the 3rd dynasty) gives results that are 600 years earlier than expected. In findings from the time of King Den (the 1st dynasty) the difference was even greater. [181]

Also in the Land of Israel the received results do not match accepted dating. In recent years 46 results were published of Carbon-14 sites where the accepted date placed them in the 3rd millennium BCE, though 41 of them were dated to the 2nd millennium BCE. [182]

What do senior archaeologists write about the lack of correlation?

"For the prehistoric period, Carbon-14 dating is very important. In later periods, this method is less and less credible because of its inaccurate results, until in the second millenium BCE its credibility has entirely ceased ... For example the scholar Millart objects to accepted chronological agreement for the 3rd millenium BCE, relying on carbon-14 dating, and the scorn it almost universally illicited from among all of the scholars." [183]

---

[180] H. Tadmor, Biblical Encyclopedia, Vol 5, p. 61-62. (Hebrew)

[181] A. Ben-Tor, Problems in the Early Bronze Age II-III in Palestine, Thesis submitted for the Degree Dr of Philosophy, Jerusalem 1968, pp. 147-148. (Hebrew)

[182] D. Segal, Results of Carbon-14 Test of Samples from Early and Middle Bronze Age Sites in Eretz Israel and Neighboring Areas, in: R. Cohen: The Ancient Settlements of the Central Negev, Vol. 1, The Israel Antiquities Authority, Jerusalem 1999, p. 338-339. (Hebrew)

[183] A. Ben-Tor, The Archaeology of Ancient Israel in the Biblical Period, unit 4, p. 13. (Hebrew)

Laboratory results are therefore considered accurate only if they fit the expected dating. If not, "its credibility has ceased entirely".

The true check is not what the date of the finding is (since it is of already known before the test) but if the carbon-14 dating check succeeded or maybe failed.

As researchers in this field write: "we can check the reliability of the carbon-14 in two ways... the second way is to compare it to the estimated age given by other archaeological methods...the dates can be strengthened by examining them in their archaeological context." [184]

Understandably, scholars in this field will attempt to reach a 'correct' result, which has produced the calibration method. The Calibration method asserts that differences in cosmic radiation have occurred over thousands of years, and so a certain number of years must be added to every test in such a way that the results correlate with the accepted date.

Calibration is presented as a pure science, based on research into ancient tree rings (Dendrochronology). However, there are many ways of calculating them and the method chosen is the one which fits the accepted dates.

One archaeologist wrote: "I submitted my findings for Carbon-14 dating and I had the estimated date. The physicists told me that if I have an estimate based on the date of the findings, that is highly valuable for that gives them the key to calibrating their Carbon-14 examination." [185]

In summary: Generally, the results of Carbon-14 dating do not correlate with accepted dating which means they have to be calibrated, a process that precedes the results. Consequently, we cannot bring proof from it to the accuracy of the accepted dating.

(Furthermore, we should relate to these tests with suspicion because absurd results have been received at certain sites, where earlier strata received later dates than the later strata.) [186]

---

[184] Y. Karmi & O. Bar-Yosef, carbon-14 Dating, *Qadmoniot* 89-90 (1990), p. 24-25. (Hebrew)
[185] Z. Meshel, the Biologenic Weathering of Limestones - A Tool that requires improvement and Caliberation, Cathedra 28 (1983), p. 148. (Hebrew)
[186] Y. Karmi and Gofer, Archaeology and the science of nature 8 (April 2000), published by the Weitzman Institute, p. 63-66. (Hebrew)

Chapter 11: The Egyptian Astronomical Tables – Science or Sorcery?

Ancient events can apparently be dated by correlating astronomical calculations and reports of astronomical events. This is meant to remove all possible doubt about their accuracy, since astronomy is a reliable science that is able to predict events such as solar eclipses reliably.

A closer look reveals that things are not as simple. For example Breasted writes: "Astronomical calculation places the beginning of the 18th dynasty with fair precision in the year 1580 B.C.E." [187] Redford fixes it in the year 1569 BCE [188] and Kitchen sites the year 1550 BCE. These are not the only opinions. [189]

From this we realize that astronomical calculations are far from exact. This is because the astronomical events we are speaking of recur every few years and we have to know the time period in advance in order to match it up with the astronomical event.

Obviously, these calculations don't have much value; however, another calculation based on the Egyptian Astronomical Tables can apparently give us an exact dating. What are we talking about?

In the year 4242 BCE the Egyptians fixed their calendar year as having 365 days and the New Year to fall on the day the star Soti, known to us as Sirius, shone for the first time.

Since the true length of a solar year is not 365 days but 365 and 1/4 days, it follows that after four years they will be one day off, after eight years two days off, and so on until after 1461 years the Egyptian New Year will return to fall on the day of Soti's sighting. (365.25 is 1461 divided by a quarter)

This period of 1461 years is called 'The Great Year'.

Consequently, the years 2781 and 1320 BCE and 140 CE should be years in which the 'Great Year" ended. This calendar date of 4242 is defined as the "The earliest fixed date in the history of the world!" [190]

Let us not dwell on this problematic way of calculating dates based on this calendar, but on the question: how do we know that in the above mentioned years the Egyptians were observing Soti's cycles?

---

[187] J. H. Breasted, A History of Egypt, New York 1951, p. 22.
[188] D. B. Redford, The Oxford Encyclopedia of Ancient Egypt, Oxford 2001, p. 519.
[189] see: H. Tadmor, The Chronology of the Ancient East, in: B. Mazar (ed.) the Patriarchs and the Judges, Jerusalem 1967, p. 52 (Hebrew)
[190] J. H. Breasted, A History of Egypt, New York 1951, p. 32.

Do we have any inscriptions remaining from the year 4242 ("The earliest fixed date") that will confirm this? Certainly not, since we're talking about a date which is more than one thousand years before the invention of writing. In the words of Neugebauer:

"There's no proof for this and there cannot be one. We are talking about an extremely early period, hundreds of years before the invention of writing...

The 'early fixed date' forces us to create absurd fantasies about the knowledge of those who founded the calendar. The earliest astronomers, before the invention of writing, did not yet even know about clay tablets." [191]

Is there any testimony from the years 2781 or 1320 when the following cycles began, or at least from 140 CE, when the last cycle ended? No.

This fact is amazing as Velikovsky asks:

"The event (the end of the final Great Year) must have occurred in the lifetime of Claudius Ptolmey, the greatest astronomer of antiquity.

Nowhere in his writing is the event evermentioned; neither did he display an awareness of a Sothic computation though he dealt in great detail with astronomical and calendar matters of his own age and of preceding centuries...

How could he remain unaware of or silent about the advent of the new Great Year in Egypt in his lifetime?" [192]

The earliest source that Egyptologists can bring is from the Roman historian Cansorinos who lived in the 3rd century CE. [193]

Tens of thousands of records remain from ancient Egypt, but no mention of Soti's cycles teaches us that this method should be left to scholars of fables. We need more reliable information to support astronomical calculations.

Moreover, Soti's cycle of 1461 years is an impossible story. Today we know that the length of a year is not 365 and 1/4 days exactly, as was thought in antiquity (the Julian calendar), so it will be off by nine minutes. [194]

---

[191] O. Neugebauer, Die Bedeutungslosigkeit der Sothisperiode Für die älteste ägyptische chronologie, Acta Orientalia 17, Oslo 1938, pp. 177, 182, 183.

[192] I. Velikovsky, Peoples of the sea, New York 1977, p. 230-231.
About other problems in the calculation of the Soti's cycle see Velikovsky, ibid.

[193] A. Gardiner, Egyptian Grammar, Oxford 1978, p. 205.

[194] Someone who knows the development of the calendar will wonder maybe how things happen, since the length of the known year today is *shorter* than the Julian calendar by some 11 minutes. How could we then say that it is longer?
To answer we must explain that there are two types of years: the Sidereal e Sun year and the Tropical year. This is what it means: the Earth makes a circuit of thin one year

The star Sirius, because of its celestial position, has a year which is longer than the Julian year by only one minute. [195] However, even the difference of one minute means that if there was such a thing as Soti cycles the length would not be 1461 years, but a number of years less than that. [196]

The testimony about Soti's cycle gives incorrect numbers, destroys its credibility, and we must ignore it when we come to calculating timelines.

---

and these circling causes: a. The stars (in the majority of cases) to disappear and then reappear. and b. differences in the seasons of the year.

The Cideral year is longer by nine minutes than the Julian year, and despite this, the period of time for the four seasons of the year is shorter by some 11 minutes. This difference (of some 20 minutes) is because of slight annual changes in the tilt of planet Earth towards the sun it takes an extra 20 minutes before the Earth reaches the point where it was the previous year.

This phenomenon is called Preceding. The time taken to complete the circuit is called the Sidereal year, the time of the four seasons of the year is called the Tropical year. In the past it was thought that the length of the year was 365.25 days exactly, both as far as the stars were concerned and also the seasons of the year. That was when they fixed in the Julian calendar that the length of the year should be exactly 365.25 days.

When it became clear that this was not true, the Gregorian calendar was introduced to fit the length of the tropical year which is shorter. Astronomers changed their calculating according to the Sidereal year, which is longer.

[195] Sirius is a southern star which in the aforementioned period precedes every year by going a bit further North, so that it starts to be seen earlier each year in the northern hemisphere. This is why Soti's year in those years was shorter than the normal sidereal year.

[196] The length of Soti's cycles (if they existed) are: 1455, 1456, 1458 (O. Neugebauer, Ibid, p. 175).

Chapter 12: The Late Bronze Age - an Imaginary Period

Identical findings from the Late Bronze Age I (LB I) and the Middle Bronze Age – Dying Rich and living Poor – Inscriptions of Thutmose III prove: the periods should be consolidated– The Settlement Pits – Why the period of 'El-Amarna' is not found in the mountains? - What is the source of the 'Collar rim' Jugs? - How did the Seals from the Middle Bronze Age reach the people of the 'Collar rim'? – An imaginary gap in the lowland – Summary

The timeline which appears in history books is much longer than reality because many parts of it were recorded more than once.

Unnecessary periods should be removed and a whole period should be erased from the archaeology of the Land of Israel. This is the Late Bronze Age (1550 -1200 BCE) which is only a copy of the periods that came before and after it.

Middle Bronze Age	2000-1550 BCE
Late Bronze Age I	1400-1550 BCE
Late Bronze Age II	1200-1400 BCE
Iron Age I	1000-1200 BCE

Accepted Timeline for the 2nd Millennium BCE

This is the accepted timeline, but the truth is that the Late Bronze Age I (which we will refer to as LBI) is really the same period as the Middle Bronze Age that preceded it, and the Late Bronze Age II (LBII) is really Iron Age I that came after it.

Our claim may seem surprising, however the proof we will bring later removes all doubts.

Identical findings from the Late Bronze Age I (LB I) and the Middle Bronze Age

Late Bronze Age utensils dating to the period LBI are identical with those vessels ascribed to the period that preceded it, the Middle Bronze Age IIB.

"As far as the creation of earthenware vessels is concerned there is a notable continuation from the Middle Bronze Age, a characteristic that we have identified also in household dwellings." [197]

---

[197] R. Gonen, The Archaeology of Ancient Israel in the Biblical Period, Unit 7, p. 129. (Hebrew)

This creates a problem for archaeologists, since the tool used to date each stratum is the style of the vessels that are found in it. If during two periods they used the same type of vessels they have no way of knowing to which of the two periods their findings belong.

Therefore, they decided that imported vessels are specialties of LB1, and in this way they managed to differentiate between the two periods. A site at which they found imported utensils belongs to LB1; a site where they did not find imported utensils belongs to the Middle Bronze Age. [198]

Imported utensil (Bichromeware) from the LBA.
The Institute of Archaeology of Hebrew University.

One investigator of the period writes: "Since a continuity is generally recognizable among local earthenware vessels between the Middle Bronze and the Late Bronze Age, investigators decide to base themselves on the appearance of new vessels of a superior type marking the beginning of the Late Bronze Age 1." [199]

---

[198] R. Gonen, ibid, p. 133.
[199] S. Bunimovitz, The beginning of the Late Bronze Age in Palestine, Eretz Israel 23 (1992), p. 22. (Hebrew)

This distinction meant that the production of earthenware vessels in the Land of Israel was frozen for the whole of the Late Bronze Age I, and there was absolutely no change in them compared to the preceding period of the Middle Bronze Age. The only difference is that in the Late Bronze Age vessels were imported and in the Middle Bronze Age they were not.

This explanation is unacceptable. Is it illogical that for 200 years the creation of clay vessels continued exactly the same as if their style was frozen?

Even if we ignore this question, as the investigations continued it became increasingly clear that remains found in the stratum of the Middle Bronze Age already belonged to imported vessels. "Paradoxically," the same scholar continues, "the chronological picture becomes foggier with the progress of the research. Imported vessels already appear among the stratum of the Middle Bronze Age." [200]

If the decision to import began before the period of LB1 it has no remains that can divide it from the Middle Bronze Age, so LB1 is the Middle Bronze Age by another name.

Dying Rich and Living Poor

What was the general situation in the Land of Israel during the period of LB1? There are contradictory sources. As one investigator testifies many settlements were abandoned. "The reduction of the population shows us that this was a period of dissent and fragmentation." [201]

---

[200] ibid.
Bichromeware were imported vessels principally from Cyprus in the Late Bronze Age I and also copied in the Land of Israel: "bichromeware vessels were typical of the LB I and their presence serves as a measuring stick for the existence of settlements during this period".
These vessels show that the Middle Bronze Age ended, and the Late Bronze Age 1 began. On the contrary, the findings show that there is no basis for this chronological distinction: "The presence of bichromeware and ceramicware in the Middle Bronze Age shows that it is related to this period... Furthermore, the roots of the chocolate on white style of ceramicware in the LB1 period are rooted deep in the traditions of potters from the Middle Bronze Age. How could the dated ceramics be a sign of the new period?" (ibid)
Albright showed that this ceramicware is found in Megiddo and Tel el-Ajul and is absent from Jericho and Beth Mirsim. He concluded from this that Megiddo and el-Ajul are later and this explains the difference between Jericho and Beth Mirsim.
However there can be a different reason: Jericho and Beth Mirsim are inland, and so imported vessels did not reach them, whereas Megiddo and el-Agul are much closer to the beach.
This distinction is extremely shaky since, in the words of another investigator, Mewly: "the established chronology of the two-color ceramicware is based on quicksand" (quoted by Butnimovitz, ibid.)
[201] Z. Hertzog, The Canaanite City between Ideology and Archaeological Reality, in: A. Faust & A. Meir (eds.) Material Culture, Society and Ideology, Ramat Gan 1999, p. 48. (Hebrew)

However, surprisingly, in many of these abandoned settlements, very splendid graves were found. In Gezer for example: "The Late Bronze Ia period is scarsely represented... However, imported Cypriot pottery, Egyptian glass, alabaster and ivory vessels, all indicate international trade, even in this era." [202]

Imported jugs from the LBA that was found in Gezer.
The Institute of Archaeology of Hebrew University.

---

[202] W. G. Dever, The New Encyclopedia of Archaeological Excavations in the Holy Land, Jerusalem 1993 pp. 501-502.

This is quite amazing! If the city was empty, who was running the flourishing businesses?

Also in Hebron: "In the period of LB there are no remains of settlement in Tel Hebron... but rich graves were unearthed from this period." [203]

Similarly, in many other places we find that: "During the period of the LB in the mountain area a very bad crisis existed among the settlements, but the number of graveyards actually increased in proportion to the number of sites." [204]

The period of LB is one of death more than life. How can it be that in such a period, there are so many splendid tombs? Scholars were unable to give a convincing answer to this question. [205]

As we have said, the period of LB1 is characterized by imported vessels. It does not pay to transport over long distances produce that is heavy and cheap, and so when it came to imports, only expensive products like perfume bottles, works of art and the like are worth the cost. Such vessels have little day-to-day use, but they were given a special place in the graves.

It so happens that the main revelation of the period of LB1 is the amazing discrepancy between the amount of riches in the graves and the poverty of life.

Actually, the Middle Bronze Age was "a period of economic plenty of which there are not many other examples", [206] and the period LB1, which is a period of flourishing business, that is revealed in the graves of the dead, are both one period.

Inscriptions of Thutmose III prove: the periods should be consolidated

Another proof that the periods LB1 and the Middle Bronze Age are all one period is given in an inscription by the Egyptian King Thutmose III, who conquered the Land of Israel during the period of LB1.

Thutmose wrote in his inscription the names of the 75 cities of the Land. However, the archaeological investigator found only 22 inhabited settlements from the

---

[203] A. Ofer, The Mountains of Judah in Scripture, and in: N. Na'aman and I. Finkelstein (eds.) From Nomadism to Monarchy, Jerusalem 1990 p. 190. (Hebrew)

[204] A. Zertal, The "Ainun Pottery" - History, Meaning, Future, in: Y. Eshel (ed.) Judea and Samaria Research Studies 12, Ariel 2003 , p. 11. (Hebrew)

[205] R. Gonen, Tel el-Ajjul in the Late Bronze Age – City or Cemetery? Eretz Israel 15 (1981), p. 77 (Hebrew); S. Bunimovitz, The Problem of Human Resources in Late Bronze Age Palestine, Eretz Israel 25 (1996), p. 49. (Hebrew)

[206] N. Na'aman, The History of the Land of Israel – vol. 1, Jerusalem 1982, p. 166. (Hebrew)

period LB1, particularly in the coastal area, while the mountain areas were almost completely unsettled. [207]

This, of course, created a contradiction between the two which scholars try to resolve. "We should be surprised by the number of settlements listed by Thutmose III, since many of these places could be little more than lookout points or sites of ruins." [208]

However, the inscription notes that all the cities had a King at their head so that if we're talking about a lookout point or the site of ruins, why would there be a King? In fact, the period of LB1 is the same as the period of the Middle Bronze Age IIB (which, as if to say, preceded it) which was marked by many inhabited settlements.

When was a decision taken to separate these periods from places where they found imported vessels and integrate them into the new period LB1, which created a period with sparse settlements mostly in the coastal area where we would expect imported vessels are more common.

This does not fit the inscription of Thutmose. But when we combine the two periods we find a correlation between the original findings and the inscription.

Up to now we've dealt with the first part of the Late Bronze Age (LB1) and we have shown that it is the same as the preceding period Middle Bronze Age IIb.

Turning to the second part of the Late Bronze Age (LB2) we find that it is exactly the same as the following period Iron Age 1.

Settlement Pits

The vessels from LB II and Iron Age I are similar to each other, [209] which leads to the conclusion that it is really the same period. However special vessels were produced in each period:

LB II - imported vessels.

Iron Age I - huge jugs (up to 110 L) named 'Collar rim jugs' (in the mountain area), and decorative vessels known as 'Philistinian Ceramics' (in the coastal area).

---

[207] R. Gonen, The Archaeology of Ancient Israel in the Biblical Period, Unit 7, p. 15. (Hebrew)

[208] ibid.

[209] A. Mazar, The Archaeology of Ancient Israel in the Biblical Period, Units 8, p. 70 (Hebrew); R. Frankel, Upper Galilee in the Late Bronze I transition, in: N. Na'aman and I. Finkelstein (eds.) From Nomadism to Monarchy, Jerusalem 1994 p. 23; I. Finkelstein, The Archaeology of the Israelite Settlement, Jerusalem 1988, p. 323; S. Bunimovitz & Z. Lederman, Six Seasons of Excavations at Tel Beth Shemesh, Qadmoniot 113 (1997), p. 26-27 (Hebrew); S. Bunimovitz, The Beginning of the Late Bronze Age in Palestine, Eretz Israel 23 (1992), p. 22. (Hebrew)

These vessels are supposed to give dates to different strata, and to designate which strata are pertinent to LB2 or Iron Age1. Vessels of Iron Age 1 are found even in later strata than the strata where we found vessels from LB 2, but in practice the vessels are found together. How can this be?

This can be explained by the fact that the people of Iron Age I dug pits into the stratum of LB2 so that vessels from the two periods were mixed.

Uncovered Collar rim jugs

In many cases, apart from these wells we do not find any signs of building from the period of Iron Age1. In Tel Dan, we found vessels of the Collar rim jars (Iron Age 1) together with imported vessels (LB II). In the initial publication the scholar wrote: "Iron Age pottery was found together with Late Bronze material, indicating that the pit was dug into the destruction levels of the Late Bronze Age." [210]

In a later article the theory of pits has become a fact. The scholar writes about the level of the Iron Age 1 in Dan: "The first Israelite level is represented mainly by pits... The pits were sunk into the Bronze Age strata." [211] and the reader receives the impression that real pits had been found.

---

[210] A. Biran, Excavations and Surveys in Israel 1984, Vol 3, (1985), p. 20.
[211] A. Biran, The New Encyclopedia of Archaeological Excavations in the Holy Land, Jerusalem 1993, p. 326.

Can the same problem on the mountain also occur on the coastal plains where the Philistinian ceramics were found, which points to the existence of the Iron Age1?

Indeed so. Philistinian ceramics from Iron Age1 mingles with vessels from LB, which are explained as pits. The excavator of Tel Aphek writes about Bronze Age1 as follows:

"The ground level was not used for building, because in the whole area of our digs we found nothing but pits that were dug into the remains of the ruling leader's palace." [212]

This phenomenon repeats itself in many places, [213] and is nicknamed 'settlement pits'. So why didn't the inhabitants of Iron Age1 who dwelt in these places build their own dwellings, but make do with digging pits alone?

One scholar responds like this: "The architectural achievements of Iron Age1 among highland settlers were quite modest. The small communities invested as little as possible energy and materials as possible in permanent structures. Building for the use of the nuclear or extended families, and even more so, public structures appear to have been of secondary importance." [214]

Another scholar writes: "It is possible that at some sites only sectors devoted to storage to have been excavated, and this would be the explanation for the seeming lack of houses." [215]

However, if we are speaking about pits for storing wheat, we wouldn't expect to find vessels in them, in the words of the excavator of Hatzor: "The pits were not intended for storing earthenware vessels. We have to find an explanation for this phenomenon." [216]

The correct answer is that the vessels of the Iron Age were not found in pits at all because the Iron Age and LBII are in truth only one period. This conclusion is drawn not only from archaeological findings in the Land of Israel but also from Egyptian records.

---

[212] M. Kochavi, Aphek - Antipatris, Tel Aviv 1989, p. 78. (Hebrew)
[213] In Hatzor, in Tel Hefer, in Tel Poleg, in Beth Mirsim and others.
[214] B. Rosen, Subsistence Economy in the Iron I, in: N. Na'aman & I. Finkelstein (eds.) From Nomadism to Monarchy, Jerusalem 1994, p. 343.
[215] I. Finkelstein, the Archaeology of the Israelite Settlement, Jerusalem 1988, p. 266.
[216] S. Geva, The Settlement Pattern of Hatzor Stratum XII, Eretz Israel 17 (1984) p. 158. (Hebrew)

Why the period of 'El-Amarna' is not found in the mountains?

The Royal Egyptian city of "El-Amarna" existed for only a short time during the period of LB II. Its association to this period is found in the imported vessels which have been uncovered there.

In the Royal Library many letters from the rulers of the Land of Israel reveal that there were two big kingdoms in the mountain area: the southern Kingdom of Jerusalem ruled by King Abdi-Hepa and the northern Kingdom of Shechem ruled by King Lebaya.

The Kingdom of Shechem was particularly aggressive toward neighboring kingdoms whose kings asked Pharaoh to save them from the provocations of the strong hand of Lebaya, the King of Shechem.

According to the findings at LB2 investigators were dispatched from El-Amarna to the Land of Israel to search for the clues that were told in the letters of El-Amarna. But the result was a great disappointment as the excavations did not reveal any settlement in Jerusalem during the period LB 2. [217]

The same applies to all the nearby area. Agricultural settlement during most of the period of Iron Age1 was near Jerusalem, but in the period of LB "this settlement disappeared altogether." [218]

If no one was living in Jerusalem and in the nearby area at the time of El-Amarna, who was Abdi-Hepa ruling over?

Excavations in the area of Shechem also did not match with what is told in the El-Amarna letters about the strong kingdom of Lebaya. As another scholar wrote:

"For years I have lived with the contradiction between the colourful stories told about Lebaya and the poor settlement that he had...In my 21 years of research we methodically mapped the whole settlement. The result is too depressing; compared to some 200 or more settlements and dwellings from Iron Age 1 we found only 35 from LB 2. Was it possible that with the help of only a few people Lebaya was able to threaten the cities of the state around him?...We discovered a great number of settlement sites in Iron Age 1 on the borders of the desert,in the valleys and in the mountains to the east. But in all these places during the period, El-Amarna was a black hole." [219]

He sums up the subject in these words: "We need to think again about the matter with an open mind. In particular the calculation of the dates which is the key to

---

[217] A. De-Groot, The "Invisible City" of the Tenth Century BCE, in: A. Faust & E. Baruch (eds.) New Studies on Jerusalem – Proceedings of the Seventh Conference, Ramat Gan, 2001, p. 29-34. (Hebrew); E. Mazar, Jerusalem - 4000 Year old Capital in the Light of Recent Archaeological Excavations, Eretz Israel 28 (2007), p. 128. (Hebrew)

[218] A. Faust, Jerusalem's Hinterland and the City's Status in the Iron Age, Eretz Israel 28 (2008), p. 165. (Hebrew)

[219] A. Zertal, A People is Born, Tel Aviv 2000, pp. 361, 363. (Hebrew)

it all. In the meantime I am leaving things over for the next generation, maybe they will find a solution."

Therefore, to find the period of El-Amarna we just have to fix the dates, and to unite the period of LB 2 with the period of Iron Age1. Then it will become clear to us that Lebaya the King of Shechem had not only 35 settlements but more than double this number and we will suddenly find the remains of Abdi-Hepa the King of Jerusalem.

We also see that the Egyptian records direct us to unite the period of LB2 with the period of Iron Age 1.

What is the source of the 'Collar rim' jugs?

The Late Bronze Age is really an imaginary period that should be erased from the timeline, and after the Middle Bronze Age immediately comes Iron Age I.

Jugs from the Middle Bronze Age

Support for this is the collar-rim jugs which were used during the first Iron Age, and continue resemble the jugs used during the Middle Bronze Age.

According to the accepted timeline 350 years separate between the two periods – the Late Bronze Age.

How can there be an unbroken continuity between populations separated by hundreds of years? In his response Finkelstein writes: "We cannot ignore the resemblance between the collar-rim store jugs and MB pithoi ...We therefore cannot preclude the possibility that the new settlers copied older pithoi, whose shards were scattered all over these sites." [220]

It is hard to believe that utensil manufacturers were motivated throughout the entire mountainous area by the desire to make them like pottery shards from hundreds of years earlier. If we want to make use of strange explanations, the similarity between the two periods proves that the Middle Bronze Age and the Iron Age are two periods that followed one after the other.

This is another proof that we should erase the Late Bronze Age from the timeline.

How did the Seals from the Middle Bronze Age reach the people of the 'Collar rim'?

Evidence to our conclusion that the use of the 'Collar Rim' jugs began toward the end of the Middle Bronze Age, is provided by seals from 'Collar rim' jugs that were found in the stratum dating to the Middle Bronze Age.

The same applies to Aphek. There founded burial caves from the period of the 'Collar rim' jugs about which the excavator writes: "It is surprising to find that a number of these scarabs (seals) on finger rings that were buried were of the type that was common during the Middle Bronze Age."

How did seals from the Middle Bronze Age reach the fingers of people from the time of the 'Collar rim'? The scholar's answer is: "The jewellery was preserved and handed down from generation to generation and the Canaanite aristocracy carried scarab seals created 300 years before their time!" [221]

Let's examine this explanation with the following question: what are the chances of finding a woman today who wears a ring created 300 years ago? This is extremely unlikely. It is difficult to imagine that in ancient times the situation was any different.

If in one grave dating to the 'Collar rim' jugs we found a number of seals from the Middle Bronze Age this is a sign that we are speaking about two consecutive periods.

---

[220] I. Finkelstein, The Archaeology of the Israelite Settlement, Jerusalem 1988, p. 283-284.

[221] M. Kochavi, Aphek -Antipatris, Tel Aviv 1989, p. 78. (Hebrew)

The same applies to the results from Tel Shilo. On-site excavations revealed a storage room with a row of 'Collar rim' jugs together with a jug from the Middle Bronze Age.

How did the inhabitants of the 'Collar rim' period possess a jug from the Middle Bronze Age? To this the scholar responds: "The new settlers reused jugs found still intact". [222]

These arguments are strange since earthenware jugs break easily and have a short lifespan. Nor does it seem likely that the people of Shilo used jugs made hundreds of years earlier.

If they also used jugs from the Collar rim period and jugs from the Middle Bronze Age this is only because these two periods are continuous.

Summary: The discovery of utensils from the Middle Bronze Age among findings from the 'Collar rim' period shows that the Late Bronze Age did not really occur.

An imaginary gap in the lowlands

In the mountains we find many remains from the first Iron Age, and almost no remains dating to the Middle Bronze Age. On the other hand in the lowlands between the mountains and the coastal plains the situation is the opposite: there are many remains from the LB period, and no remains dating to Iron Age 1: "in most of the Judean lowland no remains from Iron Age 1 have been found". [223]

The lowland is easy to inhabit and was emptied throughout the entire period of Iron Age 1 so that hardly any remains were found.

What caused people to abandon it throughout this time?

The truth is there are no gaps in the settlement of the lowlands, and the reason we have no findings from the period of Iron Age 1 is because vessels defined as coming from Iron Age 1 are the collar-rim jugs that were used in the mountains, and Philistinian ceramics were used on the coastal plains.

In the lowlands they used neither and therefore all the sites were defined as the LB 2 and not from Iron Age 1. So a gap occurred in settling the lowlands during Iron Age 1, which parallels the gap in settling the mountains during LB 2. In fact LB 2 and Iron Age 1 are different names for the same period, and so the settlement gap disappears.

---

[222] I. Finkelstein, The Archaeology of the Israelite Settlement, Jerusalem 1988, p. 284.
[223] Y. Dagan, Map of Lakhish, Jerusalem 1992, p. 18. (Hebrew)

Vineyards in the Judean lowland

Summary

Ancient artefacts are divided into periods separated by the form of earthenware vessels used and accordingly, archaeologists date their findings.

Into this system an artificial Late Bronze Age was inserted which has no special pottery. To give it credence imported vessels were transferred to it from preceding and anteceding periods to create a strange period of poverty and disintegration, but also a period "superb in its imports to great lengths" [224] - a period of many graves and very few signs of life. This period takes place mainly in the coastal plains, and disappears in the mountain areas.

The second part of this period was separated from the succeeding period, by the local vessels, where a portion of them (Collar rim and Philistinian ceramics) moved to the following period which also posed additional difficulties.

When we erase this period from the calendar, and transfer its findings to the prior or subsequent period, the difficulties disappear and the findings are understandable. Why, then, do archaeologists continue to keep this period with all its problems? This is because, in the words of one scholar, archaeologists need this timeline to synchronize with the archaeology of the Land of Israel and the historical timeline of ancient Egypt.

"Parcelling up is intended to help recreate the history of the states... It is logical that the use of these historical – political events will create artificial discrepancies between the previous culture and the culture after it." [225]

---

[224] R. Gonen, The Archaeology of Ancient Israel in the Biblical Period, units 7, p. 129. (Hebrew)

[225] Y. Gadot, Continuity and Change: Cultural Processes in the Late Bronze and the Early Iron Age in Israel's central coastal plain, A Dissertation Submitted in fulfillment of the Requirements for the Dr of Philosophy, Tel Aviv 2003, p. 261. (Hebrew)

One investigator gave this an exact definition: "The Late Bronze Age, more than it is an archaeological creation, is in fact a specifically political creation." [226]

If so, the real problem is with Egyptian history, and we will deal with this in the next chapter.

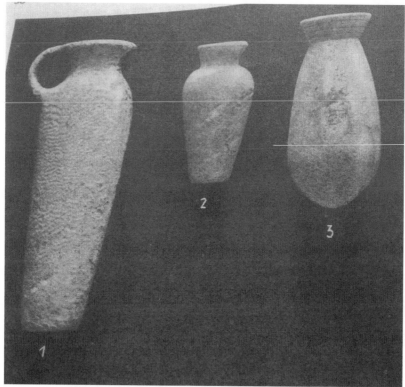

Egyptian alabastar tools that were found in the land of Israel

---

[226] Y. Portugali, Space, Time and Society in Ancient Eretz Israel, part 1, Tel Aviv 1999, p. 24. (Hebrew)

Chapter 13: The New Kingdom in Egypt - an Imaginary Kingdom (Part 1)

'Reconstructed Period' – Complementary Records – Matching the Kings from Two Periods – The Middle of the New Kingdom

Period of glory – Middle Kingdom	12th Dynasty	1750-2000
Period of Crumbling	13th -14th Dynasties	1650-1750
Foreign Rule (the Hyksos)	15th -17th Dynasties	1550-1650
Period of Glory – Beginning of the New Kingdom	Beginning of the 18th Dynasty	1400-1550
Period of Glory – Middle of the New Kingdom	End of the 18th and 19th Dynasties	1200-1400
Period of Glory – End of the New Kingdom	Beginning of the 20th Dynasty	1200 -1170

The accepted timeline in Egypt. All dates BCE.

'Reconstructed Period'

After concluding that the Late Bronze Age in the Land of Israel is a copy of the period before and after it, the New Kingdom in Egypt - which supposedly took place during the Late Bronze Age - is also only a copy of the kingdoms before and after it.

In this chapter we will deal with the first part of the New Kingdom – the beginning of the 18th dynasty, which is only a copy of the 12th dynasty and the evidence for this which lends a likeness to the findings of the two periods.

Hundreds of years separate the 12th from the 18th dynasties according to the accepted timeline, marked by chaos and the darkness of the 13th and 14th dynasties, foreign domination by the Hyksos in the 15th and 16th dynasties and, despite all this, the findings are similar:

"From the standpoint of artwork, architecture, language and books, Egypt after the reign of the Hyksos is extremely similar to Egypt during the Middle Kingdom." [227]

After the vicissitudes of past centuries, it is unlikely that Egypt would continue to function unchanged in the style of the 12th dynasty (the Middle Kingdom).

---

[227] J. Wilson, The History of the People of Israel, vol. 1, Jerusalem 1966, p. 192.

Consequently, if the findings from the beginning of the 18th dynasty are identical with those of the 12th dynasty, it is clear that we are referring to the same period broken into two under different names.

This is because the kings of this period bore dual names. (The double-record doesn't begin in the modern research. It in existence already in the 19th dynasty's kings-lists.)

Complementary Records

The Kings of the 12th dynasty are all called by the names Amenemhet or Senwosret and the Kings at the beginning of the 18th dynasty are generally named Amenhotep or Thutmose.

They all left many incomplete records so the type of records found from the 12th dynasty, are missing from the beginning of the 18th dynasty. And the type found in the 18th dynasty, are missing from the 12th dynasty.

A multitude of inscriptions from clerks and aristocrats, as well as heads of delegations acting outside Egypt and dating to the 12th dynasty have been found, but Egyptian royal inscriptions from this period are missing.

This is what Breasted writes: "The achievement of kings outside the limits of Egypt, have left more adequate records in these regions than their beneficent and prosperous rule in Egypt itself." [228] As to the capital city of Memphis, he continued: "Memphis and its ancient god were doubtless not neglected, but chance has left little evidence of the kingdom there." [229] The Royal City has disappeared and "the exact spot cannot now be identified". [230]

The lack of royal inscriptions recalls the obscure history of the 12th dynasty for "despite the many details we know from the literature of the period, we only know little of the acts of government in general." [231]

By contrast, at the beginning of the 18th dynasty, the capital cities are full of inscriptions from the Kings and their officers, but non-royal inscriptions that are so common during the 12th dynasty, have hardly been found.[232] "There was a whisper of public opinion." [233]

What caused the lack of non-royal inscriptions?

---

[228] J. H. Breasted, A History of Egypt, New York 1951, p. 180.
[229] ibid p. 196.
[230] ibid p. 157.
[231] T. Lambebin, Biblical Encyclopedia, Vol. 5, entry for Egypt, p. 254. (Hebrew)
[232] J. H. Breasted, A History of Egypt, New York 1951, p. 154.
[233] Ibid.

Breasted's answer was difficult because the "landed nobility had disappeared".[234] Could it really be true that there were no more aristocrats and people of standing to make inscriptions?

The situation during the 12th dynasty is even more surprising. Were there so many members of the aristocracy who glorified themselves, above the King who became overshadowed and didn't write anything?

In fact, the 12th dynasty and the beginning of the 18th dynasty are one dynasty, and the families of the King had two different sets of names. The Kings of the 12th dynasty bore the names Amenemhet and Senwosret which were used mainly by the subjects, and the names that are known to them as the names of the Kings at the beginning of the 18th dynasty were used by the Kings and his people.

This is why inscriptions from the 12th dynasty are in general inscriptions by clerks and aristocrats, and inscriptions at the beginning of the 18th dynasty are the Royal inscriptions.

Matching the Kings from Two Periods

These are the Kings of the Middle Kingdom and their parallels at the beginning of the New Kingdom:

XII Dynasty	Start of XVIII Dynasty
Amenemhet I	Ahmose I
Amenemhet II[235]	Amenhotep I
Senwosret I	Thutmose I
Senwosret II	Thutmose II
Senwosret III	Thutmose III[236]
Amenemhet III	Hatshepsut
Amenemhet IV	Amenhotep II

---

[234] ibid. p. 245.

[235] As for Amenmahet II, we have deviated from the normal order that sees him as the son of Senwosret I.

[236] Thutmose III was the fifth King of the 18th dynasty. However he was shunted aside after a short time by his partner Queen Hatshepsut. He remained King in name without any real authority, and he began to reign in practice only after the death of Hatshepsut.

The First King: Amenemhet I and Ahmose I

Amenemhet I began as the ruler of Thebes and took control of all the land through "Expulsion of some unknown enemy from Egypt". [237]

Ahmose I began as the king of Thebes and took control of all the land: "Ahmose I... the deliverer of Egypt from her foreign lord". [238]

The Third King – Senwosret I and Thutmose I

Senwosret I widened Egyptian rule beyond its borders, and when he set out on a journey of conquest in the south (Sudan), he reached the 3rd rapids of the Nile.[239]

Thutmose I is considered to be the founder of the Egyptian Empire. In his conquest in the South he is known to have reached past the second rapids. [240]

The Fourth King – Senwosret II and Thutmose II

The statues of Senwosret II show that he had a large body.

Thutmose II's body was found and indeed "he was heavyset". [241]

The Fifth King: Senwosret III and Thutmose III

Egyptian tradition shows Senwosret III was the greatest conqueror: "Around Senwostret III's name people forever clustered stories of war and conquest." [242]

The modern scholar on the other hand crowns Thutmose III with this title: "Thutmose... built the first real empire." [243]

In the channel that bypasses the first rapids of the Nile lies an inscription recording that it was dug by command of Senwosret III. [244] Another inscription at the same place proclaims that the same channel was dug at the command of Thutmose III. [245]

Further south in a place called Semneh are the ruins of a temple where there are two inscriptions of Senwosret III, which specifically detail the King's commandments concerning the sacrifices. [246]

An additional inscription recalls the same things which appear in the names of Thutmose and Senwosret together. The accepted explanation among scholars is

---

[237] J. H. Breasted, A History of Egypt, New York 1951, p. 154.
[238] ibid p. 225.
[239] M. R. Bunson, Encyclopedia of Ancient Egypt, New York 2002, p. 362.
[240] Ibid, p. 414.
[241] M. R. Bunson, Encyclopedia of Ancient Egypt, New York 2002, p. 363, 415.
[242] J. H. Breasted, A History of Egypt, New York 1951, p. 189.
[243] Ibid p. 320.
[244] J. H. Breasted, Ancient Records of Egypt, I. pp. 291-292.
[245] ibid 2, p. 260.
[246] ibid 1, p. 293.

that Thutmose renewed the boundary and the temple of Senwosret and he combined the older inscription in the new temple. But the problem is that "Of Senwosret III`s original temple nothing has ever been found, unless the 'second semneh tablet' was a part of it". [247]

Thutmose III wrote the names of the dead Kings that preceded him in his temple in Karnak. Missing from here are the names of the Kings of the 18th dynasty that preceded him and Kings Senwosret III and Amenemhet III from the 12th dynasty. [248]

Scholars find it hard to explain the inscription which is considered "a shortened list of the Kings and therefore has reduced value." [249]

When we identify Senwosret III with Thutmose III, this inscription is understood perfectly.

The Sixth King: Amenemhet III and the Queen Hatshepsut

Compared to all his predecessors **Amenemhet** III was the King during whose rule peace and prosperity reined in Egypt and the mines in Sinai became permanent dwellings. [250]

Unlike all her predecessors it is said of Queen Hatshepsut that during her rule there was peace and plenty in Egypt and she changed the mines in Sinai to permanent dwellings. [251]

In the temple built by Amenemhet III there is an inscription which describes his divine birth and how he inherited the kingdom from his father.

This inscription is identical, word for word, with one that was found in the temple of Hatshepsut with only one difference: instead the name of Amenemhet III the name Hatshepsut appears; therefore it would be correct to say: "The accompanying narrative of these events they copied from the old 12th Dynasty records of Amenemhet III`s." [252]

The likeness between Hatshepsut and Amenemhet III is especially evident when it comes to the artistic domain. The statues of Hatshepsut are considered to be an imitation of the statues of Amenemhet III. [253]

In a place called 'Serabit el-Hadem' in the Sinai Desert inscriptions written in ancient alphabetic scripts (proto sinaitic) have been discovered about whose date scholars disagree.

---

[247] ibid 2. p. 69.
[248] D. Redford, Pharaonic King-lists, Annals and day-books, Mississauga 1986, pp. 29-43.
[249] T. Lambedin, in Biblical Encyclopedia, Vol 5, p. 245. (Hebrew)
[250] J. H. Breasted, A History of Egypt, New York 1951, p. 190.
[251] ibid. p. 279-282.
[252] ibid. p. 273.
[253] C. Aldred, Egyptian Art, London 1994, p. 148,153.

Gardiner and his followers date them to Amenemhet III. Albright and his disciples date them to Hatshepsut and both schools offer persuasive proofs. [254]

If Hatshepsut was Amenemhet III, then both are right.

Statue of Amenemhet III - Hatshepsut

Summary: a comparison between the Kings at the beginning of the New Kingdom with the Kings of the Middle Kingdom shows a great likeness. This strengthens our view that we are speaking about the same Kings with different names.

The Middle of the New Kingdom

Until now we have dealt with the Kings at the beginning of the New Kingdom (the beginning of the 18th dynasty) and we have shown that they are only a copy of the Kings of the Middle Kingdom (the 12th dynasty) with different names.

---

[254] See: B. Sass, The Egyptian Middle Kingdom System for Writing Foreign Names and the Beginnings of the West-Semitic Alphabet, Eretz Israel 20 (1989), p. 44. (Hebrew) Compare with : Y. Beit Aryeh, New Discoveries in mine L at Serabit el-Hadem, Qadmoniot 53-54 (1981) , p. 37. (Hebrew)

What about those Kings who come after them (the continuation of the 18th and the 19th dynasties)?

From what we said above in chapters 8 to 9 ('reconstructed periods' and 'Kings and their doubles') it is clear that these Kings who apparently reigned only during the 14th and 13th centuries BCE, in fact ruled during the seventh and sixth centuries BCE, which is to say they are identical with the Kings of the 26th dynasty.

In the Fourth section we will deal with this period at length and bring more evidence.

[Consequently the 18th dynasty was not one entity, and there is significant discrepancy between the first and the last part of it.]

The 20th dynasty (12th century BCE) closed the last part of the New Kingdom. However, we have strong evidence that in reality this dynasty ruled during the 4th century BCE, and parallels the 28th to the 30th dynasties, which we will address in the next chapter.

Chapter 14: The New Kingdom in Egypt – an Imaginary Kingdom (part 3)

Evidence in the 'Peoples of the Sea' for dating the 20th Dynasty in the Persian Period – Evidence in the 'Peoples of the Sea' for dating the 21st Dynasty in the Persian/Hellenistic period - Additional Supports

The accepted date of the 20th and 21st dynasties in Egypt is the 12th to 10th centuries BCE, respectively. In his book: *'Peoples of the Sea'*, Velikovsky brings convincing arguments to prove that these dynasties are identical with the 28th to the 30th dynasties from the 4th century BCE marking the end of the Persian period and the beginning of the Ptolemic period. [255]

From here on we will quote the essence of his words, and bring additional supports that the Kings of the 20th dynasty lived during the Persian Period.

Evidence in the 'Peoples of the Sea' for dating the 20th Dynasty in the Persian Period

The 20th dynasty is identical with the 28th dynasty that rebelled against the Persians a few years before 400 BCE and ruled Egypt until 343 BCE. The proofs for this are as follows:

1. The best-known King of the 20th dynasty was Rameses III. According to the accepted view, he lived during the 12th century BCE, however in his palace there are Greek letters in the style of the 4th century BCE. (Greek writing only existed from the 8th century BCE).

From here we determine that Rameses III lived during the 4th century BCE.

2. Inscriptions showing a Greek influence have been found in graves on the seals of Rameses III, and his predecessor (King Sethnakhte). Excavators at the site disagreed whether to date it to the 12th century BCE which was the time of Rameses III (Griffis), or to the Greek period, as the inscriptions show (Nabil). However, if Rameses III lived during the 4th century BCE the findings are easily understood.

3. A papyrus from the time of Rameses IV tells what happened before the 20th dynasty began: "Yarsu, a certain Syrian chief. He set the whole land tributary before him."[256]

---

[255] I. Velikovsky, The Peoples of the Sea, New York 1982.
The quote here is with the generosity of Mrs. S Cogan, the daughter of Dr. Velikovsky.
[256] J. H. Breasted, Ancient Record of Egypt, part 4, London 1988, p. 199.

This corresponds to the situation in the generations before 404 BCE: The land was conquered by the Persians in 525 BCE, and afterwards a governor named 'Arsham' was appointed over all of Egypt. During the long reign of Arsham from 463 to 410 BCE he exploited the land.

4. Rameses III, who also bore the name 'Nakht-a-neb', tells in his inscriptions that he fought against the PRST and the Sea Peoples (Greek people) and he drove them out of Egypt.

On the other hand, the historian Diadorus tells us of an Egyptian King named Nactanebo I from the 4th century and his victory over the Persians and the Greeks. The commander of the Persian army was the governor of the Greek province of Tyaiy Drayahna, which means 'those from the sea'. Many details in the description of Diadorus are the same as those told in the tablets of Rameses III.

[We understand from this that the *PRST* against whom Rameses III fought were not the Philistines, as described in the history books, but the Persians.]

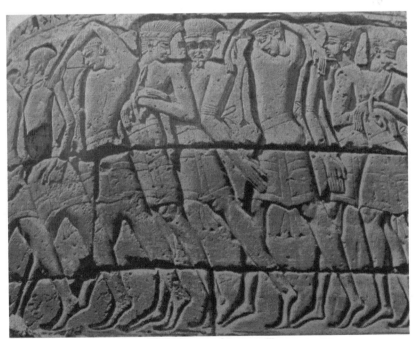

PRST prisoners of Rameses III

5. The main inheritors of Rameses III were his son Rameses IV and afterwards his nephew Rameses VI, who rebelled against his uncle. The main inheritors of

Nactanebo were his son Teos and his nephew Nactanebo II who rebelled against his uncle.

6. The Temple of Rameses III was built in a style extremely similar to the Ptolemeic Temples.

The likeness between them tells us that there wasn't a great difference in time between that of Rameses III and the Ptolemeic period.

Evidence in the 'Peoples of the Sea' for dating the 21st Dynasty in the Persian/Hellenistic period

The 21st dynasty is known as the priestly dynasty, and their period is considered to be a very poor period. Apart from sprucing up a few temples and dealing with those who had been embalmed, the Kings did almost nothing.

In truth we are talking about Egyptian governors under Persian rule during the 5th and 4th centuries BCE. They could glory in the title King of Egypt, because the Persian King ('King of Kings') did not worry about this.

The Evidence:

1. The records from the beginning of the 21st dynasty speak about the journey by a man named Wen-Amon to foreign lands to buy wood for the Temple of Amon. Similarly in the temple of Amon from the Persian period an inscription tells that the place was built by a great leader to the foreign lands, 'Wen-Amon'.

2. The second King in the 21st dynasty was Psusenne. His grave was discovered in Tanis and apparently it was built above the remains of a building from the Persian period, and from this it follows that it certainly was not earlier than this period. The man who investigated the site was forced to say that: "the Temple of Tanis was re-built anew many times until not even one stone remained from the original period".

3. Among the objects buried with Psusennes were inscriptions in the accepted style of the Ptolemein period (from the 4th to the 1st century BCE).

4. An inscription from the 21st dynasty tells at length how the priest Men-Heper-Ra received god, who came to visit the Temple of Amon. The description is identical to the smallest details with the writings of the historians about the visit of Alexander the Great to the Temple of Amun where he was decreed a god.

5. The last of the 21st dynasty was Siamun (whose name already then was not written as the name of a King), hid away all the mummies of the earlier Egyptian Kings. On the other hand, a very splendid grave was discovered from the Hellenistic period in which a very important man named Siamun was buried.

The Egyptologists do not identify Siamun from the 21st dynasty with the Siamun from the Hellenistic period, and see them as two completely different people. However, the decorations that crown the grave of Siamun the Hellenist are the same as the decorations in the papyrus written according to the command of Siamun from the 21st dynasty and from this we see that we're speaking about the same person.

Additional Supports

1. In the Temple of Khnum on the island of Yeb (Elephantine) in southern Egypt there is a gravestone of King Sethnakhte (the founder of the 20th dynasty), which tells of his rise to power. In it is told that he overcame his enemies, who were helped by the Asiatics (Sutu) and drove them out of Egypt. Accepted research doesn't tell us who these enemies were and which Asiatics fought beside them.

On the other hand, the situation at the beginning of the 4th century BCE when Egyptians drove the Persians out of Egypt fits the inscription exactly. At this time there was an army of Jewish mercenaries in the service of the Persians, who bore a deep grievance for many years for the priests of Hnum.

The victory over the Persians was also a victory against the Jews whom they hated, and these are the Asiatics (Sutu) mentioned in the inscription in the Temple of Hnum.

A letter from the Jews in Yeb to the Peha (governor) of Judah

The Egyptologist who investigated the inscriptions saw a strong likeness between the text in the inscription and what was known about the Jewish community of Yeb, but she was forced to abandon it because of the date.

"There are testimonies about the dispersal of the Jews of Yeb who acted as a mercenary army in Egypt, but to compare this reality with the inscription of Set-nacht is anachronism." [257] Nevertheless, it is not anachronism because Set-nakhte lived at the beginning of the 14th century BCE.

2. A statue of King Rameses III of the 20th dynasty was found in the fifth strata in Beth Shean. A great gate was found in the preceding 4th strata. FitzGerald (the

---

[257] P. Galpaz-Feller, "and I will give this people favour in the sight of the Egyptians", Beit Mikra 169 (2002), p. 137. (Hebrew)

investigator of the site) notes that "the gate was constructed with hewn stones in exactly the same style as the palace of the Kings of Israel in Samaria," but he did not try to explain how this could fit with the dating of the fifth level to the reign of Rameses III. [258]

This finding indicates that Rameses III lived during a later period in the palace of the Kings of Israel.

According to accepted dating there is no way to understand how the King of Israel (the 9th and 8th centuries BCE) could precede the days of Rameses III (12th century BCE).

In the section on the period of the Restoration we will see that the palace of the Kings of Israel in Samaria was in fact a palace from the middle of the Persian period (5th century BCE). The similarity with the great gate in Beth Shean teaches us that the great gate of Beth Shean is also to be dated to the middle of the Persian period.

From this we see that the later strata attributed to Rameses III, were at the end of the Persian period (4th century BCE).

To sum up the two chapters: 'The New Kingdom' in Egypt, which ruled continuously from the 16th to the 12th century BCE never existed, and is simply a reconstruction of Kings from three different periods.

The first part includes kings of the 12th dynasty, the middle part from kings of the 26th dynasty, and the last part from the Kings of the 28th to 30th dynasties.

---

[258] E. Yannai, Aspects of the physical culture in the Land of Israel during the period of the 20th Egyptian Dynasty, doctorate, Tel Aviv 1996, p. 59. (Hebrew)

Summary of Section 2

It is agreed that history began at the beginning of the first dynasty in Egypt in about the year 3000 BCE. All time lines have been set according to this date by archaeological researchers resulting in many contradictions with biblical accounts.

However, as the number of findings grows it becomes clearer that the true timeline is shorter. We have shown this in particular concerning the Late Bronze Age in the Land of Israel and the New Kingdom in Egypt, and further on we will see this in relation to other periods.

In order to keep this long timeline, they make apologetic excuses such as "a period from which there remain no grave stones and records" or, "a period in which past borders were supreme" or, "periods in which a person wore jewelry from 300 years previously", and so on.

It is clear that these excuses do not express the true reality; if we want to be honest we cannot escape the conclusion that the findings show that the ancient timeline must be reduced in length.

When we remove irrelevant parts from the timeline, we should look for traces of the biblical stories in findings from periods earlier than those in which it is accepted to search. Having done this we will reveal many details from what is told in the Bible, in the details of research.

Section 3: The Era of Israel and Judah

Chapter 15: In the Footsteps of Velikovsky - An analysis of the stories about King Shishak and the Queen of Sheba

The Journey of Shishak – Megiddo – Makat is Shechem – Why was Rehoboam in Shechem? - A proof from an Egyptian papyrus - Why was the Queen of Egypt called 'Queen of Sheba'?

The Journey of Shishak

In the Book of Kings, it is told how Jeroboam, the son of Nevat, rebelled against King Solomon and found refuge at the court of Shishak the King of Egypt. After the death of Solomon, he came back to the Land and established the Kingdom of Israel in Shechem.

Shishak conquered the Land a number of years later from Rehoboam the son of Solomon, and took spoils from the Temple.

In the chapter 'The Period of David and Solomon' we identified Shishak as the King Senwosret III, from the 12th dynasty. In the chapter 'The New Kingdom in Egypt – part 1' we showed that in the royal inscriptions this King is called Thutmose (III).[259] We should therefore expect that in the inscriptions of Thutmose III there will be a description of the looting of the holy Temple.

Indeed, Thutmose III tells about his conquest of the Land of Israel from the King of the city of 'Kadesh', who was extremely rich. The list of booty features gold and copper- rimmed altars, golden tables and golden lamps.

Particularly persuasive is the parallel between a disk that appears in the inscription of Thutmose III with the additional sign that 300 objects like this were taken as booty.

In the Scriptural description of the spoils seized by Shishak we read: "He took away all the treasures... including the gold shields Solomon had made", (Kings1, 1:26) "Solomon made... 300 smaller shields". (ibid 10:17)

According to this the King of Kadesh ('Kadesh' mean 'the holy'), against whom Thutmose was warring, is Rehoboam the King of Jerusalem 'The holy city' and the pictured vessels are the vessels of the Temple as Velikovsky already demonstrated.[260]

---

[259] In the paragraph: 'Matching the Kings from two periods'.
[260] I. Velikovsky, Ages in Chaos, New York 1952, p. 143-174.

Thutmose III

Megiddo

However, there is one surprising detail in the story of the Egyptian King. The inscription says that the King of Kadesh returned to Megiddo (at the furthermost point of the Jezreel Valley).

Thutmose conquered Megiddo, and with its fall he captured the whole northern part of the Land of Israel. However, the King of Kadesh managed to flee in good time. Several years later, the city of Kadesh was also conquered.

If Rehoboam was King of Kadesh this means that Rehoboam was hiding in Megiddo. This is not understood. Why did Rehoboam leave Jerusalem and move to Megiddo?

This is not all in the inscription of Thutmose. There is a long list of the cities in the Land of Israel headed by Kadesh (Jerusalem) and Megiddo. Where do the Scriptures hint that Megiddo was more important than the other cities and had a status almost equal to Jerusalem?

However, did Thutmose really conquer Megiddo?

Makkat is Shechem

The name of the city in the Egyptian inscriptions is Makkat, and since the letters are sometimes switched between K and G, or T and D, the investigators came to the conclusion that we are discussing Megiddo.

The incident further records that on the way to Makkat the Egyptian army turned north until they reached the spring of *Kana* river which is south of Makkat. Since Makkat has been identified with Megiddo, they identified the *Kana* river with the el-Fah stream which flows south of Megiddo (and therefore its name on today's maps is Kina river). [261]

However, there is a stream in the Land of Israel known as Kana river and it flows south of Shechem and not south of Megiddo (Joshua 17:7-9). From here we see Makkat is Shechem and not Megiddo.

This indicates that we should look for the name Makkat in the area of Shechem where we found in the wording of the verse: "Mikhmetat, that lieth before Shechem... And the border went westward unto the river Kanah" (Joshua 17:7-9).

The Mikhmetat of Shechem, is Makkat in the Thutmose inscription.

Why was Rahoboam in Shechem?

If Makkat is Shechem we understand that Rahoboam came there to carry out the coronation ceremony, as it is written: "Rahoboam went to Shechem because where all the people of Israel had gathered to make him King". (Kings I 12:1)

---

[261] There are those want to identify the *Kina* with the *Gina*, which according to their opinion is *Jenin* [Na'aman, Royal Estates in the Jezereel Valley in the Late Bronze Age and Under the Israelite Monarchy, Eretz Israel 15 (1981), p. 143 (Hebrew)].
On this we can only say, that the River that comes out of Jenin does not pass south of Megiddo, and therefore no connection can be made between them.

We also understand why the city had such an important standing, since it was supposed to be the Royal city. In the Book of Kings, it says how Rahoboam fled from Shechem and rule over the entire north of the Land passed to Jeroboam, who came from the court of the King of Egypt.

Several years later Jerusalem also surrendered to Egypt (ibid 25). This is similar to what is said in the inscription of Thutmose about the escape of the King of Kadesh from Makkat and the defeat of Kadesh afterwards.

The Book of Kings and the Thutmose's inscription tell the same story.

Proof from an Egyptian papyrus

An inscription in another Egyptian document contains a riddle about knowledge of the Land of Israel, leads to the conclusion that Makkat is Shechem. This is what it says: "The crossing of the Jordan River, how to ford it? Show me the way to Makkat, which is above it."

'Makkat' therefore is found above the crossing over the Jordan. If Makkat were Megiddo the sentence would not be understood, since Megiddo is not located above the Jordan River crossing. Therefore, someone wanted to change the text in the record: "The papyrus has mixed up the name Kina with the name Jordan." [262] One given answer is that the Jordan is found "Under 'the umbrella' of Megiddo. However the distance is almost 35 km". [263]

The plain answer is that Makkat is Shechem. The crossing over the Jordan River (the Damiya Bridge) indeed goes up to Shechem.

The record we have brought from the chapter 'The period of David and Solomon' also shows that the place which the Egyptian army besieged is Shechem: "His Majesty proceeded with great success in the direction of the King's Palace of Yeh, and Shechem fell together with the Rethenu (Land of Israel) miserable".

Why was the Queen of Egypt called 'Queen of Sheba'?

In the generation that preceded Thutmose III the ruler over Egypt was his stepmother, Queen Hatshepshut.

If we have proven that King Thutmose III reigned during the rule of Rehoboam, the son of Solomon, so Hatshepsut reigned during the time of King Solomon.

During the rule of King Solomon, the Queen of Sheba visited Jerusalem. This is how Josephus Flavius explains it to us: "During those days the Queen was a

---

[262] Y. Aharoni, Eretz Israel in the late Canaanite Period and in the Age of Israeli Settagements,   in:
Y. Rapel (Ed.) History of Eretz-Israel, Tel Aviv 1979, p. 120. (Hebrew)
[263] D. Amir, The Galilee in the Bronze Age (The Canaanite Period), Dan 1997, p.117. (Hebrew)

woman who ruled over Egypt and Cush - Ethiopia. She was gripped by a desire to see Solomon and set out on the journey towards him." [264]

From what we have said up until now it is clear that the Queen of Sheba is Hatshepshut. On this subject there is a wonderful correlation between the Egyptian records and what is told in the Scriptures. On the walls of a grand temple that Hatshepsut built, the great events of her life are explained in vast pictures.

This was not a tale of conquests or victories, but a royal journey the Queen made to a foreign land 'Punt' that took place on the same basis as is described in the Scriptures: the visit of the Queen of Sheba, as Velikovsky shows at length. [265]

The Royal journey to Punt

However, a serious question remains here, waiting for an answer: The land of 'Sheba' is in the southwestern part of the Arabian archipelago (today part of Yemen). [266] Why then do the Scriptures call Hatshepshut the Queen of Sheba, and not 'the Queen of Egypt'?

What made her different from the other rulers of Egypt who were called by the name of the land they ruled over? It is likely that the reason for this change is the special present the Queen brought with her: gold and perfume.

---

[264] Josephus Flavius, Antiquities of the Jews, Book 8, 1:5.

[265] I. Velikovsky, Ages in Chaos, New York 1952, pp. 103-141.

[266]There are those who identified the land of Sheba with Somalia in Africa, west of Yemen across the Red Sea. Nevertheless whole parts of Yemen and Somalia grow Morr and Lebona (the perfumes of antiquity).

The Scriptures give this present much importance: "almost five tons of gold and a very large quantity of spices and jewels. The amount of spices she gave him was by far the greatest that he had ever received at any time." (Kings1, 10:10)

The primary source of spices during antiquity was 'the land of Sheba' in the south of Arabia: "The south of Arabia was the main supplier of many types of spice." [267] And 'Sheba' was also the source of gold and jewels. (Isaiah 60: 6; Ezekiel 27: 22; Psalm 72:15)

This explains to us the moniker 'the Queen of Sheba' that was given to the Queen of Egypt, since as we have seen, the Scriptures attach great importance to her presence, and see her coming as an unparalled event. Since this gift was bought from 'the land of Sheba', they called the queen who bought them the Queen of Sheba.

---

[267] I. Efal, Biblical Encyclopedia, Vol. 7, p. 461. (Hebrew)

Chapter 16: Who was the Woman that Murdered when built Jericho?

Murder in the middle of construction– Hiel from Bethel – the End of the Matter

Murder in the middle of Construction

In the above chapter referring to Joshua's conquest of Jericho, excavations have uncovered findings from the time of the city's conquest by the Children of Israel which show that the place was desolate until it was rebuilt hundreds of years later.

The excavations revealed that the walls of the new city were built in a form that raises eyebrows:

"There is another curious feature which suggests that the building of this great bank was spread over an appreciable period of time... Between the period at which the bank was thrown up, and its final completion, there was a pause long enough for the rooms to be built and lived in for quite a little time... For some reason its construction was suspended." [268]

What was the cause for the delay in the building? This is not known.

"A shocking thing was revealed, in these rooms adding a final touch of mystery" by the discovery of a skeleton in one of the rooms. It is the skeleton of a woman of about thirty years of age, and she met her death by decapitation, the vertebre of the neck being severed."

Why was this woman killed? The investigator guesses: "Maybe she was responsible for building the little shack, which incurred the wrath of the builders when they returned to finish building the defences." [269]

This is surprising. Couldn't they have evicted the woman instead? Why did this woman choose to set up house inside a wall that was being built?

In any case the hut upset the building of the wall, and evidence that a murder had been committed showed that the wall's construction had not proceeded smoothly and that the builders were faced with strong resistance which they had to overcome.

Who was the woman who objected to the wall, and why?

---

[268] K. M. Kenyon, Digging up Jericho, London 1957, p. 217.
[269] Ibid.

Hiel from Bethel

This parable in the Scriptures gives a satisfactory explanation for the events that occurred when the wall was being built and of the identity of the builder of the new city.

His name is Hiel from Bethel, and the Scriptures tell us that he built Jericho during the time of King Ahab. (Kings 1, 16:34) This act came in defiance of Joshua's command forbidding the rebuilding of Jericho, and curse on anyone who dared to rebuild the city.

"Anyone who tries to rebuild the city of Jericho will be under the Lord curse. Whoever lays the foundations will lose his oldest son; whoever builds the gates will lose his youngest". (Joshua 6:26)

The Book of Kings tells that Joshua's curse was fulfilled by Hiel who buried his sons one after the other. When Hiel's wife saw what was happening to her children, she opposed with all her might her husband's plans. She waged a campaign on the building site and held back the works with her body.

This is the reason for the delay in building the wall, and the skeleton with its decapitated head teaches us how in the end Hiel overcame the problem: the woman who was murdered in the wall was his wife and it continued to be rebuilt over her dead body.

The End of the Matter

The Scriptures tell us that Tel Jericho was built at the price of Hiel's dead children and archaeological findings show also at the price of their mother's life.

The settlement on Tel Jericho continued until the end of the Middle Bronze Age (the end of the Kingdom of Israel).

The end of the city, which began its existence by spilling clean blood, was not good. Excavations reveal that in the conflagration of that era, many people were buried in it temporarily and afterwards the city was destroyed and burned. This is how the site's excavator writes:

"It seems probable that there must have been some exceptional circumstance to account for so many burials at the same time... The presumption is that it was some virulent disease. Jericho must have suffered a plague and then a fire." [270]

The excavations did not find on the tel a city from a later date.[271] Tel Jericho remains cursed to this very day.

---

[270] Ibid. pp. 254-255.
[271] Ibid p. 260-265.

Summary: the excavations at Jericho found the walls of the city built by Hiel from Bethel at the price of the lives of his sons. They found also the remains of the body of a woman who tried to prevent the building and was killed.

It seems this could be the mother of the children of Hiel, who resisted the construction of the walls with her own body and was therefore murdered.

Chapter 17: The Savior during the time of Jehoahaz

The Problem of the Inscription of Shashank –The Problem of King So – The Solution to the Problem of the Inscription of Shashank – The Solution to the Problem of King So

The Problem of the Inscription of Shashank

During the period of the First Temple, kings of Libyan descent ruled Egypt, and the 22nd and 23rd dynasties of this period are called 'the Libyan Dynasty'.

The founder of the 22nd dynasty was *Shashank* I, and in his inscription the cities of the Land of Israel are described as subjugated to him. A fragment from a gravestone that was found in Megiddo in which his name is engraved teaches us that this was not vain glory.

On the other hand, the Scriptures tell of the Egyptian King *Shishack*, who conquered the Land of Judah at the time of King Rehoboam, son of Solomon.

Because of the similarity in the name, *Shashank* has initially been identified with *Shishak* of the Scriptures, but this has presented a problem:

The Scriptures say that *Shishak* conquered the fortified cities of the King of Judah, (Chronicles II 12:4) whereas the cities mentioned in the inscription of *Shoshank* are the cities of the Kingdom of Israel and settlements of the Negev desert, while the cities of the Kingdom of Judah are missing.[272]

What is the reason for this discrepancy between the description in the Scriptures and the inscription of the Egyptian King?

The problem of King So

In the generations of the Kings of Egypt in the period of the First Temple there is an additional problem with the last King of Israel, King Hoshea.

As it is written in the Book of Kings, Hoshea was subservient to the King of Assyria. According to the Book of Kings he tried to cast off his yoke, and asked for help from the King of Egypt and was punished for this by the Assyrian king. This is the wording of the Scriptures: "Hoshea sent messengers to So, King of Egypt, asking for his help, and stopped paying the annual tribute to Assyria". (Kings II 17:4)

The problem in this story is that during the days of Hoshea (the days of the 23rd dynasty) Egypt was split into a number of principalities, and they did not have one

---

[272] B. Mazar, Canaan and Israel, p. 233-244. (Hebrew)

King. How could the Scriptures tell us about So, the King of Egypt, at the time when there was no King in Egypt?

The following answers to this question have been suggested.

1. The verse does not intend to speak about the whole of Egypt but a kingdom by the name of Masry, in Northern Arabia. [273]

2. 'So' is not the name of the king of Egypt, but the name of the city Sais. [274]

3. 'So' is the name of the Egyptian army chief and not of the King. [275]

These are all weak answers. Meanwhile the identity of So, the King of Egypt, still requires an explanation.

The Solution to the Problem of the Inscription of Shashank

The dating of the Libyan dynasty (945-718 BCE) parallels almost exactly the date of the Kingdom of Israel (945-721 BCE). [276]

Though the dynasty lasted more than 220 years, there are clear records only of the first 90 years. The remaining years, we are forced to say, were a lame-duck period without traces.

However, if we consider only the findings that exist and remove the 'dark age' from the timeline, then the Libyan Dynasty reigned only for 90 years which parallels the last generations of the Kings of Israel (805-718 BCE). [277]

If so, the founder of the Libyan dynasty, Shashank I, did not live at the time of Rehoboam at all, but more than 100 years after him, during the time of the House of Jehu.

During this period, the Kingdom of Israel suffered from the Arameans who were very cruel. As it is written of King Jehoahaz the son of Jehu: "Then Jehoahaz prayed to the Lord... And the Lord answered his prayer. The Lord sent Israel a savior who freed them from the Arameans". (Kings II, 13:4-5)

---

[273] J. H. Breasted, A History of Egypt, New York 1951, p. 549.
[274] H. Tadmor, Biblical Encyclopaedia, Vol. 4, p. 257. (Hebrew)
[275] S. Yeivin, Biblical Encyclopedia, Vol. 5, p. 1002-1003. (Hebrew)
[276] We have used the accepted numbers for the end of the period of the Kingdom of Israel. However see further on in the chapter: 'When did Sennacherib Lay Siege to Jerusalem?' and the Summary chapter.
[277] When the Libyan dynasty began, close to 804 BCE, it teaches us also the findings in the city of Byblos in Lebanon. See: D. Rohl, Attest of Time, London 1986, p. 370-371.

The Scriptures don't explain who Israel's savior was and there are those who think it was Adad-Nirari, the King of Assyria, who fought with Aram during the time of Jehoahaz. [278]

Shashank I, to whom the Kingdom of Israel was subjected, was the Savior who conquered the land at the time of Jehoahaz and freed it of Aram. His rule was beneficial, and did not last long. Afterwards "they lived in peace, as before". (ibid)

The solution to the problem of King So

Now that we discovered that the Libyans actually ruled more than 100 years later, we can also identify the Egyptian King *So* to whom Hoshea, the last of the Kings of Israel, sent for.

According to the amended timeline Hoshea's rule corresponded with the time of the Egyptian King Osorkon II, and he was the Egyptian King that the Scriptures call in this condensed form 'So'.

We have identified the King, and we have even found his footsteps in Samaria.

The excavators who dug up the ruins of the city of Samaria found the ivories that were in the palace of the King of Israel. As it is written: "Ahab... his palace decorated with ivory" (Kings I, 22:39). Among these vessels were found also "fragments of a jar on which was incised the name of the Egyptian pharaoh Osorkon II." [279]

This is the same King So whose help Shomron vainly relied upon. [280]

---

[278] Y. Aharoni, Eretz Israel in Biblical Times - A Geographical History, the revised edition edited by I. Efal, Jerusalem 1987 p. 265. (Hebrew)

[279] N. Avigad, The New Encyclopedia of Archaeological Excavations in the Holy Land, Jerusalem 1993, p. 1304.

[280] Velikovsky identified So with Shashank I (Ages in Chaos, p. 174-176).
However this identification is not logical, because a few years after the destruction of Samaria the 25th dynasty began to reign in Egypt, of which there are records in Egypt, and one of its Kings is mentioned also in the Scriptures (Taharaka). On the other hand there is a clear record that after Shoshank I, his inheritors reigned for decades. If Shoshank was So, and he lived during the period of the destruction of Samaria, when did his inheritors live?

Chapter 18: When did Sennacherib Besiege Jerusalem?

The Expeditions of Conquest by the Kings of Assyria -- the Problem with the Timeline – More Problems – A solution to the Problems – The Kings of Israel and Judah – The Mesha Stella - The 19th Dynasty in Egypt – the Gezer Calendar - When was the Exodus from Egypt?

This chapter examines the chronological problem from the period of King Hezekiah. Its solution bears implications for other biblical and historical issues.

JUDAH	ASSYRIA	EGYPT
Hezekiah 727-698	Shalmaneser 727-722	
	Sargon 722-705	
Menashe 698-643	Sennacherib 705-681	Taharaka 688-663
	681-669	
Amon 643-641	Ashurbanipal and his successors 669-612	
Josiah 641-609	Nineveh Destroyed 612	
	End of Assyrian Kingdom 609	

The timeline inherited by Hezekiah and his successors (All dates are BCE)

The Expeditions of Conquest by the Kings of Assyria

Shalmaneser, the King of Assyria, came with his army to conquer Samaria, the capital of the Kingdom of Israel. The city refused to yield and Shalmaneser laid siege to it.

This occurred during the fourth year of rule by Hezekiah the King of Judah. "In the fourth year of Hezekiah's reign, Emperor Shalmaneser of Assyria invaded Israel and besieged Samaria". (Kings II, 18:9)

After two years the Assyrians were able to conquer the city of Samaria for "in the sixth year of Hezekiah… Samaria was captured." (Kings II, 18:19)

The Scriptures do not reveal who conquered the city; however, from Assyrian records we know that it was King Sargon, the successor to Shalmaneser. [281]

Later, in the 14th year of Hezekiah's rule, Sennacherib the son of Sargon, conquered most of the Kingdom of Judah, but was forced to withdraw without being able to conquer Jerusalem. During the course of this expedition a rumor reached him that King Tirhaka had come out to fight with him. (Kings II 18-19; Isaiah 36-37; Chronicles II 32)

We learn of this matter in an inscription by Sennacherib that relates his journey to the Land of Israel during the fourth year of his reign. Here he describes his failure to conquer Jerusalem as a success: "Hezekiah himself I made prisoner in Jerusalem like a bird in a cage." [282]

The Problem with the Timeline

This story reveals a serious chronological problem, since the fourteenth year of Hezekiah was in 714 BCE, whereas Sennacherib began to rule only nine years afterwards, in the year 705 BCE.

Tirhaka (Taharaka) ruled only 26 years later in the year 688 BCE. How could the Scriptures tell us about Kings Sennacherib and Tirhaka at a date much earlier than the beginning of their reign?

A number of explanations have been offered, [283] but no solutions have been found that fit the language of the biblical verses.

Furthermore, it appears from the Scriptures that from Shalmaneser's siege (during the 4th year of Hezekiah's rule) until Sennacherib's expedition (in the 14th year of Hezekiah's rule) 10 years passed; but from Assyrian sources it appears that at least 20 years passed (from the time of Shalmaneser until the 4th year of Sennacherib, in which the expedition took place).

---

[281] L. Oppenheim, Babylonian and Assyrian Historical Texts, by: Pritchard (ed.) ANET, Princeton 1969, p. 284.

[282] Ibid, p. 288.

[283] H. Tadmor, The History of the People of Israel, vol. 2, p. 47-48; I. Efal, Byblical Encyclopedia, Vol. 5, p. 1065-1069; G. Galilee, Israel and Syria, Haifa 2001, p. 100-111. (Hebrew)

More problems

The chronological problems during these generations are not restricted to the Scriptures alone. We can add another two:

1. Assyrian records testify that during the second year Ashurbanipal (667 BCE) the Assyrian king fought Taharaka, and drove him out from northern Egypt to which he could never return.

Yet we find there an inscription from 664 BCE which cites Taharaka as the King.
[284]

How could the inscription call Taharka King when Ashurbanipal was ruling over the land?

2. The Assyrians named their years after ministers of the kingdom, each year in the name of another minister.

A register has been found listing the names of the years from 910 to 649 BCE. The names of the years from then on are not mentioned in the list but are revealed from other records and there is no correlation between the number of years and the number of names:

"However, 648 to 612 requires 37 eponyms while the number at attaste PC eponyms is ~50." [285] How could 50 years fit into 37 years?

A Solution to the Problems

The answers to all these problems are that Israelites have two New Years: in the month of 'Nissan' in the spring and in the month of 'Tishrei' in autumn.

Also the Babylonian New Year (the Aquito) is celebrated twice a year at certain periods.

It seems logical that for a number of the Israelite and gentile kings, a year of six months was used, from Nissan to Tishrei and from Tishrei to Nissan, such that these 55 years of the kingdom of Menashe were in fact only 28 years.

This year was to be used by the kings of Assyria: Shalmaneser, Sargon, Sennacherib, and Ashurbanipal (or his successors).

The custom was to celebrate the New Year every six months and to give a new name to the year. We now get the following dates:

---

[284] J. H. Breasted, A History of Egypt, New York 1952, p. 557.
[285] R. Whiting,The post canonical and extra canonical eponyms, by A. R. Millard, The Eponyms of the Assyrian Empire, Helsinki 1994, p. 72.

JUDAH	ASSYRIA	EGYPT
Hezekiah 699-670	Shalmaneser 699-696	
	Sargon 696-688	
	Sennacherib 688-676	Tirhakah 688-663
Menashe 670-642	Essarhedon 676-664	
Amon 642-641	Asherburnipa and his Successors 664-612	Psametek 663-610
Josiah 641-609		

Chronological Timeline for Hezekiah and his successors - An adjusted timeline (all years are BCE).

Now all the problems disappear, and this is the order of events. During the year 696 BCE, which was the 4th year of Hezekiah, Shalmaneser laid siege to Samaria and in the year 694 the city was conquered by Sargon.

In the year 686 which was the 14th year of Hezekiah's rule and the 4th year of Sennacherib's (in half years), the journey of Sennacherib to Judah took place, during which Sennacherib fought also against Tirhaqa. In the 663rd year, Ashurbanipal drove Tirhaqa out.

From here on begins the period of Psametek I who, as mentioned later on, (in the chapter on the generations after El-Amarna) this was not the name of a single king, rather a period in which a number of kings reigned.

The explanation for the high number of years emerges from the records of the last days of the Assyrian empire; the registered years, or part of them, do not mean a complete year, but rather half a year of six months.

[We will show that this was also the custom in much earlier periods, during the time of Zimri Lim, King of the city of Mari in Mesopotamia (the time of Hammurabi). From a comparison of the inscriptions of other kings it seems that he reigned no more than 18 years, but in his city we find an inscription that he reigned 32 years. [286] How can this be? Evidently he also counted his years in periods of six months.]

The Kings of Israel and Judah

The Children of Israel also had periods in which they counted years in sequences of six months. We have shown this above for the king *Menashe*, though this was also the custom during the time of Uziyahu, King of Judah, and Jeroboam II King of Israel until the time of Ahaz, King of Judah and Peckach, King of Israel (inclusive).

Evidence for this is found in the verse: "During the 27th year of Jeroboam, the king of Israel, Azariayahu reigned". (Kings I, 50:1) The commentator, known as the *Redak,* asks: "Behold in the year 14 of Jeroboam the king Azariah ruled?" While the *Malbim* adds: "In this verse all of the mighty men have not found their hands".

Each commentator explains it in his own way. However, after having said that in the time of Jeroboam every year was numbered as two separate years, it is clear that the 14th year has been renumbered into the 27th or 28th year. Another mystery is also solved from the Book of Kings where it is written that at least 20 years separated kings *Menachem* and *Hoshea,* yet these two kings appear in the inscriptions of the Assyrian king Tiglat Pileser who reigned only 18 years, and this is of course impossible.

Once again the explanation is that during the time of Menachem and his successors years were counted as short years, whereas Tiglath Pileser counted them as long years.

Accordingly, only 10 years separated *Menachem* and *Hoshea,* so they could both be mentioned as ruling at the time of Tiglat Pileser.

Pepole Exailed. Scene from a relief of the wars of Tiglat Pileser.

---

[286] H. Tadmor, The History of the People of Israel, vol. 2, p. 47-48.

The Mesha Stella

Our proposition that sometimes the year lasts only six months, also solves the well-known problem from the time of the First Temple of the inscription known as the 'Mesha Stella'.

The Book of Kings tells us how the Moabite king, Mesha, who was subservient to Israel, liberated himself after the death of Ahab. Jehoram the son of Ahab unsuccessfully tried to restore his rule over Moab. (Kings II, 1:1; Ibid 3:4-27) Several years later Jehoram died, and the whole royal household was wiped out. (KingsII, chapters 9-10)

On the eastern side of the Jordan River a stone was discovered bearing a Hebrew inscription of Mesha the King of Moab, which says "As for Omri, King of Israel, he humbled Moab many years, and his son followed him and said I will humble Moab, but I beheld his fall and his house fall."

Omri, it seems, is Ahab, [287] and his son is Jehoram who, when he died the house of Omri passed from the world. The inscription continues: "Omri occupied the land of Medaba and dwelled there in his time and half the time of his son, forty years".

This is astonishing, since all the days of Ahab and Jehoram together do not add up to 40 years. [288]

The scholars solve the contradiction lightly. One scholar writes that "forty years is a common expression that means one generation".[289] Another scholar writes: "This number is doubtful, we cannot use it to teach us about the time Israel ruled over Moab." [290]

After seeing in a number of ancient inscriptions that the term 'year' means six months, the Mesha inscription is easy to understand. Mesha means forty years, the half short years of six months or, twenty full years. This was exactly the time that Ahab and his son ruled Moab.

---

[287] In Assyrian inscriptions all the Kings of Israel are called by name: "The Kings of the House of Omri," including the House of Jehu, who were not descendants of Omri.

[288] One explanation is that Mesha's inscription is about Omri and Ahab and not about Ahab and Jehoram, is that we are discussing the Moabite rebellion halfway through Ahab's reign (after which Ahab went back and re-conquered Moab). The words: "I beheld his fall and his house fall" do not support this explanation.
As far as we are concerned it makes no difference since the reign of Omri and Ahab also did not reach forty years.

[289] A. Mazar, Biblical Encyclopedia, Vol. 4, p. 922.

[290] J. Leever, ibid, p. 717.

The 19th Dynasty in Egypt

Until now we have seen that in the Hebrew and Assyrian inscriptions the word year, often means a year of six months and this is also true in the Egyptian inscriptions.

This was so in the 19th dynasty in Egypt, which as we will see in Part 4 lasted less than 60 years, whereas documents from this period speak of at least a 108 years. Here too, the answer to this dilemma lies in two types of years.

Inscriptions of the 19th dynasty also used the typology of counting six months to a year and this is why we find a double number of years.

The Gezer Calendar

Our discussion of the system of counting that calls for six months 'year' begs a question: why hasn't a clear ruling been reached on this matter?

In order to answer this question lets look at the 'Gezer calendar' which prescribes the method of counting used in the past, but for which, too, no evidence was preserved.

In this calendar, discovered in excavations in 1908, the names of eight agricultural months of the year are inscribed:

1) yarcho (2 months) of harvesting.

2) yarcho (2 months) of sowing.

3) yerach (month) of late sowing.

4) yerach (month) of picking the flax.

5) yerach (month) of harvesting barley.

6) yerach (month) of harvesting (wheat?).

7) yarcho (2 months) of harvesting grapes.

8) yarcho (2 months) of harvesting pigs

Looking at the list we see that there are four ordinary months (yerach) and four double months (yarcho) altogether 12 months.

Before this calendar was uncovered we knew nothing about the existence of a double month (yarcho) and yet there is no doubt that it existed.

A year of six months also existed, but without analyzing ancient writings, we did not know of its existence.

When was the Exodus from Egypt?

Solomon started to build the holy Temple in the fourth year of his reign, which was 480 years after the Exodus from Egypt. (Kings I, 6:1) If we calculate the number of years in which the Kings of the First Temple ruled, it emerges that if the construction of the Temple began approximately in 965 BCE, then the Exodus from Egypt can be fixed around the year 1445 BCE.

However, following on from the previous chapter it appears that during the time of Uziahu to Ahaz and during the time of Menashe it was customary to count a year of six months.

If the periods of Menashe and Uziahu to Ahaz are reduced by half this shortens the timeline of the First Temple by 40 years and fixes the start of its construction to approximately 925 BCE.

From here we see that the Exodus from Egypt occurred 480 years before the construction of the Temple, and should be dated around 1405 BCE.

Summary: If we recognize that several Kings in antiquity had a year of only six-months this solves the chronological dating of Sennacherib's expedition and other chronological problems, and shortens the length of the ancient period of history.

(For further see Appendix 15)

"2 months of harvesting. 2 months of sowing..." – The Gezer Calendar

Section 4: The period of El-Amarna

Chapter 19: 'Habiru'

The El-Amarna letters –Theory A: Habiru are the Hebrews - Theory B: Habiru are People without an Identity - Solution to the Mystery of the Habiru – Summary

The El-Amarna Letters

One of the most well-known discoveries from the ancient era is a bundle of letters in the Akkadian language referred to as the El-Amarna Letters belonging to the archives of King Amenhotep IV, which were unearthed in Tel-el-Amarna in Egypt.

One El-Amarna Letter

Amenhotep III and Tiy – parents of Amenhotep IV

This King who, according to the accepted timeline, lived during the 14th century BCE also ruled over the Land of Israel and Syria. His reign was undermined because of an invasion into from the North by an army of Hittites (a people who dwelt in Anatolia – Turkey) who conquered many cities and burnted them down as well as by the kingdoms of Babylon and Mittani.

Most of the El-Amarna letters are from the Kings of the cities in the Land of Israel and Syria, addressed to their master the King of Egypt. In their letters they continuously complain about their country folk who were becoming traitors, and they were rebelling against the King.

A number of the letters mention an enemy by the name of Habiru or Sa-Gaz (some read Apiru instead Habiru) who was burning the cities of the land.

Who are these Habiru?

Theory A: Habiru are the Hebrews

According to the Scriptures the Land of Israel was conquered during the 14th century BCE. Hence some identify the Habiru/SA.GAZ as the Hebrews who were conquering the Land under the leadership of Joshua.

The identification of the Habiru with the Hebrews runs into a number of difficulties:

1. The Habiru fought in places which the Hebrews did not reach. For example, one of the main complaints against the Habiru comes from the King of the city of Byblos (Gubla) north of Beirut, who tells how the Habiru conquered all of the surrounding cities, and they were already laying siege to his walls. [291]

The land of Byblos was never conquered by the Children of Israel as it is written: "This is the remaining country...and the land of Byblos (Giblites)" (Joshua 13: 2-5).

2. The Habiru were at peace with several cities, such as with the Kings of Gezer, Ashkelon and Lachish which are mentioned as collaborating with the Habiru. [292]

Tel Lachish

These things don't match with what is said about the Children of Israel at the time of Joshua: "There was not a city that made peace with the Children of Israel, save the Hivites inhabitants of Gibeon". (Ibid 11:19)

3. The Book of Joshua does not mention or even hint that the Land was under Egyptian rule.

Theory B: Habiru are People without an Identity

Another opinion is that the Habiru are not a people, but a moniker given to people that does not belong to any ethnic group, state or geographic entity.

---

[291] W. Moran, Amarna Letters, 1992, p. 142 ff.
[292] Ibid, p. 328 (letter 287)

This explanation, even though it is current in research studies today, is problematic, because the letters show that these Habiru had a strong army including ships, something that does not fit in at all with a leaderless rabble but is characteristic of a well-organized state entity. Let us quote a number of sentences.

The King of Jerusalem writes: "The strong hand of the king took the land of Nahrima and the land of Kasi, but now the Apiru have taken the very cities of the king. Not a single mayor remains to the king." [293]

A message was sent even from the Lebanese coast: "so they go on taking (territory for themselves)". [294] "if this year no archers come out, then all lands will be joined t(o the Apir)u. If there are no archers then let a ship fetch your men." [295]

On the other hand, one of the kings, who rebelled against Pharaoh and tried to join up with many of the Habiru, sent this message: "let us drive out the mayors from the country so that (it can) be joined to the Apiru... Then will our sons and daughters be at peace forever." [296]

It is unconvincing to our minds that these sentences can be referring to roving bands of robbers. The Habiru must be one of the great powers competing with Egypt. Who are they?

Solution to the Mystery of the Habiru

An analysis of the other records leads to the conclusion that the Habiru are the Hittites. In a prisoner exchange agreement that was made between the King of the Hittites and King of the city of Ugarit the King of the Hittites obligates himself:

"If a subject of the King of Ugarit departs and enters the territory of the Habiru of my Majesty. I, Great King, will not accept him but will return him to the King of Ugarit." [297]

If the King of the Hittites obligates himself to bring back all the people who ran away to the lands of the Habiru it is logical that the Habiru are the Hittites.

Also in other El-Amarna letters it is shown that the Habiru were the Hittites. In the area called Amqu in Lebanon one of the Kings reports: "Apiru (Habiru) forces waged war against me and captured the cities of the king, and sent it up in flames." [298]

---

[293] Ibid, p. 330 (Letter 288).
[294] Ibid, p. 145 (letter 75).
[295] Ibid, p. 148 (letter 77).
[296] Ibid, p. 143 (letter 74).
[297] G. Beckman, Hittite Diplomatic Text, Atlanta 1996, p. 178.
[298] W. Moran, Amarna Letters, 1992, letters 185, 186.

In another letter from the same area they report: "Look, we are in Amqu, in cities of the king, and the ruler of Kinsa, assisted the troops of Hatti and set the cities of the king on fire." [299]

So we see that the Hittite army is the Habiru army.

The letters from the Lebanese coast also prove this. They frequently mention a ruler by the name of Abdi-Ashirta who is accused of making a covenant with the Habiru. His fellow countryment write:

"What is Abdi-Ashirta, servant and dog, that he takes the land of the king for himself? What is his auxiliary force that it is strong? Through the Apiru his auxilary force is strong!".[300]

"The Apiru killed the king of Irqata, but there was no one who said anything to Abdi-Ashirta, and so they go on taking territory for themselves...

May the king be informed that the king of Hatti has seized all the countries that were subordinate to of the king of Mittani. Behold, he is king of Nahrima and the land of the great kings, and Abdi-Ashirta is taking the land of the king." [301]

We see that the letters dealing with the treachery of Abdi-Asihrta are bound up with the Habiru and the king of Het. From here we see that the King of Het is the King of the Habiru.

After the death of Abdi-Ashirata his sons ruled. In one letter they are accused of making a covenant with Habiru, and in another they are accused of making covenant with the Hittites. In one it is told "Who are the sons of Abdi-Ashirta the servant the dog?... They have gone to Ibirta, and an agreement has been made with the Apiru." [302]

And in another letter: "Now they are mobilizing the troops of the Hittite countries to seize Gubla... The sons of Abdi-Ashirta give gold and silver to the strong king, and accordingly they are strong." [303]

In yet a third letter the two names appear together "... The King of the Hittite countries, so that the lands of the king belong to the sons of Abdi-Ashirta, servants and dogs...They are against me; they have won the lands for the Apiru." [304]

---

[299] Ibid, letters 174, 175, 176, 363.

[300] Ibid, p. 140 (letter 71).

[301] Ibid, p. 145 (letter 75).
The Lebanaon coast belonged to the Mitani King: "The Mittani King came out as far as Sumur." (Sumur − the city next to Byblos.) p. 157 (letter 85).

[302] Ibid, p. 177 (letter 104).

[303] Ibid, p. 206 (letter 126).

[304] Ibid, p. 166 (letter 129).

If so, the Habiru are the Hittites.

Types of Hittite allies – relief in Egyptian temple

Summary: It emerges from the El-Amarna letters that in the 14th century BCE the Land of Israel was ruled by Egypt; however, it was prized away from them by the Hittites, who are called also the Habiru (Apiru), or the SA.GAZ and they destroyed and burned the cities.

Apparently, the Book of Joshua tells us about the same period and what comes out is a completely different picture. Therefore, we must clarify: what is the true date of the El-Amarna period?

Entrance to a Hittite palace

Chapter 20: When were the El-Amarna letters written?

The Stratigraphic Evidence – The Philological Evidence – The Tipological Evidence – The Letters from the Kings of Mesopotamia – The Intruders from the North – The Akkadian language – The Limping King

The Stratigraphic Evidence

The El-Amarna Letters can be dated by a method of assembling archaeological layers known as Stratigraphic,

In the El-Amarna period the Hittites lived in Anatolia. It is also known that in the 8th century BCE a kingdom called Phrygia existed in that area, until it was destroyed at the beginning of the 7th century (approximately 690 BCE).

Later on in the middle of the 6th century (around 550 BCE) the place was conquered by the Persians. What entity ruled that area between the destruction of Phrygia and the Persian period? Excavations in Gordion, the capital city of the Kingdom of Phrygia did not uncover any substantial findings from this period.

"Thus there is a lacuna of about a century and a half in the stratification and history of the site...The Gordion between circa. 690 and 550 has evaded us thus far, though it seems unlikely that the main site was entirely deserted over this long period." [305]

Is it really true that nothing at all was found? Not exactly! Between the layers from the time of the Kingdom of Phrygia (the 8th century BCE) to the Persian period (at the end of the 6th century BCE) a layer 2.5 to 4 meters wide separated the two, and was full, mainly with Hittite earthenwares.

This apparently teaches that during the 7th to 6th centuries BCE the Hittites were living here. However, the Hittites lived during the time of El-Amarna, which are dated to the 14th century BCE, some 700 years earlier. So, what is the explanation for this Hittite earthenware in the levels from the 7th -6th centuries BCE?

The answer given by the excavator of the site is as follows: "The filling was all of clay which had been brought from elsewhere to raise the level of the entire mound... The clay layer, varying from 2.50 to 4.00 meters thick, has been spotted in other tests at various places on the mound...The builders appear to

---

[305] R. S. Young, The Campaign of 1955 at Gordion: Preliminary Report, AJA 60 (1956), p. 264.

have taken no account of labor (costs), for the supply must have been plentiful and cheap." [306]

Why did the mound need lifting? The excavator says: "to make an important strategic post, and at the same time to provide a more secure bedding for the buildings."

However, even if we accept these explanations, why did they need to import tens of thousands of tons of material full of archaeological material from the Hittite period?

If the layer between the Phrygian level and the Persian level was full of Hittite earthenware that leads to the conclusion that the Hittite kingdom came after the Phrygian kingdom and before the Persian conquest, during the 6th to 7th centuries BCE (from approximately 690-550 BCE), the period in which the El-Amarna letter should be placed.

The Philological Evidence

Excavations in the Canaanite city Ugarit uncovered a great library. Acording to Egyptian items from the El-Amarna period that founded there, the library dated to the 14th century BCE.

In the library revealed, among other things, religious texts that have similation to Biblical texts.

About this subject was written a wide literaturation, and we only will qoute the folowing sentenses that belong to our matter:

"Nearly all the close stylistic and verbal parallels between Israelite and Canaanite literature belong to the **Exilic and early Postexilic periods**... Poems, didactic works, and songs would become so familiar to the Jews of the **7th and 6th centuries BC**." [307]

So, the Ugarit texts, that was written in the El-Amarna period, also supports that the El-Amarna period was not in the 14th century BCE, but about 700-800 years later.

---

[306] idem, Preliminary Report, Gordion, AJA 59 (1955), p. 12.
Our thanks are to Mrs Shulamit Coggan who pointed us in the direction of these sources that also appear in her father's books: Dr. Emanuel Velikovsky.
Velikovsky himself dated the period of El-Amarna to the 9th century BCE, at the time of Ahab and Jehoshafat. From the evidence we have presented it is clear that this dating is also too early.
[307] W. F. Albright, Recent progress in North-Canaanite research, BASOR 70 (1938), pp. 23-24.

The Typological Evidence

One branch of archaeological science is called Typology, which classifies vessels according to their form. The typological evidence also shows that the El-Amarna period dates between the 7th and 6th centuries BCE.

The ruins of El-Amarna have yielded many imported vessels originating in Greece (Mycenaean) identical to the vessels found at Greek sites from the 7th to the 6th century BCE. Since the accepted date of El-Amarna is placed in the 14th century BCE, this creates a conflict between the two dates.

The ruins of El-Amarna

This problem was recognized already in the early stages of research, and much was written about it by the investigator Murray who excavated in Ankomi in Cyprus, and found it difficult to date the findings there.

"Among the patterns," Murray writes, "that of a running ivy leaf on a vase appears to be unique in the series and is, at all events, interesting because of its relationship, on the one hand, to the fragmentary vase of Tel-el-Amarna; and on the other hand to the pattern of the early 6th century B.C.E." [308]

Another finding was a necklace from El-Amarna period. "The same process in the same patterns abounds in a series of gold ornaments which were found along with a large scarab of the Egyptian King Psametek I (664-612 BCE)." [309]

---

[308] A. S. Murray, Excavations in Cyprus, London 1900, p. 6-7.
[309] Ibid, p. 18.

A third finding was a golden bell from this period: "The execution and shape of the ring alone affords a clue, somewhere in the 8ᵗʰ or even the 7ᵗʰ centuries BCE, as we understand." [310]

Also, glass utensils from the El-Amarna period "seen in our glass vases from cameiros of the 7ᵗʰ and 6ᵗʰ centuries BCE". [311]

There is a fundamental rule in archaeology that the style of the utensils (The Typology) decides their dating. Therefore, when we see utensils that are dated to the 14ᵗʰ century BCE similar to those dated to the 6ᵗʰ and 7ᵗʰ centuries BCE this is a sign that one of the dates is mistaken.

From what we have said above about the empty holes in Greek Archaeology (In the chapter: Periods without Remnants), it follows that the earlier dating is mistaken. The true date of the utensils is the 6ᵗʰ to the 7ᵗʰ centuries BCE.

Since these utensils were in use in El-Amarna, this is additional evidence to fix their date to the 6ᵗʰ and 7ᵗʰ centuries BCE.

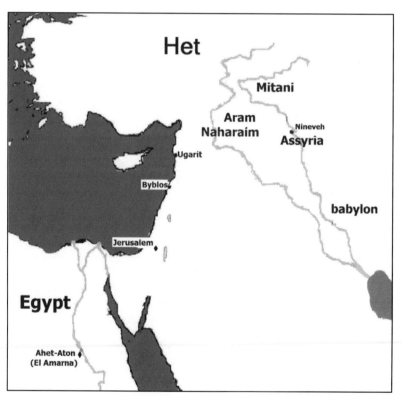

The Middle East in the period of El-Amarna

---

[310] Ibid, p. 20.
[311] Ibid, p. 24.

Letters from the Kings of Mesopotamia

Until now we have brought proofs that the El-Amarna letters should be dated to the sixth or seventh centuries BCE. To obtain an exact dating, let us compare the information stated in these letters with that which is known about this period.

During the 7th century BCE the entire Middle East was conquered by the Assyrian Kingdom (northern Iraq).

Very slowly, the power of the Babylonian King in Southern Iraq increased, until it challenged the Assyrians and supplanted them as the regional superpower. Meanwhile, for a short period, Egypt ruled the Middle East.

This is how the Babylonians took control over Assyria:

In 612 BCE the Babylonian King, Nabo-Pileser, conquered Nineveh, the capital of Assyria, and killed its King. The Assyrians retreated westwards, where they continued to hold their state in Aram Naharaim (the land to the west of Assyria), with the Egyptians supporting them from a distance.

Ashur-Uballit, the son of Essarhedon, was appointed King of Assyria, and his Kingdom continued until 609 BCE the year Nabo-Pileser the Babylonian King conquered the rest of Assyria.

Necho, the King of Egypt, came to help the Assyrians (and on his way killed Joshiah the King of Judah), but was unable to prevent their defeat and the kingdom of Assyria ceased to exist.

Necho took control over the Western territories that belonged to Assyria (the land of Israel and Syria), and held onto them until the year 604 BCE, during which Nebuchadnezzar, King of Babylon (the son of Nabo-Pileser) defeated him and the Land of Israel passed to the Babylonians.

Let us compare this to what is written in the El-Amarna letters. One letter that reached the King of Egypt was from the King of Babylon who complains: "Now, as for my Assyrian vassals, I did not send them to you. Why on their own authority did they come to your country?"[312]

The complaint of the Babylonian King was justified: The Egyptian King was keeping his connections with the Assyrians, as we can see from the letter of Ashur-Uballit, the King of Assyria, which was also found in the archives of El-Amarna. "Great King, King of Egypt, my brother: Thus Ashur-Uballit, king of Assyria, Great King, your brother... When I saw your messengers, I was very happy. "[313]

---

[312] Ibid. p. 18 (letter 9).
[313] ibid. p. 19-21 (letter 16).

In this letter Ashur-Ubalit asks for gold, and from it we understand that the Kingdom of Assyria was not as it had once been. The letter states as follows:

"When Ashur-nadin-ahhe, my ancestor, wrote to Egypt, 20 talents of gold were sent to him. When the King of Hanigalbat wrote to your father in Egypt, he sent 20 talents of gold to him. Now I'm the equal of the king of Hanigalbat, but you sent me (...) of gold, and it is not enough."

Ashur-Ubalit writes therefore that he is not equal to his father but only to the King of Hanigalbat, and Hanigalbat is a moniker for Aram Naharaim. [314]

In the words of Ashur-balit: "Now I'm the equal of the King of Hanigalbat" hinting that he was exiled to Aram Naharaim.

All this boils down to the fact that the Babylonians conquered the Assyrians, and the King of Egypt was supporting the King of Assyria who had been exiled to Aram Naharaim, to the disappointment of the Babylonians.

These things match the situation between 612-609 BCE and it is plausible that these letters are from around the year 610 BCE. The Babylonian King (his name in the letters is Burra-Buriyash the King of Karaduniyash) is Nabo-Pileser, Amenhotep IV is Necho (Ame**nho**tep) and Ashur-Ubalit is Ashur-Ubalit. [315]

Thus, the letters from the Land of Israel are from 609-604 BCE when all the land was controlled by Necho.

The Invaders from the North

Another matter discussed in the El-Amarna letters which supports the dating we established, is in regards to the invaders from the North. In their letters, the Kings are continually complaining about the Egyptian army, which is not stopping the cruel Hittites from burning the cities of the Land.

Another name for the Hittite is SA.GAZ, as we have proposed above.

On the other hand, the historian Herodotus tells us that after the fall of Nineveh in 612 BCE the Scythians invaded from the North and destroyed the land:

---

[314] Hanigalbat is the name of the Mitani kingdom, to the North-East of Mesopotamia. This Kingdom ruled for a long period over Aram Naharaim, and therefore in Egyptian records the name Nahrima is also used as the name of the Kingdom of Mitani.

[315] In the El-Amarna letters, the name of the father of Ashur-Ubalit is Ashur-Nadin-Ache, which is almost identical with the name of the father of Ashur-Ubalit from the 7th century: Ashur-Ache-Idin (in the Scripture: Essar-Hedon). These two names have an identical meaning: the God Ashur gave a brother.

"during which time their insolence and oppression spread ruin on every side". [316]

Another name for the Scythians is Ashkenaz or Ishgaz,[317] and they are mentioned in the Scriptures as one of the powers at the time of the Babylonian Empire. (Jeremiah 51:27)

The Scythians/Ishgaz who destroyed the Land of Israel and burned down its cities around 610 BCE, are the Hittites/SA.GAZ from the El-Amarna letters.

Here also is a match between the El-Amarna letters and what is known about the fall of Assyria. [318]

The Lion Gate in Hatushash – the capital of the Hittites

[316] The History of Herodotos, translated by G. Rawlinson, Book 1, p. 41.
According to these words of Herodotus there are some who explain the words of Jeremiah: "the destroyer of the Gentiles is on his way, and he is gone forth from his place to make thy land desolate, and the cities shall be laid waste" (Jeremiah 4:7) was said about this Conquest.
[317] H. Tadmor, The Hebrew Encyclopedia, Vol. 26, p. 475.
[318] The compatibility is strengthened in the description of the conquest of the Land of Judea by Nebuchadnezzar in the Babylonian records: "The King came to the land of the Hittites".
The matter is amazing, since the land of the Hittites is to be found in the North West of Syria, which is where the Kingdoms of the Hittites were.
[As mentioned in an inscription of Shalmaneser III: "I took all the land of the Hittites from the mountain of Amana until the mountain of Lebanon."]
The fact that the land of Judah is included in the lands of the Hittites teaches us that during this period the Hittites conquered all of the land of Judea until Nebuchadnezzar came and took it from them.

The Akkadian language

The El-Amarna letters which are dated to the end of the First Temple period answer one of the great wonders of the Akkadian language in which the material was written by the Assyrians and the Babylonians.

According to conventional dating the El-Amarna letters are dated to the 14th century BCE. The Land of Israel was then already one hundred years under almost continuous Egyptian occupation, while the Assyrians and the Babylonians never had any control over it. So, why are the Egyptians writing to their subjects in the Land of Israel in the Akkadian language?

The scholars can only say that Akkadian was apparently the international diplomatic language of the time, yet it is not clear how when the Egyptians are the occupying rulers the diplomatic language is imported from another place.

If the El-Amarna letters were written at the end of the First Temple this makes sense because this is after one hundred years of Assyrian hegemony over the Middle East, during which time the Assyrians also conquered Egypt. This meant that the Egyptians as well as the citizens of the Land of Israel knew Akkadian, which was the Imperial language of Assyria.

The El-Amarna letters were written in Akkadian a few years after the fall of Assyria, as Akkadian was the language common to Egypt and its subjects.

The Limping King

We have said that Amenhotep IV was Necho. Let us compare what is known to us about him.

Amenhotep IV reigned for 17 years. "The strange treatment of the lower limbs by his artists is a problem which still remains unsolved." [319] in one picture he is leaning on a stick and from here we understand that he had a defected leg.

His kingdom was limping as well. At the beginning he ruled over the whole of the Land of Israel and Syria, though at a certain point he shut himself up in his capital. He doesn't seem to have given any attention to events in Asia until Egypt lost all its foreign possessions.

This is how the Egyptologist Breasted described it: "The faithful vassals showered dispatches upon him, sent special ambassadors to represent to him the seriousness of the situation! But they either received no replies at all... to deal with the situation which demanded the pharaoh himself and the whole available army." [320] "We may censure him for the loss of the empire." [321]

---

[319] J. H. Breasted, A History of Egypt, New York 1951, p. 378.
[320] Ibid, p. 389.
[321] Ibid, p. 392.

Amenhotep IV leans on his staff

Necho ruled 17 years (610-593 BCE) and was called by the Jewish Sages: 'the limping Pharaoh'.[322]

Originally he ruled over the Land of Israel and Syria but he shut himself up in his homeland, and in the end he ruled only over Egypt alone. This is how the Book of Kings describes him:

"The King of Egypt stayed at home and no longer left his country, because the King of Babylon took control over the lands from the River of Egypt to the Euphrates, all that pertained to the King of Egypt." (Kings II 24:7)

The comparison is complete.

Summary, Amnhotep IV is Pharaoh Necho who lived during the last years of the First Temple period. The El-Amarna letters from the Land of Israel date from 609-604 BCE when Pharaoh Necho reigned over the Land.

---

[322] Babylonian Talmud Tractate Megilla 3A; Moed Katan 28B. Vayikra Rabah 20, 1.

Chapter 21: Jerusalem during the Period of El-Amarna

Letters from the King of Jerusalem – Abdi-Hepa – Is it possible to see the palace of Abdi-Hepa/Jehoyakim?

Letters from the King of Jerusalem

After demonstrating that the El-Amarna letters date to the end of the period of the First Temple, we can better understand the letters sent by the King of Jerusalem:

In the letters dispatched by the King's subordinate to the King of Egypt, we find many words of deference, like: 'I fall at the feet of my Lord, the King'. The King of Jerusalem further added: "Neither my father nor my mother put me in this place, but the strong arm of the king brought me into my father's house." [323]

This sentence sounds strange even as flattery, though it can be understood if the letters are re-dated to the end of the 7th century BCE. Why?

As we said, during the years 609-604 BCE Necho ruled over the land of Judah. His first act was to depose King Jehoahaz, the son of Joshiyah and to appoint his brother Elyakim to the throne and change his name to Jehoyakim.

According to the date we have mentioned, the King of Jerusalem in the days of El-Amarna was Jehoyakim and he indeed ascended his father's throne by the authority of the Egyptian King. Therefore, he says "the strong arm of the king brought me into my father's house".

However, dating the El-Amarna letters to the time of Jehoyakim raises a question. If the King of Judah ruled over the whole land, why do the El-Amarna letters suggest that the King of Jerusalem ruled only over his immediate surroundings while other areas like Lachish had their own King?

How do we explain the reality of independent Kings in the kingdom of Judah?

Yet when we look in the written text we see that in the days of Jehoyakim there were a number of Kings in Judah, exactly as Jeremiah says: "and Jerusalem and the cities of Judah and their Kings". (Jeremiah 25:18)

In this verse we see that during the days of Jehoayakim there were Kings in other cities of Judah, not only in Jerusalem. (In the appendix 20 we explain how it happened that the Kingdom of Judah had split into a number of Kingdoms.)

---

[323] W. Moran, The Amarna Letters, 1992, p. 326 (letter 286).

Abdi-Hepa

The King of Jerusalem in the El-Amarna letters is Abdi-Hepa, which is the Accadian name of Jehoyakim. [Just as the Accadian name of Azariah who lived during the time of Jehoyakim was Abdi-nigo (Daniel 1:7).

Hepa was the name of the Horite sun-oddess, and if Jehoyakim called himself Abdi-Hepa, this proves that he would bow to worship her.

Do the Scriptures hint to this? It seems that they do, because in the Book of Jeremiah (who lived at the time of Jehoyakim) we are told that in the land of Judah people were increasingly worshipping a deity called the 'Queen of the Heavens', and from the writings it seems that she was the most popular goddess.

"The boys are collecting wood and the fathers are burning the fire and the women are kneading the dough to make cakes for the Queen of the Heavens".

"To burn incense unto the queen of heaven, and to pour out drink offerings unto her, as we have done, we, and our fathers, our kings, and our princes, in the cities of Judah, and in the streets of Jerusalem." (Jeremiah 7:18. ibid 44:17)

The name Abdi-Hepa by which Jehoyakim is called teaches us about the goddess named in the Scriptures 'Queen of the Heavens'.

Is it Possible to see the Palace of Abdi-Hepa/Jehoyakim?

Scholars agree that there are no actual remains of Abdi-Hepa, the King of Jerusalem. However, after we have identified Abdi-Hepa with Jehoyakim, we can easily reveal his palace. Let us first of all cite the Scriptures about Jehoyakim.

Jehoyakim built himself a large palace: "I will build me a wide house with large upper chambers." (Jeremiah 22:14)

The story of the 'burning of the scroll' took place in this palace:

"And it came to pass in the fifth year of Jehoiakim, that they proclaimed a fast before the Lord to all the people in Jerusalem. Then read Baruch in the book the words of Jeremiah in the house of the Lord, in the chamber of **Gemariah the son of Shaphan** the scribe, in the ears of all the people.

When Michaiah the son of **Gemariah the son of Shaphan** heard from the book all the words of the Lord. Then he went down into the king's house, into the scribe's chamber. and, lo, all the princes sat there... and **Gemariah the son of Shaphan**, and all the princes...

And the King sent Yehudi to fetch the scroll, and Yehudi read it in the ears of the King. And he cut it with a penknife, and cast it into the fire until all the roll was consumed in the fire." (Jeremiah 36:9-23)

Where did the house stand? From the text we learn "he went down into the King's house" we see that the house of the King was located in a place lower than the Temple. [324] It follows therefore that the great palace was in the east-old-city below the Temple Mount.

Can we find in the east-old-city a royal palace of very large proportions from this period?

Indeed, a huge 18 meters high wall designed to support a building. "A building of this size is not known amongst the ruins of all the buildings in the Land of Israel...It is extremely unique and it is very powerful and it teaches us about the special status of Jerusalem as the center of government." [325]

Further excavations uncovered the remains of "a vast building that covers the entire area... the building is no longer another public building, It is a vast building that could only be built by someone with great powers of ruling and economy...The building left us amazed, since it was so great in size, much bigger than we could estimate." [326]

We have another clear evidence that Jehoyakim dwelt here. Fifty-one seals were found in one room used as an archive for letters. One of the seals belonged to **Gemayahu the son of Shafan**, one of Jehoyakim's ministers.[327]

This archive, it seems, was in the scribe's chamber where Gemaryahu sat with his friends, and the royal palace above it was where Jehoyakim sat and burned the scroll.

When Jehoyakim built his great palace he acted dishonestly "He built his house without righteousness, and its top floors without justice. He made his neighbor work for free, and he did not give his workers what they deserved." (ibid, 13)

---

[324]Another prophecy of the House of the King is also said in the language of descent "So says the Lord, go down to the house of King Judah". (ibid, 2:1)

[325] A. Mazar, Jerusalem in the 10th Century BCE – the 'Half-Full' Glass, in: E. Baruch and A. Faust (eds.), New Studies on Jerusalem, Vol 10, Ramat Gan 2004, p. 17. (Hebrew). The earthenware in the foundations of the building are from the Late Bronze Age, so that the building is from the period of El-Amarna. Earthenware from Iron Age I has also been found, according to which, the building has been dated to the transition from the Late Bronze Age to the Iron Age. This is a later period than at the time of El-Amarna. However according to the evidence quoted in the chapter about the Late Bronze Age, these two periods (the Late Bronze Age and Iron Age I) are the same, which is the El-Amarna period.

[326] E. Mazar, It Looks Like King David's Palace, in: E. Baruch et al (eds.) New Studies on Jerusalem, Vol 11, Ramat Gan 2005, p. 13 (Hebrew); idem, Excavations at the City of David (2006-2007), in: E. Baruch et al (ed.), New Studies on Jerusalem, Vol 13, Ramat Gan 2007, p. 9. (Hebrew)

[327] Y. Shilo, A Hoard of Hebrew Bullae from the City of David, Eretz Israel 18 (1985), p. 75, (Hebrew)

The palace stood for only a few years and the remains of its destruction are displayed to visitors in the east-old-city, who see the fulfillment of the words of Jeremiah: "I have sworn, says the Lord, that this house will be a ruin." (ibid, 5)

If so, we have found the palace of Abdi-Hepa, the King of Jerusalem.

The hige retaining wall in old Jerusalem

Chapter 22: An Altar to the Lord in the Land of Egypt

The Monotheistic King – "He did not harken to the words of Necho from the mouth of the Lord" – the Wonderful Oath – Pharaoh Necho changes his name

The Monotheistic King

King Amenhotep IV, unlike the kings who came before and after him that worshipped strange gods, served the only one deity who, to use his own words, revealed himself to him.

This god was Aton, the sun god, and it is emphasized in the king's inscriptions that he does not mean the sun itself, but rather he who gave it life.

Amenhotep IV and his family offers to Aton

Queen Neferetity – Amenhotep IV's wife

The King built two cities in honor of Aton; Ahet-Aton which is El-Amarna, in central Egypt, and Gem-Aton at the southernmost point. The worship of Aton reached its ascendance during the time of Amenhotep IV and there is a connection between this religion and the religion of Israel.

In the city of Ahet-Aton a psalm of praise (written by Amenhotep IV to Aton) has been preserved which strongly reminds us of the song 'Bless My Soul' in the Book of Psalms. In the words of Breasted: "The 104th Psalm of the Hebrews shows a notable similarity to our hymn, both in thought and in sequence." [328]

This faith had already begun to take hold in Egypt even in the generation before Amenhotep IV, as the Egyptologist Giveon writes about a list from the days of his father: "This list contains the special name of the God of Israel...The Asiatic roots of the religion of El-Amarna had penetrated into Egypt...We have here a kind of preparation for the El-Amarna period." [329]

Amenhotep IV believed in a faith close to Israel's faith. We have identified Amenhotep with Pharaoh Necho. Is there any hint in the Bible that Necho believed in the God of Israel? Yes, indeed, as we will see later.

"He did not harken to the words of Necho from the mouth of the Lord"

In the Book of Chronicles, it is told that when Pharaoh Necho passed through the Land of Israel, on his way to war with the Assyrians, he sent a message to Josiah, the King of Judah, and warned him not to bar his way. This is the wording of Necho's message.

"What have I to do with thee, thou king of Judah? I come not against thee this day, but against the house with which I am at war. For God commanded me to make haste: forbear from meddling with God, who is with me, so that he does not destroy thee." (Chronicles II, 35:21)

Josiah did not listen to Necho's warning, and set out for a war against him, during which he was killed. This is how the Scriptures describe it:

"Nevertheless, Josiah would not turn his face from him, but he sought an opportunity to fight with him, and he did not hearken to the words of Necho from the mouth of God, and came to fight in the valley of Megiddo. And the archers shot at King Josiah… and he died."(Chronicles II, 35:22-24)

When the Scriptures say "The words of Necho from the mouth of the Lord", it appears as if Necho merited hearing the words of the Lord, because when the Scriptures talk about 'The Lord' it means the Lord of Israel.

How can the Scriptures tell us about the King of Egypt who received word from the Lord of Israel?

When Necho, who is really Amenhotep IV, believed in the Lord of Israel and that he revealed himself to him, we understand the verse: "The words of Necho

---

[328] J. H. Breasted, A History of Egypt, New York 1951, p. 371.
[329] R. Giveon, The Footsteps of Pharoah in Canaan, p. 12. (Hebrew)

from the mouth of the Lord". This is because Necho believed in the same God of Israel.

Summary: The Scriptures leave a reminder that Pharaoh Necho (Amenhotep IV) believed in the God of Israel and even merited his revelation to him.

The Wonderful Oath

During the first days of his Kingdom, Amenhotep IV worshipped Aton, but also Amon (who was the main deity of Egypt).

In the fifth year of his rule he changed directions and began to serve only Aton, and he erased all mention of Amon and the other gods of Egypt:

"The official temple-worship of the various gods throughout the land ceased, and their names were erased wherever they could be found engraved on the monuments." [330]

He changed his name from **Amen**hotep to Akhn**aton** and even erased the name of his father Amenhotep III from the inscriptions, so no memory of Amon would remain.

There is no comparative precedent to this religious zealousness amongst the ancient peoples, whose practice was to serve many different gods at one time.

Akhnaton did not only make do with destroying all mention of Amon from the inscriptions, but also chose to uproot himself from the city of No-**Amon** (Thebes) to his new eponymous city of Ahet-**Aton**.

After moving there, he made an oath never to leave it again, as the inscriptions that were found in the city inform us:

"His Majesty raised his hand to heaven, saying: I have demarked Akhetaton. I shall not pass beyond the southern landmark of Akhetaton toward the south, nor shall I pass beyond the northern landmark of Akhetaton toward the north." [331]

What is the explanation for this strange oath that Ikhnaton made, which obligated him to remain imprisoned in this city, unable to leave?

The key to answer this question lies in the date that his behavior radically changed. Amenhotep IV changed from an easygoing, tolerant person to a zealot in the fifth year of his reign, and soon moved his capital to Ahet-Aton and shut himself up there.

Since we have identified Amenhotep IV with Pharoah Necho, it follows that the fifth year is 605 BCE. In that year the second battle of Carcamish took place, in

---

[330] J. H. Breasted, A History of Egypt, New York 1951, p. 363.
[331] Ibid, p. 365.

which the army of Pharaoh Necho was defeated by Nebuchanezzar's forces. How could his defeat bring about the change that came over Amenhotep IV?

The Prophet Jeremiah explains the defeat of the Egyptian King in the battle of Carcamish as punishment for having killed Josiah. "For this is the day of the Lord God of hosts, a day of vengeance, that he may avenge him of his adversaries." (Jeremiah 46:10)

Amenhotep IV, who held strong religious opinions, also came to understand in the disaster which befell him a sign from Heaven that he must atone for his sin in slaying Joshiah. From now on he zealously adopted the ways of Joshiah before the Lord and did not suffer the presence of other gods. As the Scriptures tell us:

"And when he had broken down the altars and the asherim, and beaten the carved idols into dust, and cut down all the sun images throughout all the Land of Israel". (Chronicles II 34:7).

This is the explanation for the zealousness of Ikhnaton who sought to atone for killing Josiah by destroying all reference to other foreign deities except for 'Aton'.

Accordingly, we also understand why he uprooted himself and went to live in another city, under oath to stay there, and not to leave. For in the Torah of Israel the atonement given to a murderer is to be exiled to another city and not to leave it. (Numbers 35:28)

In light of these words Ikhnaton went in the footsteps of his 'spiritual mentor' King Josiah and destroyed all the idols, and in order to receive atonement for his killing he exiled himself to another city.

Pharaoh Necho changes his name

As we have said before Amenhotep IV changed his name from Amenhotep to Akhnaton. A hint of this is given in the Book of Kings:

"In his (Josiah) time **Pharaoh-nechoh**, king of Egypt went up against the king of Ashur to the river Perat: and King Josiah went against him: and he slew him at Megiddo…

and the people of the land took Yehoahaz, the son of Josiah, and anointed him and made him king in his father's stead... And **Pharaoh-nechoh** put him…

And **Pharaoh-nechoh** made Elyakim, the son of Josiah, his father, king instead of Josiah and turned his name to Jehoyakim…

(Jehoyakim) he exacted the silver and the gold of the people of the land, of every one according to his taxation, to give it to **Pharaoh-nechoh**…

And the **king of Egypt** never came again out of his land" (Kings II, 23:29-35; 24:7)

Five times the Scriptures speak about Pharaoh Necho. Four times he is mentioned by name 'Pharaoh Necho'; on the fifth time his name disappears.

This is because Necho is a version of the name Ame**nho**tep by which he was initially called. After he changed his name to Akhnaton he was no longer called by the name Amenhotep or Necho, so that at the end of his days he is not called by the name Pharaoh Necho.

Even the name change of Amenhotep IV is recorded in the Scriptures!

Chapter 23: The Generations after El-Amarna

The Successors of Akhnaton – the 26th Dynasty – A number of kings hiding under one name – The Israeli Stella

The Successors of Akhnaton

After the death of King Akhnaton his son-in-law Tutankhaton whose name was changed to Tutankhamon embarked on a war expedition in the Land of Israel, and from the description of this journey we understand that his successes were limited.

"He may thus have recovered sufficient power in Palestine to collect some tribute or at least some spoil." [332]

King Tutankhamon died, and his widow was forced to marry a minister named Ay. Ay was crowned as King and at his coronation received the royal name: 'Heper-Heper-Ra'.

A mural from this period shows people who fled from the Land of Israel and came to live in Egypt. The accompanying inscription says that these people came after "Their town laid waste, and fire has been thrown". [333]

Egyptian official with semitic immigrants

Ay did not rule for long either, and he died due to unclear circumstances. A dense fog clouded Egypt during that time and when the fog cleared, there was a new kingdom in Egypt: the 19th dynasty.

---

[332] Ibid, p. 394.
[333] J. H. Breasted, Ancient Records of Egypt, III, p. 7.

The Sarcophagus of Ay

The identification of Akhnaton with Necho (who died in 593 BCE) means that these events took place after his death in the generation in which the First Temple was destroyed (586 BCE). This is the order of the events:

Tutankhamon set out to make war in the Land of Israel. It was said of him that when the Babylonians who laid siege to Jerusalem heard the rumour that the army of Pharaoh left Egypt and "they left off their siege of Jerusalem" (Jeremiah 37:5).

Tutankhamon returned to Egypt without any real achievements in hand, according to Jeremiah who said: "behold Paro's army which came out to help you shall return to Egypt to their own land" (ibid, 7).

Jerusalem was conquered by the Babylonians, who set it ablaze, (ibid 39:8), and the Scriptures say that afterwards the remaining survivors were taken to Egypt (ibid 43:7).

It follows that these are the refugees from the Land of Israel who came to Egypt and are depicted in the Egyptian mural.

The king of Egypt in those days was Hofra. He fell in a battle agains Nebuchadnezzar, who smote the Egyptians and then returned to his land. This is how the prophet Jeremiah describes Hofra: "Thus says the Lord: Behold I will give Pharaoh Hofra, the King of Egypt into the hand of his enemies" (ibid, 44:30)

Hofra was Ay/Heper-Heper-Ra, who was attacked by Nebuchadnezzar. The conquest of Nebuchadnezzar explains the chaos and darkness in the time between the death of Ay and the beginning of the 19th dynasty.

Summary: Tutankhamon is the Pharaoh who came to Jerusalem's aid, but turned out. Ay/Heper-Heper-Ra is the Pharaoh Hofra when the Jews went down to Egypt and he also fell by the hands of Nebuchadnezzar.

The 26th dynasty

From what has been said until now the end of the First Temple is also the end of the 18th dynasty in Egypt, and the exile in Babylon occurred during the 19th dynasty.

On the other hand, it is known that during these years (the end of the First Temple to the Babylonian Exile) another dynasty, the 26th dynasty, ruled in Egypt (664-525). We know the names of its Kings from the Book of Herodotus and supporting inscriptions found in Egypt.

Yet the names of the Kings of the 26th dynasty are different from the names of the Kings of the 18th and 19th dynasties. How can this be resolved?

The answer is: The inscriptions which bear the names of the Kings of the 26th dynasty are how the priests of the gods Ptah and Amon called the kings, in inscriptions connected to worship of these gods. They were not the names of the Kings themselves. [334]

This is particularly noted of the founder of the dynasty, King Psamtik I, who ruled 54 years! We have not found even one fractured statue bearing his name, and the same is true of the Kings Psametik II (593-588 BCE) and Psametik III (525 BCE).[335]

It is inconceivable that during this entire period not even a single engraved royal inscription was not issued, so we must assume that the priests of Ptah and Amon had their own terminology for naming the kings at the end of the 18th and 19th dynasties.

These names entered the book of Herodotus, who writes explicitly what he was told by the priests of Ptah and Amon (Book 2:3).

If so, there is no contradiction: the 26th dynasty is the 18th-19th dynasties by another name.

---

[334] J. H. Breasted, Ancient Records of Egypt, IX, pp. 447-520.
[335] Aldred, Egyptian Art, London 1994, p. 227.

Psamtik I worshiping the sacred bull of Ptah

Amasis worshiping the sacred bull of Ptah

Several Kings hiding under the same name

In the previous paragraph we showed that the priests had their own names for the kings of Egypt.

A similar characteristic of the names is that in a number of cases they grouped a number of kings under the same name. This is proven by the following fact.

From Assyrian records we know that in 663-661 BCE Egypt was ruled by an Ethiopean king named Tanutamon. Egypt was later re-conquered and ruled for a number of years by the Assyrian King Ashurbanipal.[336]

On the other hand, according to Egyptian priestly inscriptions, the king of Egypt in the years of 663-610 BCE was the King Psametek I.

Who, then, ruled Egypt after the year 663 BCE, Psametek I or Tanutamon and Ashurbanipal?

The answer is: Psametek is a common name for a number of kings.

If so this is the order of kings of the 26th dynasty:

---

[336] J. H. /, A History of Egypt, New York 1951, p. 558-560.

Names in Priestly Inscriptions	Names of the Kings	Date BCE
Psametek I	Tanutamon Ashurbanipal Thutmose IV Amenhotep III	663-610
Necho	Amenhotep IV	610-593
Psametek II	Tutankhamon	593-588
Afrias (Hu-eb-Ra)	Ay Harmhab Rameses I Seti I	588-569
Amasis (Ahmose II)	Rameses II Merneptah Siptah	569-525
Psamtik III	Seti II Teosret	525

(See the previous chapter 'when Sennacherib laid siege to Jerusalem' for the ruling years of the 19th dynasty.)

The Israel Stella

A number of kings from the 19th dynasty made more expeditions to the Land of Israel and left behind inscriptions that bear their names (in Beth Shean and Jaffa). These were Seti I and Rameses II.

The son of Rameses II, King Merneptah, records his victories and his journey to the Land of Israel. There is no evidence that the journey actually took place and it could be an example of his self-glorification. However, in this inscription, displayed in the Cairo Museum, we find the only Egyptian inscription in which the name 'Israel' appears!

This is the wording of the inscription: "The kings are otherthrown... Israel is desolated, her seed is not, Palestine has become a widow for Egypt".

What is the meaning of "Her seed is not" and "Palestine has become a widow"?

Until now We've established that this inscription is dated to the 6th century BCE. Thus, Merneptah's words are understood, since he wrote them after the Kingdom of Israel and the Kingdom of Judah were exiled.

Merenptah is using expressions similar to those known to us from the Scriptures. His words "Israel is desolated, her seed is not" remind us of the words of Hoshea about the exile of Israel: "Their routes are dry, and their fruits are not". (Hoshea 9:16)

And the words: "Palestine ('Kharo') has become a widow" remind us of the exile of Judah as it is understood in the Scriptures: "How does she sit apart...she was like a widow". (Lamentations1:1)

Merenptah is describing the exiles of Israel and Judah. However, in truth, at the time of Merenptah, the wheel of fortune began to turn around. These were the first days of the Persian Empire when the exiles from Judah began to rebuild their abandoned land.

Summary of Section 4

The wonderful story of the Egyptian King Akhnaton who chose to abandon all the idols of Egypt to serve the one God has stimulated the imagination of everyone interested in antiquity. To this can be added the El-Amarna letters found in his palace, which name the Habiru who are expanding over the cities of Canaan.

Much has been written about this king, maybe more than for any other king, and many explanations have been given for his actions and of those who surrounded him.

Attempts have also been made to draw parallels between what is known about Akhnaton and his generation and what is written in the Scriptures and particularly to identify the Habiru as the Hebrews. The comparison doesn't fit, and joins a long list of bad matches between the Bible and archaeology.

In this section we have brought evidence that the accepted dating of Akhnaton (14th century BCE) is incorrect. He lived at the end of the First Temple – the 7th-6th centuries BCE – and he is the Scriptural king Necho who killed Josiah the King of Judah and later in his life, he became a zealous monotheist like Josiah.

We have shown parallels in the Scriptures to the successors of Akhnaten, Tutankhamon and Ay, and we have identified the Habiru, who might also be mentioned in the Scriptures.

Now that we have found the archaeological footsteps to the First Temple, let us continue searching for the footsteps from the later periods: The Babylonian exile and the Restoration, in the next section.

Section 5: The Period of the Restoration

Introduction

This section deals with the Period of the Restoration, or the beginning of the Second Temple era, which marks the end of the Scriptural period. A multitude of records exists from this period which clearly disprove accepted research timeline.

Chapter 24: Who was LMLK?

The Hidden Periods – The Jugs of 'LMLK' and the 'Rosette' – The problem of relating to Hezekiah – The Recognition of the Symbols of the Wings – Why were the Jugs collected? – Summary

The Hidden Periods

The Kingdom of the House of David existed for hundreds of years until it was conquered by Nebuchadnezzar, the King of Babylon, who destroyed the First Temple in 586 BCE and exiled the people.

Jerusalem remained deserted until Cyrus, King of Persia allowed the Jews to return to Jerusalem (538 BCE). In the generation after him, King Darius permitted the Jewish nation to build the Holy Temple (516 BCE).

Several decades later, about 458 BCE, Ezra came up from Babylon and came Nehemiah a few years later after him and improved the State of Judah (445-432 BCE).

The years from the destruction of the Temple until Cyrus are known as 'the period of the Babylonian Exile' (586-538 BCE) and the years of the accession of Cyrus until the coming of Ezra and Nehemiah are 'the Period of the Restoration' (538-432 BCE).

Which archaeological remains do we have from the time of the Babylonian Exile? None; "There's nothing in the archaeology of the Land of Israel for a period that they call 'the Babylonian period'... The lack of findings is almost absolute." [337]

This is amazing, because though the Jews were in exile from the Land, other populations like the Samaritans remained there. Why has nothing remained of this period?

---

[337] E. Stern, The Beginnings of the Province of "Yahud" in the Persian Period, in: A. Faust & E. Baruch (eds.), New Studies on Jerusalem – Proceeding of the Third Conference, Ramat Gan 1997, p. 69. (Hebrew)
Lap, who excavated in the Tel-el-Ful (and after him Barkai and other investigators,) claims that he managed to isolate a later layer that is after the time of the First Temple and preceding the Persian period, that is the Babylonian Period.
Other investigators are skeptical: "Attempts to relate to a certain general time are problematic" (A. De-Groot, The Sixth Century BCE: a glimpse of Jerusalem, in: O. Lifshitz (ed.) is it possible to find the earthenware of the sixth century in Judah? Tel Aviv 1999, p. 24 (Hebrew)
Also those who think they have revealed findings from the Babylonian period agree that they are very sparse: "The source of knowledge about the period is, in the meantime, from the graves" (G. Barkai, the Period of the Third Iron Age – the Babylonian Period, ibid, p. 25).

From the following period – the Period of the Restoration – there are also few findings, among them a number of seals and imported vessels.

No local earthenware is dated to this period since the earlier vessels dated to the Persian period are found together with coins from the end of the 5th century BCE, that is after the Restoration period ended. [338]

Also, hardly any remains of buildings from the Period of the Restoration have been discovered in Judah. [339]

If we relied only on archaeology we would have to conclude that the Jews had not yet returned during this period to their cities: "Jerusalem was poor and miserable, not only at the time after the destruction but also at the peak of the period of the Restoration." [340]

The disappearance of the Babylonian Period and of the Restoration is one of the most serious problems in the archaeology of the Land of Israel and in the following pages we will try to provide a solution. We have been helped by one of the most well-known findings: the jugs of LMLK.

Archaeological Name	Historical Name	Date
Early Iron Age II	Beginning of First Temple	1000-900
Middle Iron Age II (LMLK)	Middle of First Temple	900-700
Late Iron Age II (Rosette)	End of First Temple	700-586
–	Babylonian Exile	586-538
–	Restoration	538-432
Persian Period	Second Half of Persian Period	432-332

Accepted Time Line (all dates BCE). There are different opinions regarding terming the periods of Iron Age II. Therefore we have chosen the attributes: Early, Middle and Late.

---

[338] E. Stern, The Material Culture of the land of the Bible in the Persian Period, Jerusalem 1973, p. 75 (Hebrew); idem, The Beginning of the Province of "Yahud" in the Persian Period, in: A. Faust & E. Baruch, (eds.) New Studies on Jerusalem – Proceedings of the Third Conference, Ramat Gan 1997, p. 69. (Hebrew)

[339] O. Lipschits, The Policy of the Persian Empire and the meager Architectonic Finds in the Province of 'Yehud', in: A. Faust & E. Baruch, New Studies on Jerusalem – Proceedings of the Seventh Conference, Ramat Gan 2001, p. 45-47. (Hebrew)

[340] O. Lipschits, Jerusalem between Destruction and Restoration - Judah under Babylonian Rule, Jerusalem 2004, p. 247. (Hebrew)

The Jugs of 'LMLK' and the 'Rosette'

Excavations in the Land of Judah have uncovered many jugs from the Middle Iron Age II which have the seal of the Hebrew word LMLK ('LaMeLeKh' - for the King), and therefore this period is named the period of LMLK.

The inscription LMLK is accompanied by a symbol with four wings that was changed afterwards to a symbol with two wings. The period of LMLK finished with a destruction of Judah.

In the following period – the end of Iron Age II – the seal 'LMLK' ceased to be used and was replaced by a new royal symbol in the form of a flower which scholars named the Rosette. This period also ended with destruction.

The four wings LMLK seal

The two wings LMLK seal

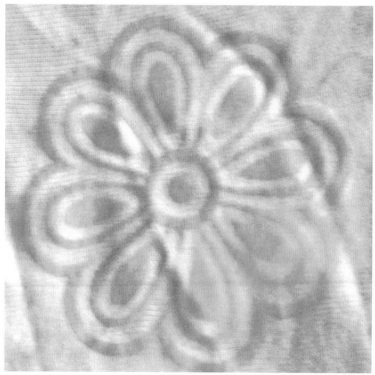

The Rosette seal

The LMLK seal has customarily been attributed to Hezekiah, the King of Judah and the Rosette to his successors.

Accordingly, the destruction of Judah by Sennacherib, the King of Assyria during the time of Hezekiah (from which only Jerusalem was saved), is the destruction of LMLK period, and the destruction of the First Temple, with which ended the period of the Rosette. [341]

What is the meaning of the four-wings symbol and why was it changed to the two-wings symbol? Why was it changed again to the Rosette? These questions remain open: "We have not found a satisfactory solution for these changes in the Royal symbol".[342]

We will try to give an answer to these questions; however first let us check if these symbols are indeed from the time of the First Temple, or from later periods.

Problems in relating LMLK to Hezekiah

The jugs of LMLK and Rosette are not from the First Temple period of Hezekiah and his successors, but from the period of the Restoration. The proofs are as follows:

1. A Jewish military community from the days of the Restoration inhabited the island of Yeb (Elephantine) in southern Egypt of which many records remain. [343] Among the findings were jugs on which the word LMLK is stamped. In the words of the scholar Sukenik:

"These inscriptions date from the end of the 6th century to the beginning of the 5th century BCE (the days of the Restoration) and are an excellent parallel to the seals found in Judah. They also have the word 'LMLK' and the symbol of the wings." [344]

---

[341] Y. Aharoni, the Archaeology of the land of Israel, Tel Aviv 1978, p. 224 (Hebrew); N. Avigad, Biblical Encyclopedia Vol. 3, p. 80 (Hebrew); A. Mazar, Between Judah and Philistia: Timna (Tel Batash) in the Iron Age II, Eretz Israel 18 (1985), p. 308 (Hebrew); Y. Garfinkel, A Hierarchic Pattern in the Private Seal-Impresions on the "LMLK" Jar-Handles, ibid, p. 112 (Hebrew); G. Barkai, The Archaeology of Ancient Israel in the Biblical Period, unit 9, Tel Aviv 1990, p. 167 (Hebrew); O. Lifshitz, Royal Judahite Jar Handles, Tel Aviv 37 (2010), pp. 7-28; E. Stern, Eretz-Israel at the end of the period of the monarchy, Qadmoniot 21 (1973), p. 15. (Hebrew)

[342] E. Stern, Eretz-Israel at the end of the period of the monarchy, Qadmoniot 21 (1973), p. 15. (Hebrew)

[343] B. Porten, Jews of Elephantine and Aramans of Syene, Jerusalem 1974. (Hebrew)

[344] E. Sukenik, The Meaning of the "Le-Melekh" Inscriptions, Qedem 1 (1942), p. 35. (Hebrew)

The Jews of Yeb lived 200 years after Hezekiah and were the soldiers of the King of Persia. From this we see that he is 'the King' (LMLK) stamped on the jugs accompanied by the symbol of the wings.[345]

Vessels from the days of Persian rule bearing the symbols of the wings and of the Rosette have also been revealed in the Land of Israel. [346] Therefore we must conclude that these jugs with the LMLK and the Rosette symbols date to the beginning of the Persian period.

2. During the Persian period the Land of Judah is known as the Province of Yahud. The earthenware that is stamped with this name - Yahud – has been revealed in various places from the period of LMLK and the Rosette. [347]

How did these vessels from the time of the Second Temple reach levels to the time of the First Temple? The answers archeologist give are: "later fillins", "pits", "scattered around on the surface", or simply "a blurred stratigraphic connection".

These poor explanations spring from the faith that the levels LMLK and Rosette are from the days of the First Temple.

---

[345] Sukenik, and in his footsteps, Stern, tried to resolve the reality of the stamps of LMLK in the Persian period with the dating to the days of Hezekiah like this: "The word LMLK and the symbol show a sign of absolute measurement. This was a custom not only in Judah as testified by their use during the Persian period." [E. Stern, Eretz-Israel at the end of the period of the monarchy, Qadmoniot 21 (1973), p. 15 (Hebrew)]
That is to say the sign of LMLK doesn't mean 'especially for the King', rather just the name of an international volume measurement.
The results that have been received from later investigations have contradicted this estimation, since it has become clear that the volume of the jugs and of the stamps is not identical, "Thus, the stamps were not meant to guarantee the volume of the vassels." (D. Usishkin, The New Encyclopaedia of archaeological Excavations in the Holy Land, Jerusalem 1993, p. 909).
However the main problem of this explanation is does not answer how this symbol, which was supposedly used during the reign of Hezekiah and ceased to be used after his death, reappears 200 years later.
Another opinion dates the jugs of LMLK to the House of Ptolemy. (Y. Etzion, the Lost Bible, Tel Aviv 1991, p. 240-245) The inscriptions of Yeb also contradict this dating.
[346] E. Stern, 'Yehud' in vision and reality, Cathedra 4, 1977, p. 20-21 (Hebrew); E. Sukenik, The Meaning of the "Le-Melekh" Inscriptions, Qedem 1, 1942, p. 36 (Hebrew); A. Negev, Introduction to the Archaeology of the Land of Israel, Jerusalem 1967, p. 172. (Hebrew)
[347] Givon - E. Stern, The Material Culture of the Land of the Bible in the Persian Period, Jerusalem 1973, p. 35-36 (Hebrew)
Ramat Rachel - Y. Aharoni, Yediot Bahaqirat Eretz-Israel Weatiqoteha IXX (1956), p. 160, 163, 165. (Hebrew) idem, Yediot Bahaqirat Eretz-Israel Weatiqoteha XXIV, (1960), p. 102, 104 (Hebrew); G. Barkai, The New Encyclopedia of Archaeogical Excavations in the Holy Land, Jerusalem 1993, p. 1265.
Tell En-Nasbeh – M. Broshy, The New Encycloaedia of Archaeogical Excavations in the Holy Land, Jerusalem 1993, p. 1102.
Rogem Ganim – R. Greenberg & E. Cinamon, Stamped and Incised Jar Handles from Rogem Ganim, Tel Aviv 33 (2006), p. 230-231.

However, when we see time and again that the stamps 'LMLK' and the Rosette meet with Yahud and occupy the same strata levels, the explanation must be that LMLK and the Rosette are from the same time as Yahud from the Second Temple era and not from the First Temple.

3. Vessels from the Persian period, for example the bowls of 'Mortaria' have been uncovered in the levels of the Rosette. The dating of these vessels (the Persian period) contradicts the accepted dating of the First Temple level.

There were those who hoped that a mistake was made here, as one publisher wrote: "These bowls are typical of the Persian period... However bowls of this type were found apparently among findings from the Israelite period – in Megiddo, in Lachish, in Tel Gema; yet this conclusion is unreliable." [348]

Yet the appearance of vessels from the Persian period in the level from Iron Age II repeats itself in a number of places. Like in the burial cave in the valleys of Judah: "The form of the cave and the inscriptions are typical of the 7th century BCE (First Temple days). On the other hand the earthenware vessels are from the 5th century BCE (the Persian period)." [349]

Similarly at Mezad Hashavya, one of the well-known sites of the Rosette period: "There is a lot of interest in many different types of vessels that the general custom is to relate them to the Persian period." [350]

Vessels from the Persian period in the Rosette levels clearly show us that this level is not from the days of the First Temple, but from the Persian period.

4. Triangular-shaped arrowheads known as Scythian arrows have been found in the Rosette levels in Jerusalem and Lachish. These arrowheads are dated to the end of the First Temple period and considered to be Babylonian those who destroyed Jerusalem. [351]

But, are they really Babylonian? The answer is no, since this common arrowhead was not found in Nineveh, which the Babylonians destroyed at this time. On the

---

[348] B. Mazar et al, Ein-Gedi - Archaeological Excavations 1961-1962, Yediot Bahaqirat Eretz-Israel Weatiqoteha XXVII (1963), p. 38. (Hebrew)
We should mention that later in these writings they report that also in their excavations at Ein-Gedi these vessels were found in the Iron Age level. So, how can they question the credibility of reports by others, when the writers themselves revealed identical findings?
[349] Ibid.
[350] E. Stern, The Material Culture of the Land of the Bible in the Persian period, Jerusalem 1973, p. 22-23. (Hebrew)
[351] Y. Shilo, The New Encyclopedia of Archaeogical Excavations in the Holy Land, Jerusalem 1993, p. 709. ; D. Usishkin, Biblical Lachish, Jerusalem 2013, p. 318. (Hebrew)

other hand incredible numbers of this arrow were "most common in the Achmeny (Persian) weaponry". [352]

We now have additional evidence that the Rosette levels date from the Persian period and not exclusively from the time of the First Temple.

5. Furthermore, a comparative likeness has been found between the LMLK jugs and jugs from the middle of the Persian period.

The types of jugs from the middle Persian period "continue clearly the trend of the 'LMLK' jugs." [353]

If the LMLK jugs date to the days of Hezekiah (First Temple period), their likeness with the jugs from the middle Persian period is amazing, since we would expect to find recognizable differences after many generations between these two periods. But because of their similarities, the LMLK jugs can be dated to the beginning of the Persian period.

6. The wings on the LMLK and Rosset stamps are identical with the main symbols for the Persian Kings as we will see later on.

This teaches that the 'LMLK' and Rosset jugs were created during the time of the Persian Kingdom and not during the time of Hezekiah and his successors.

In short:

1. The LMLK and Rosette stamps are found on vessels from the Persian period.

2. In the LMLK and Rosset levels, 'Yahud' stamps from the Persian period also found.

3. In the Rosset levels we also find vessels from the Persian period.

4. In the Rosset levels we find weapons from the Persian period as well.

5. There is a continuity of the earthenware found in the LMLK and Rosset levels to the levels of the middle Persian period.

6. The wings and the Rosette are the same symbols of the Persian Kings.

---

[352] E. Stern, The Material Culture of the Land of the Bible in the Persian period, Jerusalem 1973, p. 156. (Hebrew)
[In theory it is possible that the Scythian arrows were used not only by the Persians, but also by the Babylonians after the destruction of Nineveh. (There are studies claiming this). However it is more reasonable to say that these are Persian arrows.]
[353] E. Stern, The Material Culture in the Land of the Bible in the Persian Period, Jerusalem 1993, p. 106, 96. (Hebrew)

It can therefore be concluded that the LMLK and Rosette jugs and other findings that are customarily accepted as related to the end of the First Temple period, are in fact, from the Persian period (the time of the Restoration).

Summary: We have thus found the lost layer marking the Restoration period. (As to the Babylonian Exile, this will be dealt with later.)

Recognition of the 'Wings' Symbol

After establishing that 'the king' of LMLK is actually the King of Persia we can explain the implication the four-wings symbol, why the symbol was changed to two wings, and why the two winged symbol was changed to the rosette.

The study of the Persian kings from the beginning of the Persian period is indispensable.

The first King was Cyrus (539-530 BCE). He overcame Nabonaid the King of Babylon and created the Persian Empire. He called himself "The King of the four wings".A figure with four wings was pictured at the entrance to his palace with the inscription: "I Cyrus, the King".[354]

"I Cyrus, the King"   The tomb of Cyrus

The four wings is the emblem of Cyrus and probably that of his son Cambyses (530-522 BCE).

The Kingdom was subsequently seized by Darius (521-486 BCE) and he started a new monotheistic religion, that believed in a single god named Ahura Mazda.

In his victory inscription in Bisutun Darius is pictured receiving his Kingdom from the new god surrounded by a circle with two wings. Also on the king's seals appears the picture of the god surrounded by a circle with two wings, in some

[354] E. Porada, Ancient Iran, Methuen - London 1965, p. 144.

cases only a two-winged symbol that is identical to the two winged emblem on the stamps of 'LMLK'.

Bisutun Inscription - Darius receiving his Kingdom from Ahura Mazda.

Persian King prays to Ahura Mazda

The two-winged image designates the god Ahura Mazda and this is the emblem of Darius. Once the Kingdom was stabilized under Darius, he visited Egypt and was crowned there as Pharaoh, and as is fitting for the Egyptian customs he was announced as a god. He built his city, Persepolis, and set up a splendid palace there.

The palace walls are engraved with a picture of Ahura Mazda: A crown identical to the King's sits on Ahura Mazda's head, engraved with the sign of the rosette. This change expresses the risen status of the King, as Edith Porada explains:

"The polos of Ahura Mazda in the relief in Bisutun, differs decidedly in shape from the battlemented crown of the king, which is decorated on its circumference with a pattern of alternating rosettes and double lotus-blossoms.

In the later reliefs in Persepolis the headgear of god and king seem to have become very similar, probably owing to a conscious attempt to assimilate the image of the king to that of the god...

It is possible that the renderings at Persepolis were a deliberate iconographic innovation of Darius and express ideas about kingship which he developed in the course of his reign. Perhaps he also took from Egypt the idea of a superhuman position for the king." [355]

---

[355] E. Porada, Ancient Iran, Methuen - London 1965, pp. 158-160.

After the death of Darius his throne was taken by Xerxes (485-465 BCE). Afterwards his grandson Artaxerxes I (465-424 BCE), and the symbol of the rosette filled the walls of the palace in which they lived.

Relief with Rosettes in Persepolis

The decoration of the Rosette expresses the self-ascribed godly status by the King.

Summary: The four-winged ornament is the emblem of Cyrus and Canbuzi, the two-winged decoration is the emblem of Darius, and the Rosette motif symbolizes the Kingdom from Xerxes onwards. From this we can date anew the archaeological periods.

Archaeological Name	Historical Name	Date (BCE)
Middle Iron Age II (LMLK)	Beginning of the Restoration (Cyrus and Darius I)	538-485
Late Iron Age II (Rosetta)	Restoration cont. (Xerxes and Artaxerxes I)	485-424
Persian Period	Second Half of Persian Period	424-332

The Amended Timeline

Why were the jugs collected?

More than a thousand LMLK jugs were found in a number of places in Judah, which suggests a large-scale collection operation. Why?

First we must explain the essence (and of course the cause) of the destruction of Judah at the end of the LMLK period and the end of the subsequent Rosette period after its restoration. At first glance it seems that we have no way of knowing, since "the province of Judah from the completion of the Second Temple (-516) until the coming of Ezra (-458) is swathed in fog." [356]

However, if we will check the few hints appearing in the Scriptures we will reveal that Judah was in a difficult situation twice during the time under discussion. What does this mean?

The Scriptures tell us that the enemies of Judah tried to stop them from building in Jerusalem (Ezra 4:1-5), however King Darius did not allow them to be attacked or harmed. (Ibid 6:1-22)

After his death, the enemies of Judah wrote letters to his son Xerxes (485-465 BCE) that the Jews should not be allowed to build the city, and the Scriptures don't say what happened as a result.

The enemies remained hostile and wrote again during the time of Artaxerxes I (465-424 BCE) and here the Scriptures expand and tell us the results of the letters that were given to the King by the Samaritans:

The Samaritans were given an injunction from the King preventing the building. They came to Jerusalem "with strong arms and with an army" (Ibid 4:6-7) and Judah was hit with a difficult blow.

This is what the Scriptures tell us: "the remnant that remained from the enslavement are in a terrible condition and disgrace and the walls of Jerusalem have been destroyed and its gates burned with fire" (Nehemiah 1:2-3).

Similar things probably happened as well after the hate letters from the days of Xerxes, though the Scriptures do not expand the discussion. If nothing happened as a result of these letters, there was no reason to mention them.

Consequently there were two destructions during the period of the Restoration: one at the end of the 'LMLK' period and another at the end of the Rosette period. They came from the Samaritans and other enemies of the province of Judah. The destruction of the LMLK period was at the beginning of the kingdom of Xerxes (485 BCE), and the destruction of the Rosette period was at the time of Artaxerxes, close to 445 BCE.

---

[356] F. M. Kraus, Samaria and Jerusalem, in: H. Tadmor (ed.) the Restoration – The Persian Period, Jerusalem 1983, p. 87. (Hebrew)

[External sources tell us the Persians quashed the revolts at the beginning of the Kingdom of Xerxes, [357] and during the days of Artaxerxes I. [358] Scholars tend to find a connection between these revolts and the writing of the hate letters. [359]]

Dating the destruction from the 'LMLK' level to the year when Darious died explains the massive number of 'LMLK' jugs:

Darius amied to conquer Greece, and after he was defeated in the battle of Marathon (490 BCE) he tried a second time. To finance this military expedition he imposed a levy on the citizens of his empire for large amounts of food and equipment. [360]

It is logical that the land of Judah, which grew grapes and olives in abundance, was required to provide wines and oils to the army of Darius, and this is what the 'LMLK' jugs were intended for.

While he was preparing for war Darius died in the year 485 BCE and the Province of Judah lost a supportive leader. The jugs 'for the King' are the jugs collected by the Jews for the army of the King who rewarded them with kindness.

The levels of destruction that cover these jugs indicate that after the King's death the Jews also fell.

Summary: From an archaeological perspective the period of the Restoration is a period without remnants of buildings or earthenware vessels. This conclusion comes from a mistaken dating of the finds from the LMLK and Rosette periods (the middle and end of 'Iron Age II' period) during First Temple times.

We showed that the LMLK and rosette periods are actually from the time of the Restoration. Having found this lost period, we are able to researc much more proficiently an era about which the Scriptures tell us little, as we will see in the next chapter. [361]

---

[357] The Writings of Herodotus, Book 7, 7.

[358] Thucydides, the history of the wars of the Peloponnese, Book 1, 104-109.

[359] E. F. Rainey, The Governor of all the other side of the River, in: H. Tadmor (ed.) the Restoration - The Persian Period, Jerusalem 1983, p. 113. (Hebrew)

[360] In the words of the historian Herodotus: "He sent off messengers to make proclamation through the several states, that fresh levies were to be raised, at an increased rate; while ship, horses, provisions, and transports were likewise to be furnished. So the men published his commands, and now all Asia was in commotion by the space." (The History of Herodotos, Book 7, 1.)

[361] In the north of the Land there is also a period which is considered to be 'an empty void'; however there are different dates from the dates in the south (the Land of Judah). This void begins at the end of the 8th century BCE and continues for some 200 years until the Persian period: "It seems that this area of the land remained almost completely uninhabited. When we check the maps of these settlements from the 8th century BCE on the one hand, and from the Persian period on the other and the gap between them". (Z. Gal, The Lower Galilee between the Assyrian conquest and the beginning of the Persian

Chapter 25: The Books of Ezra and Nehemiah in the Light of Archaeology

The arrival of Ezra and Nehemiah – The difference between the time of Darius and the time of Xerxes - Where is the Nehemiah's wall? – Summary

The Arrival of Ezra and Nehemiah

The biblical account of the arrival to the Land of Judah by Ezra and Nehemiah presents the reader with one of the difficult passages in the Scriptures.

The Scriptures tell us that at the beginning of his reign the Persian King Cyrus (538 BCE) gave the Jews permission to return to Jerusalem. (Ezra 1:1; ibid 2:70)

Eighty years afterwards, in the 7th year of Artaxerxes I (458 BCE), the King issued Ezra and an additional group of people with a permit to come to Judah, and appointed him ruler over the Jews with the power to punish (Ibid 7:12-26).

In the 20th year of Artaxerxes (445 BCE) the King appointed Nehemiah Pehah (ruler) over Judah and he built the walls of Jerusalem. (Nehemiah 5:14; Ibid 2:1-4, 17)

Ezra's arrival raises the question who ruled Jerusalem until his arrival? Also the story of Nehemiah's arrival raises the question: Why was Ezra's name not mentioned from the moment he arrives in Jerusalem until the completion of the wall when he reappears to participate in its inauguration and teaches Tora to the people? (ibid 12:36; ibid 8:1-18)

If Ezra ruled over the city until Nehemiah's arrival, why wasn't he a partner in the wall's construction? This question has preoccupied many scholars whose answers have raised the unpleasant need to change the language of the Scriptures. [362]

However, in light of the above, that the period of Ezra corresponds to the period of the Rosette which ended in the destruction of Judah, everything is clear.

---

period in: D. Amit and R. Kleter (eds.), the Transition Period in the Archaeology of the Land of Israel, Jerusalem, 2007). (Hebrew)

In these areas the period of the 'Rosette' is dated correctly to the Persian period (E. Stern, The New Encyclopedia of Archaeological Excavations in the Holy land, Jerusalem 1993, p. 1303-1304), whereas the parallel period of LMLK is dated likely to the eighth century BCE.

The solution here also is the same solution: to make an 'earlier period' later to its proper place, and this will fill the imaginary void.

[362] See the summary in: A. Demski, The days of Ezra and Nechemiah, in: H. Tadmor (ed.) the Restoration - The Persian Period, Jerusalem 1983, p. 40-45. (Hebrew)

This is how it happened. In the year 538 BCE Cyrus gave the Jews self-rule and appointed a Jewish person as their leader (the Peha). (Ezra 5:4) But with Xerxes's ascent to the throne and the hate letters presented to Xerxes, the enemies of Judah gained the upper hand, Jewish autonomy was revoked, and with it ended the period of LMLK (485 BCE). [363]

Judah was now under foreign rule which continued until the Ezra arrived (458 BCE) and self-rule was restored to the Jews and they began to build a wall. [364]

Ezra received his appointment from the King, but he resisted his need for help and refrained from requesting an armed escort, "as I was embarrassed to ask from the King army and horsemen". (Ezra 8:22) Certainly, the building of the wall was also done without the cooperation of the authorities.

His actions aroused suspicion of an intention to throw off the yoke of Persian rule and set up an independent state of Judah, especially when Egypt had rebelled and for a number of years was free of Persian rule.

We should also remember that not only Persians served in the King's army, but also representatives of all the other peoples in the Empire, including Jews, and these soldiers could form the basis of an army of the new state.

Consequently, the King ordered the use of force to prevent the building of the wall and, as Judah could not stand against its opponents it was destroyed. Ezra himself survived the destruction, though he was stripped of authority and the land returned to foreign rule.

When Nehemiah arrived in 445 BCE, he didn't ask to act separately from the government and, unlike Ezra, he arrived with a royal escort: "and the King sent with me ministers of the army and horsemen" (Nehemiah 2:9), and the building of the wall was also done as a Royal action: "I said to the king… that he should give me wood to cover the gates and for the wall of the city". (ibid 7-8)

The royal umbrella helped him to overcome his enemies and to build a wall. Now when he had stabilized the independent status of Judah, Ezra was called on to guide the people (ibid 8:1) this time as a spiritual and not as a civilian leader.

Consequently, the destruction in the Rosette period is actually the destruction of Judah at the time of Ezra, which happened before the arrival of Nehemiah. Judah declined and remained in this condition until the Hellenistic period.

---

[363] Discussed the nullification of the Independence of Judah: S. Telmon, Return To Zion – consequences for Our future, Cathedra 4 (1977), p. 30; E. Stern, the State of "Yahud" in Vision and in Reality, ibid, p. 12. (Hebrew)

[364] Even though it is not written specifically who built the wall, however it is written that we are talkin about Jews who came from the King to Jerusalem (Ezra 4:12), which is a description that fits Ezra's arrival to the Land of Israel.

Archaeological remains show a sharp breakdown and a reduction in the number of settlements on a ratio of one to ten in this period relative to the preceding one. [365]

Despite Nehemiah's rehabilitation works the Jewish settlement did not recover from the blow which struck it. This explains the literary dreariness characteristic of the era after Nehemiah because the land was exceptionally poor and did not produce intellectuals of stature. And so this chapter was forgotten in the collective memory of the nation and subsequent generations knew only about the first part of the Persian era.

The difference between the Periods of Darius and Xerxes

As mentioned, in the first part of the Restoration jugs were stamped with the LMLK seal, and in the later period with the Rosette seal.

An analysis of the findings shows that the number of LMLK stamps was limited and each stamp was used to stamp a large many jugs, whereas there were many Rosette seals but small use was made of them. [366]

The large number of Rosette seals demonstrates that during this period the number of clerks appointed over the tax collection compared to the preceding period sizably increased. Why was this?

The difference between the periods is also found in the standard of living. The LMLK period was economically prosperous, and in the following period there was a fall off. [367] What caused this financial decline?

The answer lies in the differences between the ruling monarchs. In the LMLK period King Darius ruled for most of the time. He was an enterprising monarch who utilized the throne for his own powers. He organized the Empire in an efficient way and introduced a fast postal service that reached the extremities of the kingdom in a few days.

---

[365] A. Faust, Jerusalem's Countryside during the Iron Age II - Persian Period transition, in: A. Faust & E. Baruch, New Studies on Jerusalem – Proceedings of the Seventh Conference, Ramat Gan 2001, p. 83-86 (Hebrew); A. Kloner, Jerusalem Environs in Persian Period, ibid, p. 91-92. (Hebrew)

[366] R. Kelter, Aspects of the Physical culture of Judah at the end of the Iron Age, Doctorate, Tel Aviv 1995 p. 227. (Hebrew)
The seals themselves have not been found, because they were made of material that disintegrated (wood), however , according to the slight difference between the seals we can learn how many jars were stamped with the same stamp:
Consequently the number of Rosette seals, according to the number of stampings, were about 20 times or more, in relation to the LMLK seals!

[367] A. Faust, Israelite society in the period of the Monarchy, Jerusalem 2005, p. 110 (Hebrew); H. Geva, Western Jerusalem between the 8th and 7th centuries BCE, in: A. Faust & E. Bsruch (eds.) New Studies on Jerusalem, Vol 8, Ramat Gan 2003, p. 23-24. (Hebrew)

On the other hand, his son Xerxes was a weak-minded ruler, and he was drawn after those who surrounded him. This is what emerges from the scroll of Esther, and also from writings of the Greek historians. He did not improve on the wonderful Kingdom he inherited from his father. During his reign the Persian Kingdom began to decline.

King Darius and Crown Prince Xerxes behind him

This difference between the father and his son, also explains the difference between the periods: a strong and efficient ruler who maintains 'a small and wise army', whereas a weak ruler is attached to a heavy handed bureaucratic system with unnecessary 'cronies', and many people doing the work of few.

Maintaining an inflated mechanism means raising extra funds from civilian taxes, so that in general the ruling class reaps the benefits of production and the rest of the population lives with burdening taxes and a declining standard of living.

This explains how in the LMLK period (in the reign of King Darius) only a few people belonged to the state tax collection apparatus; the economic situation was good because the population was not heavily burdened.

On the other hand, during the Rosette period (at the time of King Xerxes) the number of seals greatly increased, because many people joined the bureaucracy, taxes increased and the standard of living declined.

These things are clearly written by Nehemiah when he arrived in the Land at the end of the Rosette period, "and the first rulers were before me made things heavy on the people... Also their lads ruled over the people". (Nehemiah 5:16)

In order to correct the situation, Nehemiah announced that all members of the government (the rich people) should renounce their claim to debts that were owed to them by the poor people:

"And there was a shout from the people and their wives.... We have borrowed silver to the measurement of the King, our fields and vineyards... And behold we are holding down our sons and our daughters as slaves. And I argued with the rulers and their deputies and I said to him: return to them today their fields, and their vineyards, and their olive groves, and their houses that you have taken from them. And they said: we will return it and we will not request any more from them". (Ibid 4:1-12)

So Nehemiah attempted to repair the damage done by the ruling class and the corruption left behind by Xerxes.

Summary: these seals show that Darius was not only a well-loved ruler in Judah but also a beneficial ruler, who contributed much to the welfare of his citizens. His son, apart from being hostile, was also a weak and wasteful ruler and during his reign destroyed the economy of Judah. [368]

Where is Nehemiah's wall?

Our aim here is to investigate one of the most important acts taken by Nehemiah and to reveal that the remains of the wall are in place to this day.

When Nehemiah came to Jerusalem and saw the doleful situation, he resolved to build the destroyed wall. The story of the construction is told in great detail and with it commenced the actions of rebuilding by Nehemiah. What route did the wall take?

In the middle of the City of David, on top of the slopes above the Kidron Valley, a wall was uncovered and identified as 'Nehemiah's wall'. The problem is that the findings connected to this wall are much closer to the Hellenistic period than to the Persian period that preceded it.

Not only that, findings from the Persian period indicated that the wall was exactly on the other side of where it was estimated to be: "revealed a swathe of life from

---

[368] Identical conclusions have been reached by researchers on the seals of 'Yahud' which, according to all opinions, are from the Persian period.

At an early period of the seals of 'Yahud', "A relatively large number of impressions were made from the same seal," [O. Lipschits & D. Vanderhooft, Jerusalem in the Persian and Hellenistic Periods in light of the Yehud seal Impressions, Eretz Israel 28 (2007), p. 108-110. (Hebrew)] which testifies to an efficient government. Similar to what the seals of LMLK teach us.

In the later period "a great difference in types (of seals), testify to a form of government that had not taken hold" (ibid, p. 108) close to what we concluded about the seals of the Rosette.

The seals of Yahud reveal the same process that we found in the seals of LMLK and the Rosette. In the early period, a seal was used to make many impressions, and in the later period every seal made only a few impressions, that is to say, during the reign of Darius, the government was efficient and afterwards, during the days of Xerxes became inefficient.

this period (the Persian one). Their meaning has not yet been cleared up completely, since it is found outside the walls of the city that was built in this period on the heights of the hill." [369]

Kidron Valley

The fact that during the Persian period residents lived outside 'Nehemiah's wall' shows that apparently this is not the wall, and that the wall of Nehemiah was in a much lower place. Can we find it?

Before searching for the wall of Nehemiah, let us read from the Scriptures about Nehemiah's preparations ahead of the construction: "and I woke up in the night and did not tell the people what the Lord had put in my heart to do to Jerusalem... And I went around the walls of Jerusalem where they are breached...and I went up by the valley in the night and I went around the walls." (Nehemiah 2:12-16)

After his nocturnal tour he commenced the rebuilding of the wall, and completed it within 52 days (Ibid 6:16).

From this description it is clear that Nehemiah did not come to initiate a new wall from its foundations, but to complete and close breaches in the wall that existed before he came to Jerusalem. That is to say Nehemiah only completed the wall whose building was already begun during the time of Ezra.

We can also learn from the words: "went up by the **valley** and went around the walls", that the wall passed by the Kidron Valley which courses east of the City of David.

---

[369] H. Geva, The New Encyclopedia of Archaeological Excavations in the Holy Land, p. 723.

Can we find its traces? Yes! In recent years, a wall from the end of the Iron Age was revealed along the channel of the Kidron Valley, further east than all the other walls that were uncovered. [370] This wall was built in stages, originally part of the wall was built, and later another section was erected, and then the wall was raised in two stages. [371]

This description fits the wall of Nehemiah exactly, which completed the wall whose building began at Ezra's time.

Additionally, this newly discovered wall reached the pool dug beside the Gihon spring, and Scriptures state that Nehemiah's wall reaches **"the pool that was made"** (Nehemiah 3:16). So it seems that this is Nehemiah's wall.

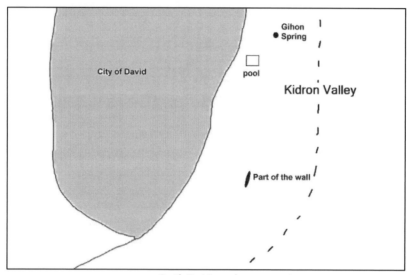

South-East Jerusalem

After finding the remains of the eastern wall of Nehemiah let us look for its western remains.

---

[370] E. Shukrun & R. Reich, A Wall from the End of the First Temple Period in the Eastern Part of the City of David, in: E. Baruch (ed.) New Studies on Jerusalem – Proceedings of the Fourth Conference, Ramat Gan 1998, p. 15 (Hebrew); idem, Channel 25, its Date, and its Relation to Waterworks in the City of David, in: A. Faust & E. Baruch (eds.) New Studies on Jerusalem – Proceedings of the Sixth Conference, Ramat Gan, 2000, p. 8 (Hebrew); idem, New Discoveries in the City of David Excavations, in: E. Baruch and A. Faust (eds.) New Studies on Jerusalem, Vol 8, Ramat Gan 2002, p.16 (Hebrew); idem, It is, after all, an Iron Age II City-Wall, in: E. Baruch and A. Faust (eds.) New Studies on Jerusalem , Vol. 13 , Ramat Gan 2007, p. 12 (Hebrew); E. Mazar, Jerusalem - 4000 Year Old Capital in the light of the Archaeology, Eretz Israe 28, p. 126. (Hebrew)
[371] E. Mazar, The Fortifications of Jerusalem in the Second Millennium BCE in Light of The New Excavations in the City of David, in: E. Baruch & A. Faust (eds.) New Studies on Jerusalem, Vol 12, Ramat Gan 2006, p. 24. (Hebrew)

Jerusalem of antiquity spanned two hills: the eastern hill ('City of David'), and the western hill ('Mount Zion').

Excavations have shown that at first Jerusalem was built only on the eastern hill. During Iron Age II houses were built for the first time also on the western hill, Later the western hill was also encircled by a wall, referred to as 'The Broad Wall', part of which can be viewed to this day in the middle of the Jewish Quarter of old Jerusalem.

'The Broad Wall' in Jerusalem

According to what we said up until now, the Broad Wall is the wall whose construction began at the time of Ezra, and was completed by Nehemiah. Therefore, Nehemiah refers to the Broad Wall when he details the route of the wall built by his people (Nehemiah 3:8).

So, we have found the wall of Nehemiah also in the west.

After we find the wall itself, we will also reveal that what was in front of the wall matches with what is said in the Scriptures by Nehemiah, and with the findings at the archaeological digs:

Nehemiah said after finishing his project: "and the city is spacious and big, few people in it and no houses are built." (Nehemiah 7:4) Scholars also say: "Large sections of the area generally remained (uninhabited)." [372]

---

[372] H. Geva, Western Jerusalem between the 8th and 7th century BCE, in: E. Baruch and A. Faust (eds.) New Studies on Jerusalem, Vol 8, Ramat Gan, 2002, p. 21. (Hebrew)

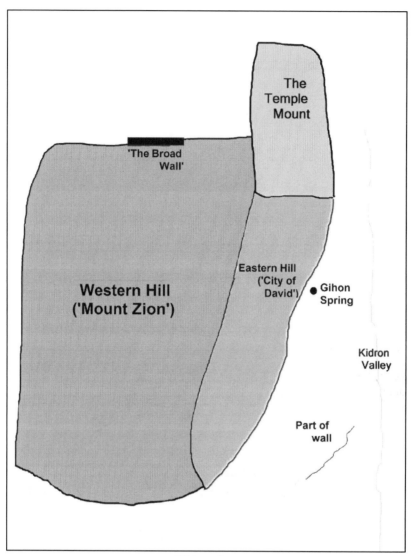

Old Jerusalem

Nehemiah's wall greatly expanded Jerusalem beyond any other previous wall, but the number of its inhabitants remained small.

Summary: The archaeological findings from the LMLK and Rosette periods match very well with what is written in the Books of Ezra and Nehemiah, and help us to understand them.

Chapter 26: Which was the Capital City?

Introduction - The Problem of the Samaria Ostraca– Which language was spoken in the Kingdom of Israel? – 'The Hidden city' Samaria of Sargon – The Royal palace in Ramat Rachel solves all the problems – The stamps of 'Yahud' teach us which was the capital – Hamitzpah, throne of the governor of the Trans-Euphrates region

Introduction

What was the capital of the Province of Judah during the time of the Restoration? Jerusalem, of course. Could there have been another city?

Archaeologists indicate that during the Restoration another city claimed the place of Jerusalem. Let us step back from this question and study the findings at Samaria, the capital of the kingdom of Israel, and in its trail we will also find the capital of the Province of Judah.

The Problem of the Samaria Ostraca

Omri, King of Israel, established the city of Samaria in the territory of the tribe of **Menashe**, and from then on Samaria was the capital of the Kingdom of Israel.

Excavations at the site revealed remains of the Palace of the Kings of Israel that stood there until the very end of the Kingdom of Israel. The Palace stored earthenware inscribed with the tax dispatches delivered from around the country. Each dispatch was inscribed with the name of the settlement from which it arrived and sometimes also included the name of the district.

It is clear from the inscriptions that these districts were all named after the descendants of Menashe: Shmidah, Helek, Noah, Hogla, and so on. (Book of Numbers 26:30-33) That is to say the taxes all arrived from the territory of the tribe of Menashe.

This fact is amazing because it means only the inheritance of Menashe was included in the Kingdom of Israel. No records of taxes from other places have been found, even though the Kingdom of Israel also included all the other tribes, except Judah and Benjamin.

Such an incongruity between the small kingdom evident in the earthenware of Samaria, in contrast to the size of the large kingdom as known from the Scriptures, is a subject that has baffled scholars.[373] We will try to find a solution later.

---

[373] B. Mazar, Cities and Districs in Eretz Israel, Jerusalem 1976, p. 242. (Hebrew)

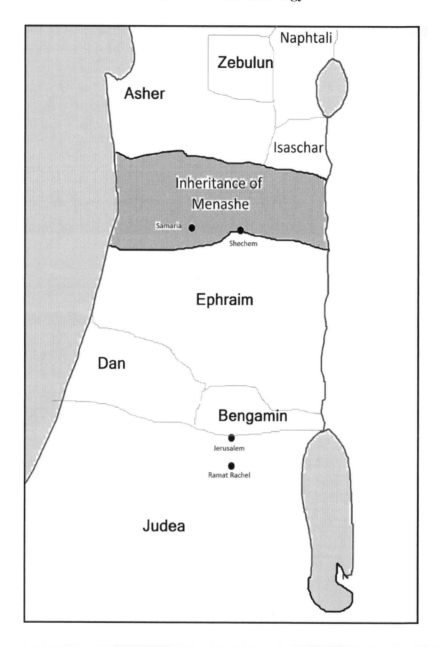

Some answer the question like this: the room in which the inscriptions were found was specificially allocated to tax revenues from the inheritance of Menashe. Mazar explains that these earthenware vessels were from the reign of King Jehoahaz. According to his opinion, during the reign of Jehoahaz the Kingdom of Israel was reduced only to the cities close to the city of Samaria.

Which language was spoken in the kingdom of Israel?

It is universally assumed that the Children of Israel spoke Hebrew until they went into exile, and then they began to speak Aramaic. This assumption contradicts inscriptions in Aramaic that have been found in Galilee, on vessels identical to those from the Palace of the Kingdom of Israel that were written during the era of the Kings of Israel. [374]

Pottery Dishes from Samaria.
The Institute of Archaeology of Hebrew University.

How do we explain the use of Aramaic in the kingdom of Israel? According to the excavator of these inscriptions, these are not Israelite ones. They were written in Aramaic because at the time of their writing the places had been conquered by the Arameans. [375]

This explanation is hard to accept. The Scriptures mention many wars between Israel and Aram and occasional Aramean victories which brought them to the gates of Samaria. (Kings I. 20: 1: Kings II 6: 24) However we do not know whether in the aftermath of such victories the Arameans settled inside the borders of the Kingdom of Israel. Therefore today the trend is to say that "Aramaic was spoken in the border areas of the Kingdom of Israel." [376]

The Children of Israel wouldn't discard the Hebrew language while they were still living in the Land. So how do we explain that Aramaic was spoken in Galilee during the monarchical era of Israel?

Here, too, we will try to answer this question later.

---

[374] N. Avigad, An Aramaic inscription on the Tel Dan Bowl, Yediot Bahaqirat Eretz-Israel Weatiqoteha XXX (1966), p. 209-211. (Hebrew)
[375] ibid, p. 212.
[376] O. Lipschits, the Consensus of the House of David, in: H. Baron and O. Lipschits (eds.) David King of Israel Alive and Enduring?, Jerusalem 1997, p. 14. (Hebrew)

'The hidden city' Samaria of Sargon

Samaria, the Capitol of the Kingdom of Israel, existed for more than 100 years, until almost the end of the 7th century BCE. Then Samaria was conquered by Sargon King of Assyria, who exiled all the inhabitants of the city and replaced them with other peoples. His inscriptions of Samaria read: "The town I rebuilt, better than it was before, and settled therein people. "[377]

We could expect that the excavations in Samaria would uncover this grand city built by Sargon; however "we have not revealed a level of the building from the Assyrian period". [378]

Later in the Persian period, Samaria was the provincial capital. The remains of this city also have not been found: "We have not succeeded during two seasons of widespread excavations on the site to bring up any sign of anything that hints of the city, which was probably one of the most important in the Land of Israel." [379]

Where did the city built by Sargon and the city from the Persian period disappear to? To answer all these questions let us present another royal palace, this time at Ramat Rachel.

The Royal palace at Ramat Rachel solves all the Problems

At Ramat Rachel, which is south of Jerusalem, a building has been uncovered. According to the earthenware found under its floors, it was built at the beginning of the Rosette period. Archaeologist Aharoni identified this building as the palace built by King Jehoyakim at the end of the First Temple period (Jeremiah 22:14). [380]

At this point a problem arose, because the 'palace of Jehoyakim' was built in the same style as the palace of the Kings of Israel in Samaria. [381] Many generations separate the two periods, so that it is not clear how these two palaces could be identical, as Yadin argues: "It is difficult to believe that 250 years after Ahab and 150 years after the destruction of Samaria a building in this style would be built in Judah." [382]

---

[377] L. Oppenheim, Babylonoian and Assyrian Texts, by: B. Pritchard (ed.) Ancient Near Eastern Text, Princeton - New Jersey 1969, p. 284.

[378] E. Stern, The Assyrian Impact on the Material culture of Palestine, Eretz Israel 27, 2003, p. 222. (Hebrew)

[379] E. Stern, The Material culture of the land of the Bible in the Persian period, Jerusalem 1973, p. 31. (Hebrew)

[380] Y. Aharoni, the Archaeology of the Land of Israel, p. 238. (Hebrew)

[381] idem, Excavations at Ramat Rachel, Yediot Bahaqirat Eretz-Israel Weatiqoteha XIX (1955), p. 166-167. (Hebrew)

[382] I. Yadin , The "House of Baal" in Samaria and Judah, in: J. Aviram (ed.) Eretz Shomron, Jerusalem 1973, p. 62. (Hebrew)

The similarity between the Palace of the Kings of Israel and the palace from the period of the Rosette in Ramat Rachel shows us that this building, called 'The Palace of the Kings of Israel' is not from the time of the Kingdom of Israel, but from a later period. If so, whose palace was it?

In the previous chapters we learned that the Rosette period dates to Persian rule. It is clear that the buildings called 'The Palace of the Kings of Israel' in Samaria and the building called 'The Palace of Jehoyakim' were in fact the centers of Persian rule, and this is the reason for the similarity between them.

Now we can answer all the questions:

1. The Samaria Ostraca lists only the settlements of the tribe Menashe, because Samaria in those days was no longer the capital of the Kingdom of Israel but the capital of the Persian Province Samaria which was much smaller. [383]

The Province of Samaria included only the local boroughs, that is to say, the territory of Menashe, and for this reason we did not find in the palace any records of the taxes bought from other areas.

2. In the Galilee spoke Aramaic because during this period the tribes of Israel no longer lived there. They exiled at the fall of the Kingdom of Israel: "Tiglat Pileser the king of Assyria came and took... And from the Galilee all the land of Naftali and he exiled them to Assyria." (Kings II, 15:29)

[In a way this is different from the area of Samaria where a large population remained even after the Exile, so that, Hebrew continued to be the language of the area. In the Galilee apparently only a few Israelites remained, and the new peoples who inherited their land spoke Aramaic, not Hebrew.]

3. Samaria of Sargon, like the Babylonian and Israelite Samaria exists underneath the Persian Palace mistakenly called 'The palace of the Kings of Israel'.

These strata have not been found because the excavator (K. Kenyon) did not dig deeper.

[In truth she found a more ancient layer underneath 'The Palace of the Kings of Israel' (what she calls 'period I'), but she chose to ignore the results. In the words

He himself suggested that the palace in Ramat Rachel was built by Queen Attaliah, the daughter of Ahab. With the finding of the stamps of LMLK under the floorboards, he was forced to explain that reconstructions were made at the end of the days of the Kingdom of Judah.

Aharoni, on the other hand, justified his later opinion to the end of the First Temple like this: " Hardly any development was recognizable In this building-system. There is no way to use this as a criteria for exact dating" (Y. Aharoni, The Archaeology of the Land of Israel, p. 180).

[383] I. Efal, The Assyrian rule over the land of Israel, in: A. Malamat (ed.) The Age of the Monarchy, Jerusalem 1982, p. 197-198. (Hebrew)

of N. Avigad: "Kenyon did not overlook this problem. Although she noted the discovery of two walls covered by the floors of buildings from period I, when discussing the pottery she stated that there was no trace of occupation until the time of Omri." [384]

Kenyon ignored these ancient remains because it is apparent from the Scriptures that Samaria was not built until the time of Omri. In order not to spoil a match between the Scriptures and the finds, it was decided that the strata of the 'Palace of the Kings of Israel' is the earliest level. If she had not stopped there, the excavations could have found the real Palace of the kings of Israel.]

Summary: Comparing the palace in Samaria to the palace in Ramat Rachel teaches us that the palace in Samaria should be dated to the Persian period, and not to the time of the Kings of Israel. Now we understand why only taxes from the inheritance of Menashe were received in this palace, as well as the answers that have been given to the other questions that were raised above.

Ramat Rachel

The stamps of 'Yahud' teach us which was the Capital

The Royal building in Ramat Rachel is, therefore, the center of Persian rule in Judah. Why not in Jerusalem? This is because, as explained above, during the Rosette Period (the time of Xerxes) the independent status of Judah was nullified and foreign rulers were entrusted with it. The enemies of Judah wanted to reduce the importance of Jerusalem, and therefore the government buildings were moved outside the city.

---

[384] N. Avigad, The New Encyclopedia of Archaeological excavations in the Holy Land, Jerusalem 1993, p. 1303.

The findings of the Royal seals from the time of the Second Temple, when the land of Judah was called the 'Province of Yahud', certifies that for most of the period of Persian rule, Ramat Rachel was the capital of the Province of Judah.

The Royal seals of Yahud were mostly discovered in Jerusalem and Ramat Rachel, though the number of seals found at Ramat Rachel was 48% more than the number in Jerusalem which amounted only 26% of the total seals found. [385]

These stamps show that their earliest distribution were found in Jerusalem, but in later periods more than two thirds of these stamps were found mainly in Ramat Rachel and less than 10% in Jerusalem. With continuing Persian rule most of these stamps were in Ramat Rachel (55%), though Jerusalem was well represented with 21%. During the Hellenistic period 61% were found in Jerusalem.

It can therefore be concluded that the place in which the greater number of government stamps was found is the capital; and from the distribution of the findings we learn how Jerusalem was the capital at the beginning of the Persian period, but later moved to Ramat Rachel, as a result of the hate letters at the start of Xerxes period.

Later on, at the time of Nehemiah, Jerusalem rose in status, but this did not last long and Ramat Rachel returned to be the Capital of Judah until the end of the Persian period. Only with the Hellenistic period Jerusalem returned to be the capital.

Hamitzpah, throne of the Governor of the Trans-Euphrates region

We have shown that the capital of Judah at the time of Xerxes was in Ramat Rachel, known in Arabic as Khirbet Sabkha. What was the name of the place in Scriptural times? Mazar suggested identifying the site with 'Netofa', Aharoni with 'Beth Hakerem', and Barkai with 'Mameshet'.

However, if we examine the Scriptures carefully we will discover that the government site is called "Hamitzpah Lekiseh Pakhat Ever Hanahar (Lookout of the throne of the governor of the Trans-Euphrates region)." (Nehemiah 3:7)

The name 'Hamitzpah' (lookout) suits Ramat Rachel well, for it is sited on a hill with a panoramic view and today a scenic plaza over the whole Jerusalem.

The official name 'of the throne of the governor of the Trans-Euphrates region' is also very fitting which, in the words of the excavator: "The finest techniques were

---

[385] O. Lipschits & D. Vanderhooft, Jerusalem in the Persian and Hellenistic Periods in light of the Yehud stamp Impressions, Eretz Israel 28 (2007), p. 108-110. (Hebrew)

employed in constructing the buildings and walls." [386] "A palace that had no comparison... A glory which is not recognizable in other places in Judah." [387]

The words 'Kiseh Pakhat' (throne of the governor) has been preserved in the Arabic name Sabkha, since the Arabs change the letter P to B and therefore 'Kiseh Pakhat' was changed to 'Sabkhah'.

Summary: the capital of Judah was Jerusalem until the time of Xerxes, and then another place was chosen: **'Hamitzpah Lekiseh Pakhat Ever Hanahar'** (Ramat Rachel), which remained the capital of Judah until the end of Persian rule (except for the short period of Ezra and Nehemiah).

The view from Ramat Rachel

---

[386] Y. Aharoni, The New Encyclopedia of Archaeological Excavations in the Holy Land, Jerusalem 1993, p. 1264.
[387] O. Lipschits et al, Ramat Rachel and its secrets, Qadmoniot 138 (2010) p. 64. (Hebrew)

Chapter 27: The Negev during the Period of the Restoration

Lack of LMLK stamps in the Negev - When did the Negev change from being Jewish to Edomite? - What is Mameshet? - The time of the Arad letters - Kuntilat Ajrud

Lack of LMLK stamps in the Negev

Military fortresses from the Iron Age have been excavated at Arad in the Negev (southern Israel), and many letters were revealed.

These letters teach that Jewish soldiers served in the fortress at Arad and looked after the place, against their enemies, the Edomites. One letter mentions "the evils which Edom (did?)", and in another the clerk warns: "lest Edom will come there." [388]

LMLK stamps were discovered in this fortress, as well as in another fortress in Tel Aroer; however, in the rest of the Negev very few LMLK stamps were found. In the words of the scholar M. Aharoni: "The fact that the stamps of LMLK are almost not to be found requires an answer." [389]

In the period after LMLK - the period of the Rosette - this phenomenon strengthens, not only in the settlements of the Negev there are no stamps of the Rosset but also missing in the area of Hebron. [390]

What is the explanation for the lack of LMLK and Rosette stamps in the south of Judah? The answer rests with the Edomite invasion of the Negev.

When did the Negev change from being Jewish to Edomite?

The prophets of Israel prophesied that Edom will turn into a desert (Isaiah 34, Jeremiah 49, and Ezekiel 35). This occurred shortly before the time of the Second Temple, when Nabonaid the King of Babylon destroyed the land of Edom and transformed the cities into barren wastes. In the words of the prophet Malachi: "and I hated Esav and I made his cities a desert." (Malachi 1:3)

The Edomite people emigrated westwards to the South of Judah, which became Idumaea (the land of the Edomites), and so part of Judah became a land settled by gentiles.

---

[388] Y. Aharoni, Arad Inscriptions, Jerusalem 1986, p. 48-72. (Hebrew)
[389] M. Aharoni, LMLK Stsmps, in: Y. Aharoni, Arad inscriptions, Jerusalem 1986, p. 131. M. Aharoni suggested that the stamps of LMLK indicate wine that came from the vineyards of the King, and in the Negev there were no royal vineyards, only private vineyards.
[390] R. Kleter, Aspects of the Physical Culture of Judah at the end of the Iron Age, Doctorate, Tel Aviv 1985, p. 233. (Hebrew)

When did this Edomite settlement begin in Judah? Apparently in the beginning of the Second Temple. However, Edomite ceramics and religious artefacts were found in settlements of the Negev dated to the end of the First Temple period (the end of the Iron Age).

Based on this evidence, investigators concluded that Edomite settlements in the Negev began even before the destruction of Edom, already at the end of the First Temple period. [391]

However, in fact, the Edomites did not reach the Negev at the time of the First Temple, but after it, since as we said the end of the Iron Age was not the end of the First Temple period, but at the beginning of the Second Temple era.

By then the Kingdom of Judah no longer existed, but the Jewish governorship over a small territory. The Negev, which ceased to be part of Judah, changed into an Edomite entity. That explains why the LMLK stamps were not found in the Negev.

Why were no stamps found from the Rosette period even in the Hebron area?

The Scriptures tell us that during the Second Temple period, Judah's borders retracted further and the Hebron area became non-Jewish. The lists in the Book of Nehemiah (chapter 3), show that during his time Jewish settlement in the mountain region reached only as far as the Beth Tzu area, north of Hebron. [392]

A fact that the Negev was already non-Jewish at the end of the Iron Age is given by findings from Tel Sheva (near Beer Sheva). They revealed a storage room containing inscriptions showing the names of the people from whom taxes were collected. The names are non-Jewish: "The taxed owners of these farms were generally Arabs and Edomites." [393]

---

[391] N. Na'aman, The Negev in the Latter days of the Kingdom of Judah, Cathedra 42 (1987), p. 15. (Hebrew); A. F. Rainey, Arad in the Latter days of the Judean Monarchy, ibid, p. 25. (Hebrew); Y. Beit-Aryeh, Hurvat Uzza - A Border Fortress in the Eastern Negev, Qadmoniot 73-74 (1986), p. 38-39 (Hebrew); idem, An Edomite Shrine at Horvat Qitmit, Eretz Israel 20 (1989), p. 145 (Hebrew); A. Kasher, Edom, Arabia and Israel, Jerusalem 1988, p. 9-10. (Hebrew); Z. Meshel, Iron Age Negev settlement, in: Y. Aviram et al (eds.) Eilat, Jerusalem 1985, p. 174; I. Efal, The Origins of Idumaea, Qadmoniot 126 (2003), p. 77-79. (Hebrew)

[392] The book of Nehemiah has another list that includes Hebron and even Beersheba: "The people of Judah dwelt ... and Beersheba and its surrounding hamlets". (Nehemiah 11:25-27) We see that during this time the Negev was settled by Jews, contrary to our words.

However this list does not talk about the settlements during the time of Nehemiah at all, but rather about the places in which they had lived in the past ("They dwelt" is written in the past tense) and as is written by E. Stern: "It is brought not as a real list, rather as an optimal plan. How they would need to settle the men of Judah coming back from the Exile." (E. Stern, 'Yehud' in vision and reality, Cathedra 4 (1977), p. 20).

[393] Y. Aharoni, Arad Inscriptions, p. 23. (Hebrew)

This explains the absence of LMLK stamps in the Negev and the lack of Rosset seals even in the Hebron area. The period of LMLK and Rosset correspond with the restoration. In the beginning Jews did not live in the Negev, and later not even in the area around Hebron.

However if the Negev was not Jewish during the period of LMLK, why do we find LMLK seals in Arad and Arorer?

What is Mameshet?

The LMLK seals appear with the name of one of these four cities: **Zif**, **Socho**, **Hebron** or **Mameshe**t. The first three cities of Judah are mentioned in the Scriptures, (Joshua 16:24, 35, 54) and we know where they were, but where is Mameshet?

A Nabotean city named Mamsheet existed in the Negev (Memphis); however, this Mamsheet city was established later, at the end of the Second Temple period.

No other persuasive identification can be given, and Mameshet remains a mystery.

Nonetheless, what was the significance of these four cities? One opinion is that they were the capital cities of the boroughs of Judah.[394] But Zif was only 5 km from Hebron on the edge of the desert, so it is hard to accept this explanation. (There was another Zif, close to Dimona, though it was a distant settlement it was not fit to serve as the borough capital).

The 'Spice Road' can provide an answer. What is the 'Spice Road'?

In antiquity the spices myrrh and frankincense were extremely prized commodities for which vast sums were paid. These spices were grown in Southern Arabia and brought by land to the port in Gaza from where they were shipped to the whole ancient world.

Due to the high value of these spices, fortified army posts were built along the route to protect the passage of these convoys through the Land of Israel from the Ramon crater to Gaza.

---

[394] Y. Aharoni there.

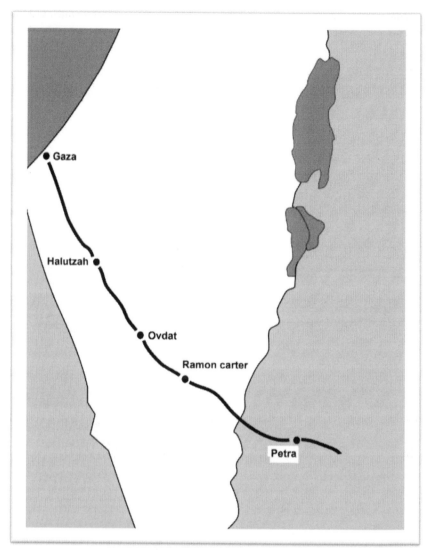

The 'Spice Road'

During the reign of Darius, Gaza belonged to the Arabs and not to the Persians.
[395] It is obvious the Persians were interested that the spice convoys did not reach
Gaza but remained under their control. How could the Persians protect the
convoys in their areas?

The Persians had a northern spice route that passed along the axis: Hatzebah-
Ma'ale Dragot.[396] On this axis sat **Mamsheet**. From Ma'aale Dragot the convoys

---

[395] E. F. Rainey, The Governors of the other side of the river, in: H. Tadmor (ed.) The
Restoration - The Persian Period, Jerusalem 1983, p. 110. (Hebrew)
[396] E. Orion, the Spice Roads, Sedeh Boker 1991, p. 15. (Hebrew)

continued to **Zif**, **Hebron**, and **Socho** and to the port at Ashdod which were all under Persian control.

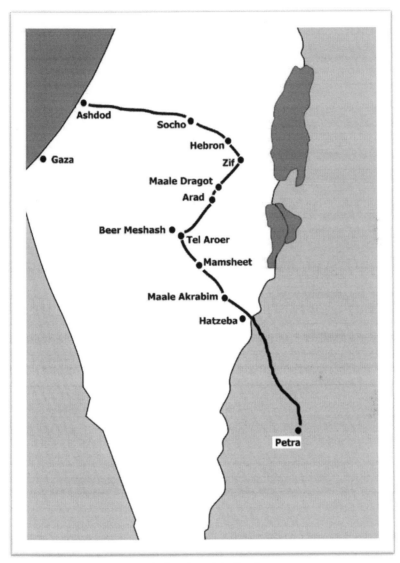

The 'Northern Spice Road'

The fortresses that were built along its length testify to the importance of this road. Surveys from the Persian period have revealed "a clear line of border fortresses westwards in the direction of the city of Ashdod, and southwards in direction of the southern Hebron mountains." [397]

---

[397] E. Stern, "Yehud" in vision and reality, Cathedra 4 (1977), p. 22. (Hebrew)

These fortresses named 'The Border Fortresses', but this name isn't true, as Z. Kalai writes "They were not located along the the real border and we have no information to help us explain the expansion of the fortresses." [398]

The protection of the spice road accurately explains the position of the fortresses. It also explains why south of the governorship of Judah we find the LMLK seals in a significant number only in Arad and Arorer, because both were fortresses that protected this route.

If the purpose of the Persian army units was to protect the Mamsheet-Zif-Hebron-Socho road, we understand why the seals are inscribed with the names of these places, and the seals weren't changed, even when they moved to another area.

This explains the names of these jugs as well as the name Mamsheet. The Nabotean city was not yet built, though the likeness between the Nabotean name and the name appearing on the LMLK seals is not an unreasonable coincidence.

So we must look for a fortress from the LMLK period. A fortress like this actually exists, and it is Tel Arorer close to Mamsheet to the north, and was inhabited during the LMLK period. [399]

The place, today is called **Tel Arorer** is apparently the **Mameshet** of the time of LMLK.

Later, when the Naboteans established their city, the name moved from Tel Arorer, which was no longer inhabited, to the new city.

During the later period a new monastery was built north of Tel Arorer, and even this place - in the language of the Arabs Beer Meshash - has preserved the ancient name of Mameshet.

Summary, the cities in which the LMLK seals were found are stations on the spice road protected by Jewish soldiers who served in the Persian army. The protection included the Negev, even though it was outside the borders of the Governorship of Judah. Mamsheet was one of these guard stations - the fortress of Tel Arorer close to Mamsheet.

The time of the Arad letters

The well-known Arad writings should be dated to the era of the Persian rule, and not as universally accepted to date it to the period of the First Temple.

The following evidence will prove that the correct time is the Persian rule:

---

[398] Z. Kalai, Judah and the Stamps of the Jewish settlement, in: H. Tadmor (ed.) The Restoration – The Persian Period, Jerusalem 1983, p. 78. (Hebrew)

[399] A. Biran and R. Cohen, *Arorer* in the Negev, Eretz Israel 15 (1981), p. 250 ff. (Hebrew)

Apart from earthenware with Hebrew inscriptions, other earthenware has been found in Arad written in Aramaic from the Persian period.

Is there a stratum in Arad from the Persian period?

According to the excavator "no buildings or floors were found that relate to this stratum". Persian earthenware was found in the stratum. How can this be?

In response they are forced to say "The Aramaic ostracons were found in garbage pits". [400]

This is a weak explanation, even if we are speaking only about one site. However, we will discover that the archaelogists are repeatedly forced to return to this excuse.

Storerooms with Aramaic inscriptions from the Persian period were also discovered at **Tel Sheva** and here too it is hard to find remains of buildings from the Persian period, and so the answer is similar: "The majority finds dating to the period stem from pits." [401]

The storerooms in Tel Sheva

---

[400] Y. Aharoni, Arad Inscriptions, p. 5 (Hebrew); idem, The Arad Ostraca, Qadmoniot 3 (1968), p. 101. (Hebrew)
[401] Z. Hertzog, The New Encyclopedia of Archaeological Excavations in the Holy Land, p. 172.

The same is said of the fortress at **Kadesh Barnea**: "Most of the finds from this period were discovered in pits dug into the earlier levels." [402]

Z. Meshel says the same of other places: "A situation like this is recognizable also in **other places in the south** of Israel. In these settlements no buildings were found from the Persian period, and in general only pits and barns filled with earthenware and ashes." [403]

It is incredible that nothing was built during the Persian period, yet the scholars made do with 'garbage pits'. So that finding these Persian objects in the stratums of 'Iron Age II' proved that these stratums are from the Persian period.

2. The connection between the Hebrew records of Arad and the Aramean inscriptions from the Persian period does not end with finding them in one layer. Apart from this "the content of a number of these earthenware pieces in Hebrew is likened to the contents of the Aramean earthenware... It is possible to suggest that the military purpose of Arad had not changed." [404]

3. in arad founded also Aramean inscriptions from the Persian period. Jewish soldiers are also mentioned in these inscriptions, even though the place lies distance from the borders of the governorship of Judah: "The Hebrew names are mostly on the Aramean earthenware... Most of the responsible workers are Jews." [405]

Amazingly even the commander's name in both periods is the same. The commander in the Hebrew records is called Elyashiv, [406] and he also appears in one of the Aramean inscriptions from the Persian period: " 'horseman of Elyashiv men 10'– meaning a unit of 10 horsemen that Elyashiv was commanding." [407]

If we accept the conventional dating for the Arad records (the First Temple period) this will force us to say that the commander Elyashiv in the Hebrew earthenware, and the commander Elyashiv in the Aramean earthenware are two different people from two different periods.

It is more logical to say that we are speaking about the same person than to assume that in two different periods two different commanders with the same name were stationed in Arad.

---

[402] R. Cohen, The New Encyclopedia of Archaeological Excavations in the Holy Land, p. 847.
[403] Z. Meshel, The Negev during the Persian Period, Cathedra 4 (1977), p. 46. (Hebrew)
[404] Y. Neveh, The Aramic Ostracons from Tel Arad, in: Y. Aharoni, Arad inscriptions, p. 212. (Hebrew)
[405] Ibid, p. 213.
[406] Ibid, P. 12, 15, 18 and others.
[407] Ibid, p. 182.

'Elyashiv Room' in Arad

4. The language in which the Hebrew earthenware is written also proves that they are not from the First Temple period: "Terms are found in the language of these inscriptions that look as if they belong to a much later period." [408]

The logical conclusion from all this is that the Arad inscriptions must be from the Persian period.

5. Additional facts are clarified when we date the Arad letters to the Persian period, such as the commands given to Elyashiv in a number of the letters, to ensure that food is provided to the 'Kittim'. (The inhabitants of the Greek city Kittie in Cyprus), and the list of items uncovered in his room written entirely in Egyptian. That is to say Greek and Egyptian soldiers also served in the Arad fortress.

According to accepted dating, it is hard to understand what the Kittites are doing here, since no known source at the end of the First Temple period records that Kittite soldiers were used, as one excavator writes: "This is the first testimony that hired soldiers of Greek origin served in the army of Judah." [409]

---

[408] Ibid, p. 150.
[409] Ibid p. 154.

The inclusion of Egyptians is even more amazing, and some very unconvincing explanations have been given for this.[410]

The Persian army, on the other hand, was a large international army in which there were many Greek soldiers. Similarly there were Egyptian soldiers, and the appearance of Kittites and Egyptians as part of the force in Arad, should not raise any eyebrows.

Summary: Kittite and Egyptian findings in the fortress at Arad, comfortably dates it to the Persian period, which adds to the other proofs that the letters are from the Persian period.

Kuntilat Ajrud (Horvat Teman)

An amazing site comprising a number of buildings called 'Kuntilat Ajrud' (Horvat Teman) was uncovered in the southernmost part of the Negev on the Sinai border.

The inscriptions in these buildings indicate that this was a very important religious center. Priests dwelt here, the visitors offered them donations and asked them for the blessing of the Lord. The inscriptions teach us about the religious world of their inhabitants.

They served the Lord of Israel but also Ashera and Baal and other gods. The blessings in the inscriptions are worded 'your blessing from YHVH', similar to those found on the Arad earthenware, though with one addition. In Kuntilat Ajrud they wrote 'YHVH of Samaria' or 'YHVH of Teman'. [411]

Who were these people who served the Lord of Israel together with other gods? Why did they establish their place of worship in such a distant place? What brought the writers to call the Lord: 'YHVH of Samaria'? Where was Teman whose name is appendage to the name of the Lord?

The earthenware on this site is from the LMLK period.[412] According to the dating we have given, we are speaking about the beginning of the Restoration and the explanation for the site is as follows:

---

[410] Yeivin argued theory that this is a supplies list to Egyptian mercenaries. Aharoni alternately argues there is no proof that Egyptian citizens were in this place. In his opinion the list this was made after the place fell into the hands of Pharaoh Necho's army. However if signs of destruction are found after the list was written, it will explain that the place fell without a fight, that the conquerors made a list of the contents, and then burned down the fortress. (ibid p. 64-66).

[411] Z. Meshel, Kuntilat Ajrud - An Israelite Site on the sinai Border, Qadmoniot 36 (1973), p. 126 (Hebrew); idem, The New Encyclopedia of Archaeological Excavations in the Holy Land, p. 1458-1463.

[412] L. Singer-Avitz, The Date of Kuntille Ajrud, TA 33 (2000), p. 209.

When the people returning from Babylon began to build the Second Temple, the Samaritans also asked to take part in its construction. These were people who were brought to Samaria by the Kings of Assyria after the destruction of the Kingdom of Israel. They undertook to serve the Lord of Israel but did not cease to serve other gods: "and these nations fear the Lord and still serve their statues." (Kings II, 17:41)

The Jews declined the request of the Samaritans to take part in the building (Ezra 4:2-3). The Samaritans were excluded from the holy Temple in Jerusalem and were forced to continue their worship in Samaria until the time of Alexander the Great of Macedonia who destroyed Samaria as punishment for their rebellion. The Samaritans moved their center of worship to Mount Gerizim, where they continue to worship to this day. [413]

Samaria was considered inferior to Jerusalem which had an ancient tradition of being a holy place and Samaria did not. The Samaritans wanted to adopt a holy place from generations ago to cover up this shortcoming, and the most suitable place obviously was on Mount Sinai, which could become a truly holy place instead of Jerusalem.

This apparently explains the site of Kuntilat Ajrud, which is located on the way to Mount Sinai. It could have been used as a parking ground for pilgrims attending festivals, but it could also be that because it was difficult for them to travel the long distance to Mount Sinai, so they identified this place as Mount Sinai.

The Samaritans are the builders of the site that served the God of Israel equally with other gods. They used the expression 'YHVH of Samaria' because Samaria was a place of sacrifice to the Lord, and also 'YHVH of Teman', because Teman is the name of Mount Sinai located in the South (Teman means south).

Summary, the religious center of Kuntilat Ajrud (Horvat Teman) in the south, was established by the Samaritans at the time when they were excluded from building the holy Temple.

The Negev during the period of the Restoration was not Jewish but Edomite, and during the time of Xerxes and afterwards the Hebron area was also Edomite.

There are three Jewish fortresses points in the Negev: Arad, Tel Ira and Tel Arorer (Mameshet) where Jewish soldiers were stationed to guard the spice road.

---

[413] There is a tradition that the temple on Mount Gerizim existed even before the destruction of Samaria. Excavations on the site do not support this, because the earliest earthenware found in the Samarian temple on Mount Gerizim is from the 3rd century BCE: "A dating that contradicts apparently the probability that the Temple was founded before the time of Alexander" [F. M. Kraus, Samaria and Jerusalem, in: H. Tadmor (ed.) The Restoration – The Persian Period, Jerusalem 1983, p. 92].

Chapter 28: The Babylonian Period

Introduction - Where has Solomon disappeared to? – 'The Gates of Solomon' in the prophecy of Ezekiel – The Lachish letters and the stamp of Jehucal - The 'Israelite fortresses' that are not Israelite – The devaluation of the shekel

Introduction

Until now we have dealt with the Middle Iron Age II ('LMLK') and the End of Iron Age II ('Rosette') and shown that the accepted dating for these periods is incorrect. In this chapter we will focus on the beginning of Iron Age II, and supply proof that here, too, the accepted timeline is mistaken.

Early Iron Age II	Beginning of the First Temple period	1000-900
Middle Iron Age II 'LMLK'	Middle of the First Temple Period	900-700
Late Iron Age II ('Rosette")	End of the First Temple Period	700-586

The accepted timeline for Iron Age II is divided into the following units (all dates BCE)

Where has Solomon disappeared to?

The findings from the beginning of Iron Age II are extremely problematic. King Solomon lived in this period, and we would expect to find remnants of Jerusalem's glory. However, excavations have indicated, this was one of the most miserable periods that the city of Jerusalem had known. [414]

Some archaeologists explain the absence of remains from the period of Solomon to Herod's massive building works that resulted in the disappearance of remains from earlier periods.

Finkelstein, on the contrary, argues that "the perfectly preserved remains of fortifications from the Middle Bronze Age and the Late Bronze Age contradict the

---

[414] A. Kloner, Surveys of Jerusalem – the Southern Sector, Jerusalem 2000, p. 11 (Hebrew); A. De-groot, "The Invisible City" of the Tenth Century BCE, in: A. Faust & E. Baruch (eds.), New Studies on Jerusalem – Proceedings of the Seventh Conference, Ramat Gan 2001, p. 29-34. (Hebrew)
Some claim that there are enough findings from Jerusalem from the 10th century BCE, however they also agree: "The cup is half full. This is not the splendid city that we see in our imaginations when we read the Scriptural texts." (A. Mazar, Jerusalem in the 10th Century BCE, in: A. Faust & E. Baruch (eds.), New Studies on Jerusalem, Vol. 10, Ramat Gan 2004, p. 17).

opinion that the building actions from the time of Herod could have totally erased all the remains of monuments from the time of Solomon." [415]

Another archaeologist, Yadin, who wholeheartedly believed what was said of Solomon, was forced to admit: "Solomon was the evader of all the builders of the land from the archaeological perspective." [416]

In other parts of the country remnants have been found of buildings from this period, however its style does not conform to Solomon's. Solomon commissioned builders from the Phoenician coastal cities – Tyre and Byblos, (Kings I, 5:32) yet the building style at the 'beginning of Iron Age II' is not like Phoenician building but closer to the style from more distant areas. In the words of Aharoni:

"What was the architectural source that penetrated the land so quickly? The accepted assumption is that it was Phoenicia. However, until now, this has not been supported by archaeological research. The best comparisons can be made with those from northern Syria." [417]

If so, in Jerusalem there are absolutely no remains from the time of Solomon and in other cities the remnants do not support what's written in the Scriptures. Is this in fact the case?

Rather, as we have explained in previous chapters, the facts we have presented show that the Iron Age is much later than it is customary to say, and should be dated as follows:

Early Iron Age II	Babylonian Period	600 -538
Middle Iron Age II ('LMLK')	The Restoration	538-485
Late Iron Age II 2 (Rosette)		485-424

Now we understand why Jerusalem was so miserable at the beginning of Iron Age II, since this is not the time of Solomon but the era of exile in Babylon.[418] This also explains the new architecture that arrived from the North during this time, a direct result of the Babylonian conquest.

---

[415] I. Finkelstein & N. Silverman, David and Solomon, Tel Aviv 2006, p. 250-251. (Hebrew)

[416] I. Yadin, Hatzor, Tel Aviv 1975, p. 187. (Hebrew)

[417] Y. Aharoni, The Archaeology of the Land of Israel, p. 185-186. (Hebrew)

[418] While the Period of Solomon is dated to Middle Bronze Age II, and the findings in Jerusalem correspond to this period: "the findings tell us about the settlement growth in the city of David during the period MB II, and prove how much stronger it was during the period under discussion" [D. Bahat, City of David Excavations 1998, in: E. Baruch (ed.) New Studies on Jerusalem – Proceedings of the Fourth Conference, Ramat Gan 1998, p. 24 (Hebrew)].

To prove this theory we can cite the gates of the cities. What are they?

'The Gates of Solomon' in the Prophecy of Ezekiel

Excavations at a number of sites in the Land of Israel have revealed that during the beginning of Iron Age II it was customary to build three cells on each side of the city gates. [419]

It is also customary to link this period to the 10th century BCE. Since Solomon is known to have lived in the 10th century BCE, these gates are known as 'the gates of Solomon'.

The 'Six Cells' Gate in Gezer

Later critics claimed that these gates or part of them, are from the time of Ahab the King of Israel (9th century BCE) and arguments around the subject were most gripping in the archaeological community in previous years. However, while there is no conclusion as to who built these gates – Ahab or Solomon – they found that the Gates of the six cells have a Scriptural connection to which there can be no disagreement, and that is the prophecy of Ezekiel which describes the gates:

"In the 25th year of our Exile ... in the visions of the Lord I was brought to the Land of Israel and put down on a very high mountain, on which there was

---

[419] I. Yadin, Hatzor, Tel Aviv 1975 p. 105 (Hebrew); idem, The Megiddo of the Kings of Israel, Qadmoniot 10 (1970), p. 38 (Hebrew); W. G. Dever, Gezer - A City Coming to life, ibid, p. 57. (Hebrew)

something like the building of a city... and the cells of the gates three from here and three from here." (Ezekiel 40:1-10)

In this prophecy Ezekiel describes the gates in the form of the 'Gates of Solomon', three cells on a side. Ezekiel lived during the 6th century BCE, could it be that during his days the gates of Solomon still existed?

According to what is accepted, the answer is no: "In the 10th century a group of 'Gates of Solomon' appears whose use was short lived... in the 8th century, the gates were already built with one room on each side. From the 7th to 6th century BCE is recognizable for the moment only a simple gate." [420]

Why would the prophet when talking about "the building of a city" describe gates that were not used for hundreds of years?

The answer is: The Early Iron Age II period when the gates of six cells are found, this was not the 10th century BCE, but the 6th century BCE in which the prophet Ezekiel lived, being the time of the Babylonian exile. Ezekiel, who spoke about a gate with six cells referred to gates that were used during his time.

The gates of six cells therefore are not the gates of Solomon, but the gates from the time of Nebuchadnezzar. The true gates of Solomon, like other findings from the time of David and Solomon were found in an earlier period (as we explained in the chapter the 'The Period of David and Solomon').

The Lachish Letters and the stamp of Jehuchal

From what we have said up to now it comes out that the destruction of the First Temple took place during the period Early Iron Age 2. In order to ratify this, let us present two findings whose attribution to the days of the destruction is almost without doubt. They are the Lachish letters and the Jehucal stamp.

The Lachish Letters

21 broken earthenware were found in Tel Lachish containing letters written on the eve of the destruction of the First Temple. Lachish and Azeqa are mentioned in the letters as cities the small settlements have stretched out their eyes to, as is written in Jeremiah "and the army of the King of Babylon is making war on Jerusalem... and Lachish and Azeqa behold there remain from the cities of Judah fortified cities." (Jeremiah 34:7).

Most of the letters were found in the doorway of an external gate, and an additional letter, written in the same style by the same scribe was found in the Tel itself. The external gate had an internal configuration of six cells that was in vogue during the early period of Iron Age II. Some 300 years separate this period from the destruction of the First Temple.

---

[420] Z. Hertzog, Biblical Encyclopedia, Vol 8, p. 241. (Hebrew)

The 'Six Cells' Gate in Lachish

Scholars who explain their findings according to the accepted timeline have been forced to separate the external gate from its internal continuation, and to place them to two different periods. Furthermore, it is not clear based on their explanation what the external gate was connected to: "The openings of the gates have not been fortified in an efficient way, and evidence is missing of the walls and towers that control the area between the gates ... inadequate protection over the hinges of the gates makes the weakness of the fortifications more prominent." [421]

In order to find a logical solution to the gatehouse of the Lachish Letters, the external gate must be reconnected to its continuation built in the design of the 'Solomon gates'. Here we have proof that the gates designated as the 'Solomon gates' are not from the time of Solomon but from the time of the destruction of the Temple.

[The letter inside the Tel originated in an earlier stratum from the Late Iron Age II which is identified with the period of Nebuchadnezzar. [422]

The scholar of these records was aware of this problem, and claimed that the stratum differed by only a few years. The letter in the Tel, he said, "was written according to the place where it was found during the Kingdom of Jehoyachin."

---

[421] Z. Hertzog, the Gates of the city in the land of Israel and its neighbours, Tel Aviv 1976, p. 124. (Hebrew)
[422] Inge, Excavations at Tel ed-duweir, PEQ 70, 1938, p. 254.

[423] (King Jehoyachin preceded the destruction of the First Temple by some 11 years).

However, according to what is agreed today, even the closest stratum in which the letter was found precedes the destruction of the Temple by some 115 years so that this answer is not possible, and the problem of fitting the letter into the accepted dateline remains open.]

The stamp of Jehucal

A seal with the stamp of Jehucal, son of Shelemiah, (Jeremiah 37:3) who was one of the ministers in the last generation before the destruction of the Temple, was found in the City of David in Jerusalem.

"Jehucal, son of Shelemiah, son of Shevy"

(Photographer Gaby Laron. in honor of Dr. E. Mazar, The Institute of Archaeology of Hebrew University)

According to the excavator it was found "in a bad stratigraphical position", [424] close to vessels from the early period of Iron Age II ('the period of David and Solomon') while the layer from the late period of Iron Age II ('the period of the destruction of the Temple') was not found in that place at all.

How could a letter from the time of the destruction of the Temple be found in a stratum from the time of David and Solomon?

---

[423] N. H. Tur-Sinai, The Lachish Ostraca, Jerusalem 1987, p. 197. (Hebrew)
[424] E. Mazar, the procedings from the lectures from the conference of the new Studies on Jerusalem from the year 2006.

Here is another proof that the layer from the early period of Iron Age II is from the period of the destruction of the Temple and not from the time of David and Solomon.

The 'Israelite Fortresses' that are not Israelite

Some 50 sites from the early period of Iron Age II were found in the arid areas of the southern Negev.

Investigators disagree on the purpose of these sites; some say desert nomads lived in them. [425] Others see them as military fortresses. [426]

An examination of the sites shows that we are indeed talking about fortresses and not civilian buildings, [427] and since it is customary to identify the period with the beginning of the Israelite kingdom, these buildings have been nicknamed 'the Israelite fortresses'.

However a number of questions remain without convincing answers:

1. The walls of these structures are very thin. If they are military fortresses why are their walls so weak?

2. The buildings were used for only a short period. Why? There was no further need to protect the southern border?

3. These fortresses are not positioned along any kind of border but spread over a wide area. If the fortresses were meant to guard the southern border, what is the logic behind their deployment?

4. Rough ceramics, known as 'Negev Ceramics', were found here distinct to all these fortresses. Similar ceramics were found at the Koraya and Tema sites in Northern Arabia. [428] If these were fortresses built by the first kings of Israel, what explanation is there for their likeness to the findings in northern Arabia?

However, after concluding that the period 'Early Iron Age II' is not the beginning of the kingdom of Israel but the period of Babylonian exile, the picture clarifies:

King Nabonaid (555-539 BCE) who ended the Babylonian period was guided not only by rational considerations, but also by his mystical experiences. [429] Among

---

[425] I. Finkelstein, The Iron Age "Fortresses" of the Negev, Eretz Israel 18 (1985), p. 366 ff. (Hebrew)
[426] Z. Meshel & A. Goren, "Aharoni fortress", Eretz Israel 23, 1982, p. 196 ff. (Hebrew)
[427] R. Cohen & R. Cohen-Amin, Ancient Settlement of the Negev Highland – volume 2, Israel Antiquities Authority Reports 20, Jerusalem 2004, p. 9. (Hebrew)
[428] B. Rotenberg and J. Glass, Midianite Pottery, Eretz Israel 15, 1981, p. 96. (Hebrew)
Certain differences exist between the vessels from the two sites: in North Arabic earthenware is decorated and in the Negev the decoration is missing.
[429] H. Tadmor, The Historical Background to the Declaration of Koresh, in: Oz Ledavid, Jerusalem 1964, p. 454. (Hebrew)

his strange decisions was to go into exile for 10 years with his army, to dwell in Tema in northern Arabia.

He stayed not only in Tema, but in one inscription he says that during these years he travelled across northern Arabia to an oasis in a distant desert. [430] Another inscription by him was recently discovered on a rock in Edom (Jordan) that indicated he arrived here as well. [431]

If during this period King Nabonaid and his soldiers, circled the deserts in this area, then they almost certainly built the Negev fortresses.

Nabonaid cylinder in the Louvre museum

Now it is clear why the buildings are of a temporary nature, since these fortresses were not meant to be used continuously. Obviously there is no need to look for a border line and the similarities with finds in northern Arabia are also obvious.

Summary, the 'Israelite fortresses' in the Negev were built by Nabonaid the King of Babylon who spent some time in this area.

The Devaluation of the Shekel

The prophet Ezekiel urged people to be honest in commerce, (Ezekiel 45:10) and he discussed with them the value of the Shekel. Also in regards to these matters we see that the dating we have chosen is correct as will be explained.

It says in the Torah that the shekel is 20 Gera (Gera – unit of weight) (Exodus 30:13). Ezekiel also said that the shekel is 20 Gera, though he added that the

---

[430] I. Efal, Biblical Encyclopedia, Vol. 8, p. 523. (Hebrew)
[431] E. Raz et al, 'Sela' - The Rock of Edom, Cathedra 101 (2001), p. 35- 36 (Hebrew); E. Ben Eliyahu, what Does 'Fair Babylon' have to do in Edom's Sela?, Cathedra 133 (2009), p. 5-12. (Hebrew)

Shekel has an added value of 20% to its weight. [432] During the time of Ezekiel (The exile in Babylon), the shekel was worth 20 Gera and it was supposed to increase by some 20% to a value of 24 Gera.

The shekel during 'the late Iron Age II' was 24 Gera. We can see this in a document of this period in which payments are listed in this language: "One shekel 22 Gera, and then 2 shekels 21 Gera, all the shekels: 4 Shekels of silver and 19 Gera." Here it is clear that one Shekel had 24 Gera. [433]

However, if the period 'Late Iron Age II' is the period of the First Temple as it is customary to say, what is the meaning of Ezekiel's words that the Shekel was 20 Gera when already in generations before his time the shekel had grown to 24 Gera?

Ezekiel's wording about one shekel being worth 20 Gera in his day proves that he lived before the period 'Late Iron Age II' when the shekel was already 24 Gera. That is to say his words prove that the period 'Late Iron Age II' comes after the Babylonian period and in the period of the Restoration.

Tel Azeqa

---

[432] This is the wording of the Scriptures: "and the shekel is twenty Gera. 20 shekels, 25 shekels, 15 shekels, the *Mannah* shall be for you" (Ezekiel 45: 12), and this is the explanation:
A Mannah is fifty shekels, and Ezekiel is saying that the Mannah is sixty shekels (15+25+20). Why? Because the measurements devalued by 20%, and therefore when we use the old shekels of 20 Gera you need 60 shekels in order to reach the new Mannah.
[433] E. Eshel, A late Iron Age Ostracon, IEJ 53 (2003), p. 157.

Summary of Section 5

The accepted dating fixes the period 'Iron Age II' (including the period of LMLK) at the time of the First Temple (the 10th to 7th centuries BCE). After the findings of this period have appeared beside findings from the middle of the Persian period (5th century BCE), no archaeological period remains for the Babylonian exile and the time of the Restoration.

Likewise many problems have been revealed in the incompatibility between the archaeological findings and the written texts.

Checking the signs on the LMLK jugs teaches us that the accepted dating is mistaken, and the correct dating should be: 'Early Iron Age II' – the Babylonian period, 'Middle/Late Iron Age II' - the Restoration period.

Now we must find archaeological remains from the missing periods, and the problems of incompatibility have been solved.

The interleafing between the Scriptures and archaeological testimonies following the period of the Restoration has been divided to two parts: The first part began during the reign of Cyrus and ended during the days of an enthusiastic King (Darius I). The second part began with a hostile king (Xerxes) and ended again with an unstable king (Artaxerxes I):

The first part began in the reign of Cyrus when he gave permission to build the Second Temple, however it did not come into being during his lifetime. Afterwards was the reign of King Darius who authorized the construction of the Second Temple and even gave the required supplies. He was an efficient ruler and Judah benefited from his reign.

The good times ended with the death of Darius and the coming to power of his son Xerxes whose negative attitude toward the Jews already meant (long before the events recounted in the Scroll of Esther) a range of anti-Semitic acts by the enemies of Judah who sent provocative hate letters leading to the partial destruction of Judah and the transformation of the area of Hebron into an Edomite stronghold.

Xerxes was a wasteful king, and his tax-collection policies enriched all his close government advisors at the expense of the rest of the population. During the time of Xerxes the capital city was set up in Ramat Rachel to replace Jerusalem and it was the governmental throne until the Hellenistic period.

After Xerxes, his son Artaxerxes I sent sacrifices to the Holy Temple and appointed Ezra the scribe to restore the Jewish religion in Judah. However when the letters from the enemies of Judah arrived and told the king that the Jews were rebuilding the walls of Jerusalem, he forcefully intervened to halt all construction. Judah was almost destroyed and the situation in the region became very tense.

Then the king gave Nehemiah permission to return to Jerusalem. The wall was rebuilt, and help was given to the population to alleviate the state of poverty; Ezra was called again to lead the people with the Torah and to renew their observance of the commandments.

Tel Aroer – Mameshet of LMLK seals

A View from Tel Aroer – Mameshet

Tel Socho

A View from Tel Socho

Section 6: The Patriarchal Era

Chapter 29: Places Associated with Tales of the Patriarchs

Introduction – The Plain of Jordan – The Dwelling Places of the Patriarchs – The War of the Four Kings – The Giants

Introduction

We have shown above that correct dating resolves problems in matching the Scriptures with Archaeology. This principle works also during the period of the Patriarchs (Abraham, Isaac and Jacob).

Subsequently we will present places where there is evidence mentioned in the tales of the patriarchs showing that they are not part of 'Middle Bronze Age II', as is customarily believed, but belong to the earlier period: Chalcolithic / beginning of the Early Bronze Age. [434]

The Plain of Jordan

When Abraham was with Lot in the mountains of Beth El he asked Lot to leave and go elsewhere. Lot searched for a worthwhile place to live and chose the Plain of Jordan because of its fertility, as it is written in the Scriptures: "And Lot lifed up his eyes, and beheld all the plain of Jordan, that it was well watered every where, before the Lord destroyed Sodom and Gomorrah, even as the garden of the Lord, like the land of Egypt". (Genesis 13:10)

The Plain of Jordan consists of a depression in the Jordan Valley, and from where Lot stood (close to Beth El), he could see the southern part of the Jordan Valle, close to the Dead Sea. Nowadays this area is dried up, (apart from the desert oasis of Jericho); however the Bible testifies that before the destruction of Sodom it was full of water "like the land of Egypt", which is to say that the Jordan River watered it just as the Nile waters Egypt.

In Abraham's time there was plenty of water in the Plain of Jordan, and it was most likely an inhabited area. What did the archaeologists find here from the period of Abraham?

Not much was found of the Middle Bronze Age II in the Plain of Jordan to match the Scriptures, because the area was desolate as nowadays. However, the remains of 17 settlements from the Chalcolithic period have been found in the dry part of the Jordan River. [435]

---

[434] For the equality between these periods – see Appendix 2.
[435] R. Gonen, The Archaeology of Ancient Israel in the Biblical Period, Unit 2, Tel Aviv 1989, p. 125. (Hebrew)

One of them is the greatest settlement in the land of that time – Tuieilat el-Ghassul – 5 km north of the Dead Sea. Very little rain falls in this area, as was also the case during the Chalcolithic period, [436] and yet olive trees which require a lot of water were grown here.

Southern Jordan Valley. Left: Jericho. Right: The Dead Sea.

Archaeologists have suggested that like the pollen of river plants found in the Tel, tell us that the waters of the Jordan at that time reached this site. [437]

Today Tuieilat el-Ghassul rises above the Jordan River to a height of almost 100 meters. If in the past the waters of the Jordan reached Tuieilat el-Ghassul it must mean that the level of the Jordan was much higher and its waters flooded the Plain of Jordan.

This waters of the Jordan irrigated the entire Plain of Jordan, just as the Nile River in Egypt floods and irrigates its surroundings. It is exactly as described in the verse we have quoted: "well watered … like the land of Egypt". [438]

---

[436] P. Bar-Adon, The Cave of the Treasure – The Findings from the caves in the Nahal Mishmar, Jerusalem 1971, p. 223. (Hebrew)

[437] T. E. Levy, The New Encyclopedia of Archaeological Excavations in the Holy Land, Jerusalem 1992, p. 509. (Hebrew)

[438] The fact that the deep dip in the Jordan was higher in the past than today has also been proven from other angles. Zoologists have reached a similar conclusion on the basis of the remains of the snail known as the: 'Melanopsis Costata' which lives only in the Jordan Valley, at a certain height above the level of the Jordan (H. B. Tristram, The Land of Israel: A Journal of Travels in Palestine, undertaken with special reference to its physical character, London, Society for Promoting Christian Knowledge, 1882, p. 218)

Also the geological survey shows that during the Chalcolithic period the level of the Dead Sea was much higher by some one hundred meters than its level today (Alon & Levy, The graphic expression and questions about the climate during the Chalcolithic period in the Northern Negev, Eretz Israel 25 (1996), p. 43).

These figures teach that the gorge which opened up in the Jordan Valley to a depth of hundreds of meters until it reached its present low level so that the settlements on its embankments remained high above it.

Archaeologists in Tuieilat el-Ghassul found evidence of tremendous earthquakes which struck the settlement until it was destroyed, and has since it remains uninhabited.

Lots of ashes were also found here. This corroborates whif what is told in the Book of Genesis about the Plain of Jordan: Before Sodom was destroyed, the Jordan Valley was full of water but when Sodom was struck the entire delta was damaged, its cities emptied of inhabitants and its vegetation dried up.

Tuieilat el-Ghassul

The Scriptures write: "And it upset these cities and the entire plane and all the inhabitants of the cities and all the plant life". (Genesis 19:25)

The Scriptures also tell us that at the time of Sodom's destruction the air was full of smoke: "the column of smoke from the land rose up like the form of a fiery furnace" (ibid, 19:28). This is the origin of the ashes found in Tuieilat el-Ghassul.

Apparently these earthquakes resulted in a deepening of the Jordan's channel, making it impossible to utilize its waters, and so the Plain of Jordan dried up making it unfit for settlement to this day.

The Dwelling Places of the Patriarchs

Isaac lived in the area around 'Be'er Lechai Roi', on the way to 'Shur', between 'Kadesh' and 'Bared' (Genesis 25:11; ibid 16:7-14) Where are these places?

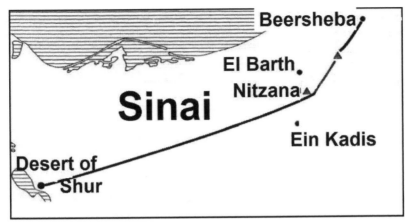

The Way to Shur

The road to Shur is the way to Egypt via the desert of *Shur* that is in the area of the Suez Canal. *Kadesh* is Ein Kadis, south of Nitzana, and *Bared* is El Barth, north of Nitzana.

'Be'er Lechai Roi', close to where Yitzhak dwelt, is located between the two of them in the area of Nitzana. However we do not find any evidence of human settlements in this dry area during the Middle Bronze Age II.

On the other hand remains of settlements were found here from the Chalcolithic period, [439] and the dating to this period for the Patriarchs matches the results.

The evidence from the Chalcolithic period in the Negev, helps us to understand a difficult verse that speaks about the dwellings places of Abraham "and he dwelt between Kadesh and Shur, and he lived in Gerar." (Genesis 20:1) Where were these places?

As we have said, Kadesh is close to Nitzana in the north-eastern Sinai, and Shur is in north-western Sinai beside the Suez Canal and between Kadesh and Shur means therefore North Sinai.

Concerning Gerar, there are different opinions about its exact location, but everyone agrees that it is in the northern Negev close to Gaza.

If so where did Abraham live, in the northern Negev or in the northern Sinai? The contradiction between the two parts of the verse has tresulted in attempts to amend the wording of the Scriptures as in the words of Y. Aharoni: "The traditional wording is, according to the opinions of many investigators corrupted, and nevertheless we do not understand it." [440]

---

[439] Heard verbally from Prof. Beno Rotenberg.
[440] Y. Aharoni, Biblical Encyclopedia, Vol 2, p. 456. (Hebrew)

However the archaeological findings in these areas show how precise the wording of the Scriptures is, since sites from the Chalcolithic period were found in the northern Sinai as well as in the northern Negev. Agricultural sites were found in the northern Sinai and shepherds sites were found in the Negev.

Given the great similarity between these sites researchers concluded that apparently we are talking about the same people: "in times of sowing and harvesting they went down to northern Sinai and for the rest of the year they worked in the pastures of the Northern Negev." [441]

This explains the verse we mentioned: Abraham divided his time, some of his days he lived in northern Sinai ("between Kadesh and Shur"), and part of the time he lived in the northern Negev ("in Gerar").

In Sinai he was a farmer and that meant "dwelling" in the one place: "and he dwelt between Kadesh and Shur". In the Negev where he was busy with grazing his livestock, which meant moving on and migrating, the wording is one of a temporary stay "lived".

[We should mention that at the Chalcolithic site in the Shikmim River the bones of a domesticated camel were found. [442]

This finding destroys claims heard from time to time: "How can it be that the patriarchs used camels when domesticating camels began only during the 12th century BCE?"]

The monument on the Tomb of the Patriarchs

[441] R. Gonen, The Archaeology of Ancient Israel in the Biblical Period, Unit 2, Tel Aviv 1989, p. 128. (Hebrew)

[442] M. Heymann, Shepherds and Agriculturalists in the Area of Kadesh Barnea, p. 151. (Hebrew)

The War of the Four Kings

The Bible tells us that in antiquity there were giants called Nefilim (ibid 6:4). A place particularly identified with the Giants was the eastern side of the Jordan river, where three nations of giants lived: Emim, Zuzim and Refaim.

In Abraham's time these people participated in a war in which they were attacked by an army 'of the Four Kings' who arrived from the East.

The Book of Genesis recounts that after they attacked the people of Refaim, the army from the East also attacked the people of "Hatzazon Tamar", that is Ein Gedi. (Chronicles II 20:2)

Is there evidence in this place of the war that was fought here?

No actual settlement was found in Ein Gedi from this period, (and if there was one maybe it is sunk nowadays under the Dead Sea). However rich findings have been discovered in caves in this area, particularly in the 'cave of the treasure' where people lived, though the access to it is difficult and dangerous.

Here are a few quotations about the findings in the caves:

"It can be concluded from the great number of finds in the caves that their dwellers led a prosperous lifestyle and a developed culture which is completly unexpected of cave dwellers in the desert." [443]

"It is hard to understand what people saw in choosing to live in such harsh living conditions ?... Maybe they were forced to abandon their places for some reason or other – fear from an attack by enemies or disease." [444]

An examination of the skeletons confirmed the assumption about an attack by enemies: "They reached the cave after they were cruely beaten. Those buried in the second cave were wrapped in blood-stained cloths. The right hand of the man was cut off... evidence of death in exceptional circumstances, maybe in war." [445]

The findings show that the men of Hatzazon Tamar (Ein Gedi) were attacked in a war, exactly as is recounted in Genesis chapter 14.

---

[443] P. Bar-Adon, The New Encyclopedia of Archaeological Excavations in the Holy Land, p. 826.
[444] R. Gonen, The Archaeology of Ancient Israel in the Biblical Period, Unit 3, Tel Aviv 1989, p. 130. (Hebrew)
[445] Ibid, p. 170.

The Giants

We are told in the Book of Genesis that Giants dwelt on the eastern side of the Jordan River. However, in the Book of Numbers we learn that Giants were to be found not only on the eastern side of the Jordan but even in the Land of Israel. (Numbers 13:33)

The peoples of the Giants on the eastern side of the Jordan were destroyed close to the time when the Children of Israel entered the Land. (Deuteronomy 2:10-21; Ibid 3:11-13) The Giants of the Land of Israel were destroyed partly by Joshua (Joshua 11:21-22), and the rest of them at the time of David and his soldiers. (Samuel II 21:16-22; Chronicles I 20:4-8)

Did the Giants leave any traces behind them?

Huge megalithic gravestones have been found throughout the world, however on the eastern side of the Jordan river tens of thousands of them. [446]

This is amazing since we are not talking about Royal gravestones, for which state resources could be invested, but normal gravestones. how did they manage to lift stones of such an enormous weight?

The answer is given in the Bible. The people who built the megalithic gravestones were the immensely strong Giants, as the researcher Karge already suggested. [447]

This phenomenon ends at the end of the Early Bronze Age,[448] during which the Children of Israel entered the Land (as we've shown in the chapter: Joshua's Conquests).

In the Land of Israel, west of the Jordan river, large gravestones are less commonplace than in the east, but here a number of graveyards like those can be found as well, especially around Safed, the Judean mountains and Ephraim.[449] These structures were built by the Giants feared by the generation of the desert. (Numbers 13:28-33)

To summarize: tens of thousands of huge gravestones (Dolmens) are reminders of the giant people who lived in the Patriarch's era.

---

[446] D. Bahat, The Date of the Dolmens near Kibbutz Shamir, Eretz Israel 11 (1973), p. 48 (Hebrew); C. Epstein, The Dolmen Problem in the light of Recent Excavation, Eretz Israel 12 (1975) p. 8. (Hebrew)
[447] Levenstein, Biblical Encyclopedia Vol. 7, p. 404 (Hebrew); M. Hartal, The Dolmens in Eretz Israel, 1987, p. 62. (Hebrew)
[448] L. Vinitzki, The Date of the Dolmens in the Golan and Galilee – A Reassessment, Eretz Israel 21 (2001), p. 167-171. (Hebrew)
[449] M. Zohar, The New Encyclopedia of Archaeological Excavations in The Holy Land, Jerusalem 1993, p. 353.

Chapter 30: The Philistines

The Origins of the Philistines - The Philistine Migration - How to distinguish patriarchal settlements from those of the Philistines - Gerar – The departure into Exile

The Origins of the Philistines

The Philistine people dwelt on the southern beaches of the Land of Israel. According to the Scriptures, the Philistines arrived from the island of Crete, called Kaftor in the Bible (Deuteronomy 2:23; Zefaniah 2:5; Ezekiel 25:16).

Has evidence of their origins been found?

Actually yes! The material culture of the Chalcolithic period in the south of Israel is similar to the material culture of the Greek islands and Crete. This is particularly striking when it comes to the statuettes, as the scholar R. Gonen writes:

"The styles are so similar, there is almost no doubt that they spring from a common conceptual grasp." [450]

In view of this she asks: "Can it be there were connections between the people in the south of the Land of Israel and people from distant places and, if so, what was the connection?" [451]

Some have suggested that the people of Canaan immigrated to Crete: "The vast number of similarities makes it likely that in reality the first settlers in Crete came from the Land of Israel." [452]

However the Scriptures present an opposite view: the population of Crete settled in the Land of Israel and brought with it the accepted lifestyle from the place of their origin.

If so, we have found remnants bearing evidence of the origin of the Philistines in the Land of Israel.

The Philistine Migration

The Book of Genesis recounts that the King of the Philistines lived in Gerar (Genesis 26:1-26) a city south of Gaza, and their land included Beersheba amongst other places. (Ibid 21:33-34)

---

[450] R. Gonen, The Archaeology of Ancient Israel in the Biblical Period, Unit 3, Tel Aviv 1989, p. 173. (Hebrew)
[451] Ibid.
[452] Vine, Biblical Encyclopedia, Vol 4, p. 334. (Hebrew)

However in the Book of Joshua it is written that the Philistines lived in five cities: Ashdod, Ashkelon, Gat, Ekron and Gaza, (Joshua 23:3), all north of Gerar and Beersheba.

This means that the Philistines changed their abode between the period of the patriarchs and the time of Joshua. Contrary to the Children of Israel who migrated south to Egypt, the Philistines migrated from Gerar north.

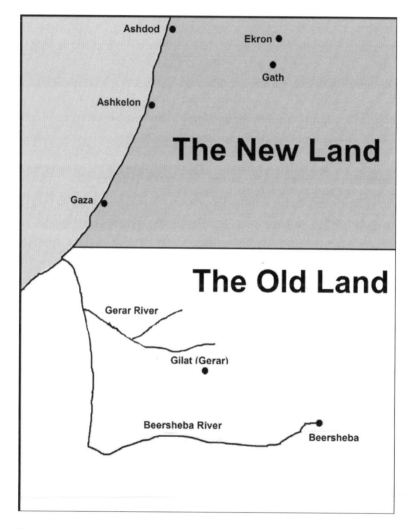

Do we have archeological evidence for this migration?

Before anser, we need know the situation in this time: The Chalcolithic culture had two main centers: in the Jordan Valley and in the Negev desert. Settlement in the Jordan Valley was short lived (because of the destruction of Sodom), whereas in the Negev it lasted for a long time.

Today, the Negev isn't a preferred living area because it is dry; however, in the Chalcolithic period the Negev was much wetter and therefore many people lived there. [453]

At the end of the period, the prevailing rainy climate gave way to the present-day dryness which led the Chalcolitheans to abandon their settlements in the Negev, in most cases forever.

It seems that the climate change produced the great famine in Joseph's time. (Genesis 42:54) This is why the Children of Israel migrated to Egypt, while the Philistines migrated north where there was more rain. Therefore in Joshua's time, the 'land of the Philistines' was from Gaza northwards.

Archaeological finds show evidence of settlements abandoned in the northern Negev at the end of the Chalcolithic period. These are reminders of the Philistine migration northwards at the end of the patriarchal period.

How to distinguish patriarchal settlements from those of the Philistines

Differences exist between the Chalcolithic settlements in the Negev. In the northern area (to the Gerar River) the bones of pigs comprised almost 20% of all bones; whereas in the southern area (to the Beersheba River) pig bones are missing.

Some explain the difference due to climate change: pigs need very rich pastures, and in the south inadequate rainfall meant that there were insufficient pastures for the pigs.[454]

However, this is only a partial explanation because in the southern settlements the bones of many cows were found. Cows, like pigs, also need rich pastures. If in the South they husbanded cattle, this is a sign that there was enough pasture there. So why weren't pigs raised there?

Northern settlements differ from Southern settlements also in their earthenware vessels, [455] and this is certainly not because of climate.

---

[453] P. Goldberg, The Geologist's Study of Changes in Climate Conditions, Cathedra 28 (1983), p. 147 (Hebrew); D. Alon & T. Levy, Demographic and Climate Problems during the Chalcolithic Period in the Northern Negev, Eretz Israel 25 (1996), p. 42-44. Hebrew)
[454] D. Alon and T. Levy, Demographic and Climate Problems during the Chalcolithic Period in the Northern Negev, Eretz Israel 25 (1996), p. 42-44. (Hebrew)
[455] D. Gazit, map of Urim, published by Israel Antiquities Authorities, Jerusalem 1996, p. 12. (Hebrew)
[Some explain that the difference between the North and South comes from the fact that the North is more ancient and the South is later, according to which only the North was settled in antiquity where there was more rainfall; and in the later period only the South was settled where there was scarce rainfall.

The difference is because the patriarchs lived in Gerar for only a short time before they moved further south to Beersheba (Genesis 21:32; Ibid 26:23; ibid 28:10) where they spent most of their time, and they had many animals but no pigs, as is written of Abraham and Jacob. (Ibid 12:16; Ibid 32:6-8)

Therefore pigs are found in the northern settlements because these were the settlements of the Philistines who raised pigs. In the southern areas there were no pigs, because this is where the patriarchs of Israel and those attached to them lived, and they refrained from raising pigs.

Beersheba River

Both the patriarchs and the Philistines were part of the Chalcolithic culture; however, the bone finds enable us to differentiate between them: The pig bone sites in the north are Philistine sites, and the non-pig sites in the south are the sites of the patriarchs.

Gerar

The Philistine kingdom of cities as we said was in Gerar, which from the Scriptures is clear that it was South of Gaza (Genesis 10:19). Gerar is not mentioned as a city after the period of the Patriarchs, and its name was preserved

---

This does not make sense. Why in the later period would people want to live only in the South which is less suitable for habitation and abandon the North where life was easier? It is more reasonable to say that the difference between the North and the South stems from the fact that we're speaking about two different populations – the Philistines and the Patriarchs.]

until the Roman period, only as the name of a province of the north western Negev (Grariky), but not as the place of a city. Where, then, was Gerar?

In the western Negev there are four large tels from the Bronze Age (Tel Haror, Tel Farah, Tel Gema, and Tel Sharah). Each one of them is identified as Gerar by one of the scholars.

However, after seeing that the period of the Patriarchs was during the Chalcolithic period, we should search which of the Chalcolithic settlements in the northern Negev was worthy of being the Philistine capital?

It is not difficult to find. This is the Chalcolithic site close to the settlement of Gilat, which was the principal site in the Negev at that time, 15 kilometers northwest of Beersheba. In the words of the excavator: "Studies indicate Gilat's importance as a regional Chalcolithic cultural center in the northern Negev." [456]

[After the excavations the archaelogists covered the site.]

We can therefore determine almost certainly that the Chalcolithic site in Gilat is the city of Gerar.

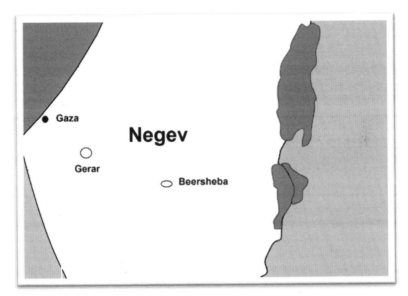

Southern Land of Israel

---

[456] T. E. Levy, The New Encyclopedia of Archaeological Excavations in the Holy Land, p. 517.

The departure into Exile

During the Chalcolithic period the Negev was divided into two parts: The Philistines lived in the northern part around Gerar, and the Patriarchs lived in the southern part around Beersheba.

At the end of the period the Philistines migrated from the Negev northwards, and the Children of Israel went down to Egypt. The archaeological signs of a migration by the Philistines are mentioned above and now we will try to trace the footsteps of the migration of Jacob's family. But let's begin by asking a question connected to the story of the departure of the Children of Israel to Egypt.

Jacob and his sons lived in the Land of Israel (Canaan) until Pharaoh invited them to live in his land. In order to persuade them to come he said "Don't let your eyes have pity on your vessels, because all the good of the land of Egypt is for you." (Genesis 45:20)

Here we see that it was hard for them to leave their possessions behind in the Land of Canaan. What objects could shepherds have of such value that Pharaoh had to say "don't let your eyes have pity on your vessels"?

Beersheba is the place from where Jacob and his family came to Egypt (Ibid 46:2). Let us examine what the archaeologists have to say.

Excavations on the site in Beersheba (next to the neighbbourhood Neve Noy) have uncovered the remains of dwellings from the chalcolithic period and with them vessels made from copper, ivory and basalt. [457]

A network of underground rooms was found under the dwelling site in which sealed vessels had been buried before the place was abandoned permanently: "All the household objects were stored in perfect order and later the openings to the rooms were sealed with large stones." [458]

---

[457] M. Dotan, Excavations in Horvat Beter, Atiqot 2 (1959), p. 1-42; D. Usishkin, The Chalcolithic Period in Eretz-Israel, Qadmoniot 12 (1970), p. 112 -118 (Hebrew); I. Gilad, Beersheva during the birth of history, Ariel 79-80, p. 22-23 (Hebrew); D. Inbar, a Journey to the Scriptural past, Tel Aviv 1989, p. 97 (Hebrew); J. Perrot, The New Encyclopedia of Archaeological Excavations in the Holy Land, p. 163; R. Gonen, The Archaeology of Ancient Israel in the Biblical Period, Unit 3, Tel Aviv 1989, p. 144. (Hebrew) The site that was excavated is found within the realms of the city of Beersheva.
The fact that the place is connected to the number seven from ancient days is testified to by the decorations: there have been found colored garments with different emblems. Each group is divided into a number which is a multiple of seven.
Also to the east of Beersheva there is a Hill which is called by mistake the "Tel of Beersheva". It has already been pointed out that this *Tel*, which is close to the Beduin settlement of Tel Sheva, is not Beer Sheva, rather the city of *Sheva,* which is mentioned in the Book of Joshua: "Beersheva and *Sheva* " (Joshua 19:2).
[458] D. Usishkin, The Chalcolithic Period in Eretz-Israel, Qadmoniot 12 (1970), p. 113. (Hebrew)

Some of the rooms were hidden and remained locked until our time.

Why was such a remarkable effort made to hide the vessels?

The reason is because of their great quality. These vessels, some which are on display in the Israel Museum, are uniquely beautiful: "The form awakens wonder in the heart of the beholder... The question is how could these fragile, vessels with exact measurements have been created." [459]

Why was Beersheba abandoned? There are no signs of enemy destruction, and so scholars believed that the place was abandoned because of a heavy famine. [460]

Where did the people migrate to? It is not known, however vessels similar to those found in Beersheba have also been found at archaeological sites from the Gerzian culture in Egypt. [461]

In Chapter 2 we saw that the people of the Gerzian culture who lived in Egypt of antiquity were the Children of Israel, and there's almost no doubt that the vessels found in Beersheba belonged to them as well. These vessels were extremely important to them, as is shown by the enormous effort made to ensure that the vessels were not lost.

Now we understand why Pharaoh said to them: "and your eyes should not have pity on your vessels".

It is reasonable that archaeologists have found the exact site in Beersheba from where Jacob's family migrated to Egypt, and from here we learn that they were expert manufacturers of vessels.

summary: The **'Chalcolithic /Early Bronze Age I' period** coincides with the **time of the patriarchs,** and at archaeological sites from that period we find many allusions to the biblical stories.

---

[459] D. Usishkin, ibid, pp. 113, 115. (Hebrew)
[460] M. Dothan, The Late Chalcolithic Period in Palestine, Eretz Israel 10 (1971), p. 171.
[461] Wanke, The Ancient Egyptian State, Cambridge University press, New York 2002, p. 227; Hoffman, Egypt before the Pharaohs, New York 1979, p. 201-205.

Chapter 31: Hammurabi

The Hammurabi codes - The Anuma Alish – The Gilgamesh epic – Mari and the Torah – Hammurabi and the Torah – The lack of credibility of the King list – When did Hammurabi live? – The Records of Mari and the Generation of the Settlements – Summary

The first people to rule in Babylon were the Shumeri people, and later on the Babylonians. The most important King of the first Babylonian dynasty was Hammurabi, who turned his kingdom into an empire and the city of Babylon into a center of learning.

In his time a new form of creative literature was born, different from ancient Shumeri literature. Portions of this new literature are similar in their writing to the Bible. These are called the Hammurabi Codes, the Anuma Alish (the story of the creation of the world) and the Gilgamesh Epic.

Writings also by another King, Zimri-Lym King of the city of Mari, from the time of Hammurabi have been found reminiscent of the Bible.

The Hammurabi Codes

The Hammurabi Codes are a collection of laws claimed to have been received from heaven to impose righteousness on the world: "So that the strong shall not exploit the weak, and to deal rightly with the widow and orphan".

Among the laws we find reminders of what is written in the Book of Exodus. Here are two examples:

"If someone will destroy the eye of his friend, his eye shall be taken out, if he breaks a limb, his limb shall be broken ... somebody who takes out the tooth of his friend, his tooth will be removed". Similar things are written in the book of Exodus (21:34): "An eye for an eye, a tooth for a tooth, a hand for a hand, a foot for a foot."

"If a person rents an ox or a donkey from his friend and a lion devours them in the field, the damages are liable on the owner". As opposed to "If a person gives his friend a donkey or an ox and they are killed he shall bring a witness and he shall not pay for the damage." (Exodus 22:9-12).

The Anuma Alish

The Anuma Alish is the Babylonian vision of the story of The Creation of the World, according to which in the beginning there was only water. The Goddess of the Sea, Tihamat and her husband gave birth to the rest of the gods, and when they could no longer stand the noise of their progeny they tried to destroy them.

In the war between them one of the gods cut the crocodile body of Tihamat into two pieces. From one part heavens and the stars were created and from the other the dry land. [462]

Scholars have drawn attention to the fact that in the Book of Genesis at the beginning the world was also all water and it mentions the *Tehom* - the depths, and crocodiles: "and there was darkness on the face of *Tehom*", "and the Lord created the great crocodiles." (Genesis 1:2; ibid, 21)

The Gilgamesh Epic

An epic poem about an ancient King combined with the story of the oldest human being, named Utnapishtim. This is the fable:

One of the gods revealed to Utnapishtim that a flood is going to happen and that he should build a boat and put in it all different types of animals. The man did as he was told and he smeared the ark with tar. The flood came and lasted for seven days.

When the flood at last subsided the man opened the window of the boat and saw the tops of the mountains. When the boat stopped moving he released a dove but it came back to the ark because it could not find a place to rest its feet. The same happened to a swallow. Afterwards he sent out a raven and it didn't come back. The man came out of the ark and brought a sacrifice.[463]

This fable of course reminds us of the story in the Torah about Noah (Genesis chapters 6-8).

Mari and the Torah

Recognizable ideas were also found with Zimri-Li, the King of Mari. If the Babylonian myth reminds us of the story about the Creation of the World, decorations in the Mari palace offer descriptions that remind us of the story about the Garden of Eden: streams of water that separate into four main rivers, and trees with angels beside them. [464]

These recall the verses: "and the river went out of Eden to water the garden and from there it separated and became four main rivers... He placed at the east of the garden of Eden angels to keep the way of the tree of life" (Genesis 2:10, ibid 3:24).

---

[462] S. Shifra and J. Klein, In Those Distant Days, Tel Aviv 1996, p. 9. (Hebrew)
[463] M. D. Kasuto, Biblical Encyclopedia, Vol 2, p. 493. (Hebrew)
[464] A. Malamat, Biblical Encyclopedia, Vol 4, p. 561. (Hebrew)

Apart from this, "the special judicial procedure in Mari contains certain lines some of which have a parallel in the Scriptures". [465]

Also by Zimri-Lim who lived in the same generation as Hammurabi, we can find similarities with the Bible.

Hammurabi and the Torah

Hammurabi apparently lived during the period of the Patriarchs, and some even identify him with the King 'Amrafel' from the time of Abraham (Genesis 14:1). That means Hammurabi lived many generations before the Exodus from Egypt and the Giving of the Torah.

What explanation is given for the similarity between the Babylonian literature in his time and the Torah?

The school of Scriptural criticism sees in these Babylonian records the source for what is written in the Torah: the laws of the Book of Exodus are a copy of the Hammurabi Codes; the story of The Creation is based on the fable of Tihamat, and the story of Noah is a reworking of the Gilgamesh epic.

The believers rejected this critique and deliberately tried to show that the Hammurabi Codes and the Laws of the Torah are similar by coincidence.

The starting point for all of them is that Hammurabi lived during the period the Patriarchs, but how do they know this?

The scientific date given to Hammurabi was the 21st century BCE and it was determined by the Babylonian records from the time of the Second Temple. Afterwards earlier records (the Mari records) were found proving that Hammurabi lived during the time of the Assyrian King Shimshi-Adad who, according to the Kings-list of Assyria is dated to the 18th century BCE.

The Assyrian lists are considered to be more reliable than the Babylonian records, and therefore the timing of Hammurabi was re-set to the 18th century BCE (though some set the date earlier or later by 100 years).

Accordingly, Hammurabi lived at a much earlier time by hundreds of years from the Giving of the Torah (the 15th or 14th centuries BCE).

Lack of Credibility in the List of Kings

The dating of Hammurabi is based as we said on the list of Assyrian Kings; however it is also not reliable for the following reasons:

---

[465] A. Malamat, ibid, p. 586.

Imaginary names have been added in the first part of this list detailing the forefathers of Shamshi Adad: "The list mentions his true forefathers and beside them imaginary forefathers ... their inclusion is intended to add to his prestige." [466]

If the beginning of the list is fraudulent, how can we say that the continuation is accurate?

2. This list ends with Tiglat Pileser which apparently dates to the time of his successor Sargon (8th century BCE). From the time of Sargon's son – King Sennacherib – an inscription exists on which the number of listed years does not correspond to what is written in the list and the same applies to his son, King Essarhedon. It only remains for the scholars to say that: "The scribes of Essarhedon edited the sums in a way whose meaning has not been made clear to us still." [467]

If so, even the scribes of the Kings of Assyria who lived close to the time when the list was created did not trust it and wrote numbers which differed from those written in the list.

This strengthens the suspicion that fictitious Kings were added to the list.

3. Another reason to doubt that some of the Kings mentioned in this list actually existed is the amazing similarity between the Kings that apparently ruled during the 13th to 11th centuries BCE (the time of the Middle Assyrian Empire) with the Kings between the 10th and the 7th centuries BCE (the time of the Later Empire).

We compare quotes attributed to Shalmaneser I and II from the Middle Empire with the quotes attributed to Shalmaneser III and IV from the Later Empire:

Shalmaneser I – "He exploited the imbroglio of the Hittites... He invaded Ararat, he attacked Carcamish and opened the trade routes to the north east."

Shalmaneser II – "a King during a period of pressure and tension."

These are the Kings of the Middle Empire, opposed to the Kings from the Later Empire:

Shalmaneser III – "He crumbled the alliance of neo-Hittites, headed by Carcamish. He also overcame Ararat. He forced his way to the sources of raw materials from Anatolia and Northern Syria."

Shalamaneser IV– "His rule was marked by a period of military attacks on Assyria." [468]

---

[466] A. Malamat, Mary and Israel, Jerusalem 1991, p. 149-150. (Hebrew)
[467] H. Tadmor, the History of the People of Israel, vol. 2 p. 45. (Hebrew)
[468] The Hebrew Encyclopedia, Vol 31, pp. 1002-1003. (Hebrew)

The Stella of Essarhedon

Also Tiglat Pileser I, who attacked Aram and whose conquests expanded the Middle Empire to the Mediterranean Sea, and for Tiglat Pileser III, who attacked Aram and whose conquests expanded the Later Empire to the Mediterranean Sea, have many things in common.

These comparisons lead to the conclusion that the Kings of the Middle Empire are merely look-alikes of the Later Empire

4. The dates that appear in the inscriptions of the kings *Shalmaneser I* and *Tukulty-Enurta I* do not fit the dates appearing in the List of Kings, and actually support the theory that the Middle Assyrian Kings never existed.

These inscriptions tell us about a very early King (before Hammurabi and Shamshi Adad) by the name of *Ilushumah*. Shalmaneser says that 739 years passed from the time of King *Erishu, the son of Ilushuma*, until the year that he began to reign. Tukulty-Enurta says that only 720 years passed from King Ilushuma until his time.

When were these inscriptions written?

It is customary to credit them to Shalmaneser I (1273-1244 BCE) and to his son Tukulti-Enurta I (1207-1243 BCE) from the Middle Empire.

Naturally, we cannot reconcile the years that appear in the two inscriptions, because if we do then the father (Ilusumha) ruled at the earliest in 1963 BCE, and the son (Erishu) in 2012 BCE, this is to say, the son ruled 49 years before his father.

A weak excuse has been given for the discrepancy between the inscriptions. "It seems that we should see the 720 years as a round number of 12 times 60 and should not be used in the chronological calculation." [469]

The situation is different when we relate this to the Later Empire, which also had kings bearing these names. Here Shalmaneser (858-824 BCE) is not the father of Tukulty-Enurta (890-884 BCE) rather his grandson, and in this way matching this is realistic was the father (Ilushuma) in 1610 BCE, and the son (Erishu) in 1597 BCE.

If Ilushuma and Erishu lived around the year 1600, Hammurabi and Shamshi-Adad lives there must be later. The longest Kings list cannot enter completely into the time left, we must cross out a number of them that is a say, the Middle Empire which is only an imaginary creation.

---

[469] H. Tadmor, the History of the People of Israel, vol. 2 p. 44. (Hebrew)

When did Hammurabi Live?

Shamshi-Adad ruled for 33 years and in his 23rd year Hammurabi began to rule for 42 years. According to the inscription of Shalmaneser, we can calculate when these kings lived.

This inscription reads, among other things, that 580 years passed from the repair that Shamshi-Adah made in one of the temples, until the beginning of the Kingdom of Shalmaneser. Shalmaneser began to rule in the year 858 BCE, so that Shamshi-Adad repaired what needed repairing in the year 1438 BCE.

Since we do not know in which of the 33 years of his kingdom Shamshi-Adad made the repair, we can only say that his kingdom began between 1471 and 1438 BCE. Here there is evidence that Hammurabi, who ruled 23 years after Shamshi-Adad, began to rule between the years 1448 and 1415 BCE. (Shalmaneser's inscriptions however should also be related to with caution though they are certainly much more reliable than the later lists.)

Hammurabi therefore lived around the year 1400 BCE and, as we said earlier, he was not the only one to compile a book of laws. Other kings did similar things in his time (Ibel-Piell the King of Eshnunna, Nidnushna the King of Dir), and "it is logical to say that this style was a sign of the period." [470] What caused the kings in that period to start compiling law books?

Maybe the language in which the laws of Hammurabi are written will explain this, since it shows many borrowings from a Western text: "The language of the codes in its structure is very close to the Aramaic. Its original language was certainly western Semitic, Aramaic (or ancient Hebrew)." [471]

The book of Hammurabi's laws resembles a similar book written in the Western Semitic language. As we mentioned the 15th century BCE was the time of the Exodus from Egypt and giving of the Torah, we can guess what 'Western Semitic text' inspired Hammurabi and other members of his generation to write the books of laws. [472]

---

[470] H. Tadmor, Biblical Encyclopedia, Vol 4, p. 76. (Hebrew)

[471] Korngreen, the Laws of the Ancient East, Tel Aviv 1944, p. 9. (Hebrew)

[472] We have used the conventional dating, however in the chapter 'When did Sennacherib lay siege to Jerusalem?' and in the appendices here we have shown that we should remove several years, both from the history of Israel and of Assyria, such that the Exodus from Egypt really happened in the year 1405 BCE. Hammurabi started to reign between the years of 1373 to 1339 BCE, that is to say several decades after the Giving of the Torah.

The Mari Documents and the Generation of the Settlements

We mentioned above Zimri-Lim the King of the city of Mari, who lived at the same time as Hammurabi. An archive of documents has survived from his time, which also mentions the Canaanite city of Hatzor with no less than 20 records.

The King of Hatzor in the Mari documents is **Yibni**-Adad which reminds us of the name of the King of Hatzor at the time of Joshua and the Judges: Yabin (Joshua 11:1. Judges 4:2).

It emerges from one of these records that Yibni-Adad's standing was extremely high: "amongst all the rulers mentioned in the documents, only Yibni-Adad and Hammurabi carry the titles of 'King' ". [473]

This is similar to what is told about the Kingdom of Hatzor at the time of Joshua: "and Joshua returned that time and conquered Hatzor, and its King he smote with a sword because Hatzor earlier was the head of all of these kingdoms" (Joshua 11:10).

Mari also traded with the Land of Israel, and in the records we find Hebrew names. This is what the scholar Malamat writes "the link is particularly strong to ancient Israeli names from the period of the patriarchs, their nomadic times and their settlements." [474]

In the Mari documents thousands of tablets have been decoded, and none of them mention Egypt which was a regional power. "The absence of Egypt from the Mari documents is very strange" [475] say scholars but they have no satisfactory explanation for this.

However in the Land of Israel there is also a single period in which archaeologists have not found any sign of a connection with Egypt, and this is the Intermediate Bronze Age. [476] The Intermediate Bronze Age was the period when the Children of Israel entered the land of Canaan (See chapter 'Joshua Conquest').

This is also approximately the time of the Mari documents. Egypt does not appear in them because it has still not recovered from the blows that landed on her, and therefore had no influence in the countries of Mesopotamia.

---

[473] A. Malamat, Mari and the Bible – A Collection of Studies, Jerusalem 1975, p. 107. (Hebrew)

[474] A. Malamat, Biblical Encyclopedia, Vol 4, p. 570. (Hebrew)

[475] H. Tadmor, The History of the People of Israel, vol. 2, p. 50. (Hebrew)

[476] M. Kochavi, The Middle Bronze Age I (The Intermediate Bronze Age) in Eretz Israel, Qadmoniot 6 (1969), p. 38. (Hebrew); E. Oren, The Interconnections between the Southern Levant and the Agean at the end of the Early Bronze Age, Eretz Israel 27 (2003), p. 10-15. (Hebrew)

Thus the writings of Mari also support the dating of Hammurabi to the generation after the Exodus from Egypt. [477]

Summary

The laws of Hammurabi are similar to the laws of the Torah. Hammurabi is dated to the period of the Patriarchs (around 1800 BCE) so that some think that the laws of the Torah imitate the laws of Hammurabi. The dating of Hammurabi is based on the list of Assyrian Kings. However, imaginary kings are in the first part of the list, but the rest of the list is considered reliable.

In this chapter our comparison of later parts of the list to early Assyrian inscriptions shows that imaginary kings were also added to later parts of the list. Based on other records we have seen that Hammurabi should be redated to the time of Joshua (1400 BCE), so Hammurabi borrowed from the laws of the Torah and not the opposite.

---

[477] There is an additional law in the Mari documents recognizable to the generation which settled Canaan, forbidding the transfer of an inheritance from tribe to tribe. This law is unusual in the laws of nations, but is known to us from the Book of Numbers (36:7), which took place only during the generation of settlement, as it was handed down by the Sages. (Babylonian Talmud, Taanit 30)

Another parallel to the generation of settlement is the procedure practised in Mari to place a ban on booty from war which forbade soldiers from seizing it for personal gain: "the ban —...would be used to prevent the army from desecrating the spoils of war." [A. Malamat, Biblical Encyclopedia, Vol. 4, p. 577. (Hebrew)]

This is also something unusual in the laws of the nations, but is known to us from the wars waged by the Children of Israel during the generation of settlement. This was the case of Arad: "and Israel made an oath and said to the Lord if you will surely give this people into my hand and I will consecrate their cities." (Numbers 21:2) Afterwards in the conquest   of   Jericho: "the   city   was consecrated, it and everything that was in it to the lord". (Joshua 6:17-18)

The place of Biblical Gerar – between Gilat and Ofakim

Neve Noy neighbourhood – the place of Beersheba of the Patriarchs

Conclusions

This book begins with determining the identity of the Pharaoh that ruled at the time of the Exodus from Egypt. And the underlying subject is: do archaeological findings corroborate with what is written in the Bible?

This is a large subject and we tried to supply as much information as possible to answer that question. The conclusion is that the findings indeed corroborate the story told in the Scriptures, provided that the mistaken timeline which has no connection to the Bible is replaced by the correct timeline, as we have shown.

The pioneering work of Dr Immanuel Velikovsky has a great importance in this subject. However, we have not accepted his dating for the Egyptian dynasties, except partially (the beginning of the 18th dynasty and the 20th to the 21st dynasty).

The difference is particularly recognizable in the dating of the Exodus from Egypt which in Velikovsky's opinion was close to the ascent of the 15th dynasty, but in our opinion was at the end of the 4th dynasty!

An additional important step was made with the book 'The Lost Bible' which deals essentially with the archaeology of the Land of Israel. We generaly accepted the first part of its dating until the period of the Middle Bronze Age [except for the date of the Exodus from Egypt which he dates at the end of the 6th dynasty, and we date it to the end of the 4th dynasty.] From here on (the Late Bronze Age), our ways parted entirely.

From what we said in our book, (and from the appendices), it appears that in the timeline of the Land of Israel the following changes should be made:

1. The Chalcolithic period is identical with the beginning of the Early Bronze Age (evidence is presented in the appendix 'When did the Gerzian culture begin?')
2. The period of the Intermediate Bronze Age is very short, and lasted for only a few decades. (Evidence is presented in the appendix 'During which dynasty was the period Middle Bronze Age IIb?')
3. The period Middle Bronze Age IIa parallels the end of the Ancient Kingdom in Egypt – Intermediate Period I in Egypt, and the period of the Middle Bronze Age IIb parallels the Middle Kingdom in Egypt – the 12th dynasty. (Evidence is presented in Appendix 'During which dynasty was the period Middle Bronze Age IIb?')
4. The period Late Bronze Age did not really exist. The first part is identical to the period of the Middle Bronze Age IIb, and the second part is identical to the period Iron Age I. (Evidence is presented in the chapter 'The Late Bronze Age – an Imaginary Period'.)

5. The period Iron Age II did not occur during the First Temple times – the 10th to the 7th centuries BCE. Thecorect time is: the first part was at the time of the Babylonian Exile – 6th century BCE. (Evidence is presented in the chapter 'The Babylonian Period'), and the second part was at the time of the Restoraion – 6th-5th century BCE. (Evidence is presented in the chapter 'LMLK', 'Whose was the Capital', 'The Negev during the time of the Restoraion'.)

In the Egyptian timeline the following changes should be made:

1. The Gerzian culture in Egypt is not pre-dynastic but from the period of the 3rd-4th dynasties. (Evidence is presented in the Appendix 'When did the Gerzian culture begin?')

2. The period of the New Kingdom in Egypt did not take place in reality. The first part is identical with the Middle Kingdom. (Evidence is presented in the chapter 'The New Kingdom in Egypt – an imaginary Kingdom – part 1').
The second part is identical with the 26th dynasty. (Evidence is presented in the chapters 'Periods without Remnants', 'Reconstructed Periods', 'Kings and their doubles', 'When were the El-Amarna Letters written?').
The last part is identical with the 28th-30th dynasties (Evidence is presented in the chapter 'The New Kingdom in Egypt – an Imaginary Kingdom – Part 3').

3. The 21st dynasty was not a Royal Dynasty but a dynasty of religious leaders from the Persian period, up to the beginning of the Helenistic period (Evidence is presented in the chapter 'The New Kingdom in Egypt - an Imaginary Kingdom - Part 3').

4. The 22nd to the 23rd dynasties reigned for only 90 years, not 220 years. It follows from this that there was no period of the 23rd dynasty. (Evidence is presented in the chapter 'The Savior during the days of Jehoahaz'.)

5. In the 25th dynasty there were only two Kings (Evidence is presented in the Appendix 'How many Kings comprised the Ethiopian Dynasty?')

An additional change that should be made in all the calendars is to shorten the years, because some Kings of Israel, Judah and Assyria, and also in the 19th

dynasty in Egypt, counted years of only six months (Evidence is presented in the chapter 'When did Sennacherib lay siege to Jerusalem?').

In view of these points the correct timeline is presented below and not the one that appeared at the beginning of section 2.

Corrected Timeline

Bible	Land of Israel	Egypt	Date (BCE)
Period of the Patriarchs	Early Bronze Age I/ Chalcolithic	1st and 2nd Dynasties	1900-1650
Joseph	Early Bronze Age II	3rd Dynasty	1650-1550
Slavery in Egypt		4th Dynasty	1550-1405
Wandering in the Desert	Early Bronze Age III	5th Dynasty	1405-1365
Joshua's Conquest	Intermediate Bronze Age		1365-1300
Period of the Judges	Middle Bronze Age IIa	6th to 11th Dynasties	1300-1000
Saul, David, Solomon-Asa	Middle Bronze Age IIb = (Late Bronze Age I)	12th Dynasty = Start of 18th Dynasty	1000-840
Jehoshaphat – Jehoash		13th -16th Dynasties	840-785
Jehoash - Hezekiah (End of the kingdom of Israel – 693)		22nd (Libyan) Dynasty	785-693
Hezekiah		24th-25th Dynasties (Ethiopians)	693-663
Menashe		Assyrian Conquest	663-655
Josiah, Jehoyakim	Iron Age I = (Late Bronze Age II)	Beginning of 26th Dynasty = End of 18th Dynasty (655-584)	655-600
End of First Temple (Destroyed 586)	Beginning of Iron Age II		600-525
Babylonian Exile (586-538)		End of 26th Dynasty = 19th Dynasty (584-525)	
Restoration	Middle of Iron Age II (LMLK)	27th Dynasty (Persian)	525-485
Mordechai and Esther, Ezra and Nehemiah	End of Iron Age II (Rosetta)		485-424
	Persian Period		424-400
		28th-30th Dynasties (20th Dynasty)	400-330

Appendices

Appendix 1: Is there a connection between Imhotep and the name Zaphnath-paaneah?

In Chapter 1 we identified Joseph with Imhotep, the deputy to Pharaoh Djoser. In the Bible it says that Joseph's name was 'Zaphnath-paaneah' (Genesis 41:45). Is there evidence that Imhotep was called Zaphnath-paaneah?

Tzofnat is identical with the name 'Tzefon' which is the name of the Egyptian god Sofed as is seen later in the appendix 'who was Baal Tzefon'. Is there a connection between Imhotep and Sofed?

Yes. After the death of Imhotep the cult of the god Sofed was centered in the city of Sacara, the city of Imhotep, and was partnered with the cult of Shmum, the god of wisdom who is identified with Imhotep and the priest was called both the priest of Shmun and the priest of Sofed. [478]

Not only that, Sofed "is depicted as a human form wearing the dress of Asiatics. In this likeness he already appears during the time of the ancient kingdom". [479]

Consequently, Imhotep is to be identified with the god Sofed-Tzofnat, and the understanding that Imhotep is Joseph explains to us very well why the Egyptians depicted Sofed as a God who had arrived from Asia.

We have found Sofed and we have seen that there is a connection between Josef-Imhotep and Tzofnat-Sofed. What is the explanation of the second part the name – Paaneah?

'Paaneah' means 'the live one', Zaphnath-paaneah means 'the god Sofed who lives'.

However, if Joseph's name was Tzofnat-Paneach, why was he known by the name of Imhotep?

The answer is that Imhotep was the name given to him as the priest of On (Heliopolis), since we found this name amongst the Priests of On in later generations. [480]

Josef is said to have received the name Zaphnath-paaneah before married the daughter of the priest of On. He received the name Imhotep later, when he inherited his father-in-law's titles of honor, including the name Imhotep which was more exclusive than the name Tzafnat Paneach

---

[478] R. Giveon, Lexikon der Ägeptologie, V, Wiesbaden 1980, p. 1107.
[479] R. Giveon, The Stones of Sinai speak, p. 126. (Hebrew)
[480] P. A. Clayton, Chronicle of the Pharaohs, London 1994, p. 81.

Appendix 2: When did the Gerzian Culture begin?

In the first chapter we identified Joseph as Imhotep, and according to this the Children of Israel migrated to Egypt during the 3rd dynasty.

On the other hand, in the second chapter we identified the emigration of the Children of Israel to Egypt with the penetration from the north of the Gerzian culture which originated began in the pre-dynastic period, which is much earlier than the days of the third dynasty.

Apparently there is a contradiction here, but we must remember how the researchers came to the conclusion that the Grtzaitic culture was pre-dynastic.

'Predynastic' painted pottery

The findings discovered in Gerza are, in part, similar to the findings from the Ancient Kingdom and in part different. Flinders-Petrie concluded that we are discussing a period close to, but not during, the Ancient Kingdom itself, possibly between the 6th-7th dynasties. Later, based on findings from the Gerza period, he revised his dating of the Gerzian to the 'pre-dynastic' period before the Ancient Kingdom.

However, this dating also has its difficulties:

1. Gardiner noticed that the registration of these immigrants from the north was not found at the beginning of the dynastic period, only later on, and he summed it up by proclaiming: "Let us frankly admit our ignorance in these matters." [481]

2. The width of the layer is very small compared to the amount of time attributed to it. [482]

Consequently, the Gerzian culture should be dated to the middle of the Ancient Kingdom (3rd-4th dynasties) and the reason for distinguishing between these and other findings of that period is the foreign source of the inhabitants.

[This also is relevant to dating the 'Chalcolithic cultures' present in the Land of Israel, which we dealt with in the chapter: 'Places Associated with Tales of the Patriarchs'.

Vessels from the second phase of the Chalcolithic period are similar to the Early Bronze Age II, [483] and vessels from the first Chalcolithic phase were found together with those from the Early Bronze Age I. From this we see that the Chalcolithic culture is from the Early Bronze Age I-II, which paralleled the early dynasties in Egypt.

However, since the Chalcolithic vessels are similar to the Egyptian vessels defined as 'pre-dynastic', they have been forced to bring back the Chalcolithic period to the pre-dynastic period, and claim that they were mixed in vessels from different periods. [484]

In fact, Chalcolithic culture in the Land of Israel is from the Early Bronze Age, just as the Gerzian culture in Egypt is from the period of the Ancient Kingdom.

The differences between the 'Chalcolithic culture' and the Early Bronze Age arise from the fact that the men of the Early Bronze Age were settled dwellers, while those of the Chalcolithic culture were a nomadic society that arrived from the North. [485]]

Appendix 3: The Pyramids

Pyramid is a Greek word. The Egyptian word is Pir-Em-Us, which the Greeks corrupted to pyramid. The word Pir-Em-Us does not have any explanation.

---

[481] A. Gardiner, Egypt of the Pharaohs, p. 397.

[482] Payne, Catalogue of the Predynastic Egyptian collection, Oxford 1993, p. 6.

[483] M. Dothan, The late Chalcolithic Period in Palestine, Eretz Israel 10 (1971), p. 170.

[484] Gufna, the Settlement Geography of the coastal plain of the Land of Israel during the Early Bronze Age, doctorate, Tel Aviv 1974, p. 164-165. (Hebrew)

[485] R. Gufna, ibid, p. 134 (Hebrew); P. Bar-Adon, The Cave of the Treasure – The Findings from the caves in the Nahal Mishmar, Jerusalem 1971, pp. 223, 218-219. (Hebrew)

Edwards, one of the greatest scholars of the pyramids, writes: "A word of uncertain meaning". [486]

Can a reading from the Scriptures about the slavery of the Children of Israel explain the Egyptian use of the word?

In the Book of Exodus we are told that Pharaoh forced the Children of Israel to build him "Misknot cities, Pithom and Ramses" (Exodus 1:11). What is the explanation of the term 'Misknot cities'?

According to the Scriptural time's sources from the Canaanite city of Ugarit, Misknot meaning gravestone, [487] so that the cities of Misknot are cities of gravestones, or the pyramid cities. [488]

(Pyramids were not standalone buildings, but the main building of a complex of buildings surrounded by a wall. That is to say we are talking about a complete city that was built as a gravestone in the memory of the dead King.)

So now, what are Pithom and Ramses? But first, why was the stepped pyramid, at the time of the 3rd dynasty, redesigned with straight lines during the 4th dynasty?

This is because of a religious revolution during the 3rd dynasty when Egyptians saw Atom as the principle god and believed that Atom threw the King from the pyramid to the heavens in order to change him into a star god. [489] In accordance with this conception the pyramids were built with steps like a staircase that rose up to heaven.

During the 4th dynasty, however, the status of the sun-god Ra was strengthened, until he identified as Atom. He was represented on the earth by a broken stone, (a Meteorite?) in the form of a straight pyramid called 'Ben-Ben' established in the Temple of Ra.

From now on the King was considered to be the son of Ra. [490] At his death he changed into a heavenly being by the name of 'Beno'. [491] Consequently, the pyramid was changed from stepped to straight lines, so that act as the representative of the son of Ra. [492]

---

[486] I. E. S. Edwards, The Pyramids of Egypt, London 1955, p. 231.5
[487] H. L. Ginsberg, The Ugarit Text, Jerusalem 1936, p. 130-132. (Hebrew)
[488] N. R. Ganor, Who were the Phoenicians, Tel Aviv 1974, p. 57. (Hebrew)
The commentators explain is that 'Miskenot' were treasure storehouses. This explanation can also be explained as the pyramids, because we're not talking about storehouses for wheat or gold and silver, rather the storehouses for Pharoah. The body of the King was a treasure for which the cities were built.
[489] Shaw and Nicholson, Dictionary of Ancient Egypt, London 1996, p. 45.
[490] Clagett, Ancient Egyptian Science, Philadelphia 1989, p. 789.
[491] Lurker, The Gods and Symbols of Ancient Egypt, London 1995, p. 95.
[492] I. E. S. Edwards, The Pyramids of Egypt, London 1955, pp. 233-235.

Pithom implies in Egyptian 'the house of Atom', and Ramses means 'the son of Ra'. The Pyramid cities were initially built for the worship of Atom and afterwards, according to their faith, for the King as the son of Ra.

Pithom and Ramses are the names of pyramids. In the Egyptian language they are called Piremus which is a contracted form of Pithom and Ramses.

Appendix 4: To which dynasty do the Papyri of Ip-wer and Nefer-Rohu refer?

In Chapter 2 we quoted from the Papyri of the Admonitions of Ip-wer and the prophecy of Nefer-Rohu warning of the disasters visited upon Egypt at a certain unexplained period.

Some scholars think the papyri refer to between the 7th and 11th dynasties, while others think they refer to between the 13th and 17th dynasties.

An analysis of these papyri shows that they refer to the fall of the 4th dynasty, because the prophecy of Nefer-Rohu opens with the prophet being summoned into the presence of King Sneferu.

The King asked him about the future of his kingdom and the prophet Nefer-Rohu began to tell him of the prophecy. The Royal household of Sneferu lasted only until the end of the 4th dynasty, so that the future disaster befalling his kingdom would not happen any later.

Furthermore, with the fall of the 4th dynasty the status of Ra as the God of Egypt was nullified. This event, that mentioned in the prophecy of Nefer-Rohu, is a one-time event that took place only at the end of the 4th dynasty and was never repeated, not even by the religious revolutionary Akhnaton (who called himself Son of Ra).

To conclude: The Papyri refer to the period in which heavy disasters befell Egypt, and which led to the fall of the 4th dynasty.

Appendix 5: Where is the land of Goshen?

We have cited several quotations from the Ip-wer papyri recounting the Exodus from Egypt from the Egyptian viewpoint. A broken sentence preceding Egyptian preparations to set out in pursuit of the fleeing people requires an explanation: "The West emptied out." [493] What does 'the West emptied out' mean?

This brings us to the question where did the Children of Israel live? Let us try and find an answer from the Scriptures.

---

[493] A. Gardiner, The Admonitions of an Egyptian Sage, p. 78.

When Joseph asked his father to come to Egypt, he said "and you shall dwell in the land of Goshen, and you shall be close to me". (Genesis 45:14)

When the family arrived in Goshen, Joseph said to them: "If Pharaoh should call you... you should say: Your servants were men of cattle... in order to settle in the land of Goshen because all shepherds are an abomination to Egypt". (Ibid 46:33-34) The brothers did as he said, and indeed they received the land of Goshen. (ibid 47:6-27)

We understand from these verses that the Children of Israel lived in a land called Goshen, where Egyptians did not live, but was close to the Royal city.

Where was Goshen that was close to where Joseph resided, and why didn't Egyptians live there?

Ancient Egypt was divided into 42 districts. None of these districts bears the name Goshen (or a name like it), however from the ancient translations and down to today's scholars all of them place Goshen in the area close to the Sinai, that is to say in the north-eastern Egypt. [494]

The paragraph that speaks about the meeting between Jacob and Joseph directs us apparently in another direction. The wording in the Scriptures is as follows: "and Joseph harnessed his chariot and went up to meet his father in Goshen". (ibid, 31:29)

This implies that the land of Goshen was higher than the place where Joseph lived, and this could not be said about the customary identifications for Goshen, because northern Egypt is a flat country almost at sea level. We must search further south, but where?

Here archaeology comes to our aid. Parallel with the course of the Nile on the west for a hundreds km is a canal called the Bahr-Yusuf (The Joseph Canal). On the banks of this canal, especially in the Faiyum Basin are many settlements by people from the Gerzian culture, including the city of Gerza itself, which sits on the Josef Canal.

---

[494] The translation of Johnathan-ben-Uziel sees the area of Pelusion (Baluza) as the land of Goshen (the north west of the Sinai). Today it is acceptable to identify Goshen with Wadi Tumiliat which is to the east of Cairo. Another identification is with the city of Per-Rameses, South of Tannis.

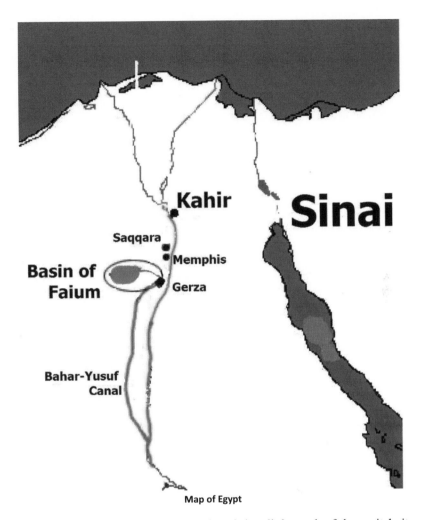

Map of Egypt

This place fits the Scriptural Goshen since it is a little south of the capital city Memphis and close to where Joseph lived, and to reach Memphis one must climb along the bank of the Nile, as in the wording of the Scriptures "and he went up to Goshen".

[On the other hand the places themselves are lower than the Nile, and in order to return to the Royal City one must go up to the Nile, as in the words of Joseph when he was in Goshen: "I will go up and I will tell Pharaoh" (Ibid, 47:31)]

We have said that not one of Egypt's districts reminds us of the word 'Goshen'. This is not exactly true, since apart from the 42 districts there was an additional borough absent from the list of boroughs, and its name does have a likeness to the word Goshen. This is the basin of Faiyum which is called in ancient Egyptian 'Tasheh' which implies 'the land of the lake'. [495]

Tasheh is Goshen.

Then why didn't the Egyptians live there? The name of the canal in which the settlements sit, the Bahar-Yosuf, testifies to the fact that it was Joseph who had it dug. When the Children of Israel went down into Egypt this was a development area just completed, and Joseph made efforts that his family received it.

This is the explanation of the words: "the West is emptied out" in the papyrus. The West refers to the Faiyum basin and the whole Josef Canal which is to the west of the Nile, is the land of Goshen. It emptied out when the Children of Israel abandoned Egypt and therefore the command was to go out to war.

Summary: The Faiyum basin west of the Nile which receives its waters from the Bahar-Yusuf canal is the land of Goshen where the Children of Israel lived. This is also the West that emptied out mentioned in the Ip-wer papyrus.

Appendix 6: Where is the land of Rameses?

In the previous appendix we identified the land of Goshen which the Children of Israel inhabited with the Fayum basin. An analysis of the Scriptures shows that the place was not easily achieved. Joseph himself did not dare to request it from Pharaoh so he told his brothers when they came to Goshen that they should request it from the King. (Genesis 46:34)

The King answered their request, but he instructed Joseph to try and settle his family inside Egypt "in the best of the land", and if they still wanted the land of Goshen, they could live there. (Ibid 47:6)

Joseph carried out his instructions to the letter "and Joseph settled his father and his brothers and gave them an inheritance in the best of the land, in the land of Rameses" (Ibid 11), and only in the end, the land of Goshen became the land of the Children of Israel. (Ibid 27)

Accordingly, the Children of Israel first dwelt in the land of Rameses when they arrived in Egypt. Where is the land of Rameses?

For this let us check the settlements of the Gerzian culture.

The findings in which point us to the connection between them and the land of Israel, however there is one place in which the resemblance is more recognisable, especially to the settlement of Beersheba from which the Children of Israel descended into Egypt (Ibid 46, 5). (See the chapter about the Patriarchal Period.)

---

[495] Arnold, Lexikon der Ägeptologie, II, p. 87.

This place is called Maadi, a little south of Cairo, opposite the great Pyramids of Giza. This is how the place is described:

"Maadi is unique among the known predynastic sites of Egypt... foreign house types and pottery... Since such structures are present at several sites around Beersheba in southern Palestine but otherwise unique to Egypt, archaeologists believe them to be imports and perhaps even the actual houses of aliens resident at Maadi." [496]

The exact similarity to Beersheba found in this place leads to the conclusion that this is Rameses, where the Children of Israel lived when they came from Beersheba.

The name "The Land of Rameses" suits Maadi well, as it is explained in the 3th appendix that 'Rameses' means a straight pyramid. Maadi is located opposite Giza, which is the main site of these pyramids.

Appendix 7: Who was Baal Tzephon?

When the Children of Israel left Egypt they passed by a place sanctified to the idol 'Baal Tzephon' (Exodus 14:2).

Can we find in the Egyptian pantheon an Egyptian God named in the Bible Baal Tzephon?

Apparently this is the god Soped (Sopdu), in the Assyrian language 'Tzefat' which, according to Egyptian belief, is "the guardian of the road along the Sea of Reeds... His main temple was beside the important route to Sinai and the Land of Israel." [497]

The city from which this road sets out is named after the god: Per–Soped (nowadays: Saft-el-Hinna), and from there the route continues to 'Theku' (nowadays: Maskhuta) which is the Scriptural city of Succoth, where the Children of Israel camped on their way to the sea. (Exodus 13:20)

The title 'Baal Tzephon' mean 'Master of the North', and is better understood when we recognize the position of Soped in the Pantheon of Egyptian Gods. He belonged to a family of gods: the father god Sah, the mother goddess Sopdet and the son, the god Soped.

---

[496] Hoffman, Egypt before the Pharaohs, New York 1979, p. 201.
[497] R. Giveon, The Stones of Sinai Speak, p. 214. (Hebrew)

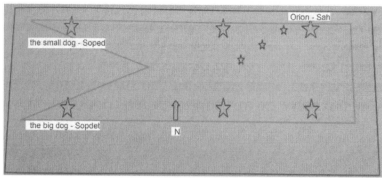

Orion star constellation

This family is identified with the Orion star constellation. Sah is Orion himself; Sopdet is the southern accompanier, the big dog (Sirius), and Soped with the northern accompanier star – the small dog. [498]

Soped and Sopdet mean is the 'sharp tip' (in the masculine and feminine) which Egyptologists found difficult to explain. [499]

They are well understood if we look at the Orion constellation. Sopdet was the southern extreme and Soped was the northern extreme, so that it is correct to give it the name 'Baal Tzephon' (Master of the North).

To conclude: The Egyptian god 'Baal Tzephon' mentioned in the story of the Exodus from Egypt is the god Soped (Tzefat).

Appendix 8: Where was the Sea of Reeds?

Where did the Children of Israel cross the 'Sea of Reeds'? This is a subject about which scholars have deliberated and many answers have been given:

[498] Shaw and Nicholson, Dictionary of Ancient Egypt, London 1996, p. 276.
[499] Giveon, Lexikon der Ägeptologie, V, Wiesbaden 1980, p. 1107.

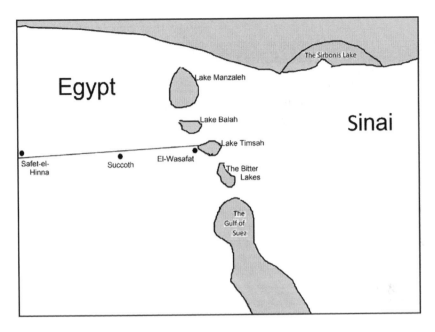

1. The Sirbonis Lake

2. Lake Manzaleh

3. Lake Balah

4. Lake Timsah

5. The Bitter Lakes

6. The Gulf of Suez

Some scholars even go so far as to suggest the other side of the Red Sea or the Gulf of Eilat.

However, as we have shown in the previous appendix, that Baal Tzephon is Sofed/Tzefat, then we can also point to the branch of the Sea of Reeds which the Children of Israel crossed at "Pi-Hahiroth opposite Baal-Tzefon" (Exodus 14:9), and this site can be easily found.

The road to Sinai sets out from Saft-el-Hinna on the way to Succoth and it ends (about 3 km away) at another place named after the god Sofed/Tzefat: "El-Wasafat" which is situated opposite the lake of Timsah,

'El-Wasafat' is Baal Tzephon, opposite which the Children of Israel began to cross the Sea of Reeds, and the lake of Timsah is the Sea of Reeds itself. We can also reveal Pi-Hahiroth. This is Sa-Hara actually located on the banks of the lake.

If we proceed to check the lake, we will discover in it reminders of the time when the Children of Israel passed by it. This is Mount Miriam (Jabbal Maryam) which rises up to the south of the lake named after Miriam who broke out in song at this place:

"and Miriam the prophetess, the sister of Aaron, took the drum in her hand, and all the women went out after her with drums and cymbals and Miriam said to them: Sing to the Lord because he has been very exalted, the horse and his chariots have been thrown into the sea." (ibid 16:20-21)

To conclude: The Sea of Reeds which the Children of Israel passed is Lake Timsah.

Appendix 9: Who were the Hyksos

The Egyptian historian, Manetho, tells us that the 15th Egyptian dynasty – the Hyksos – comprised six kings from the Children of Israel who ruled Egypt for 511 years, from the period when the god was angry, until they left by way of the desert to Jerusalem.

Manetho's comments about these Israelite rulers have always been related to with disbelief, despite the fact accepted by scholars that there were foreign rulers at this time, because the inscription of Queen Hatshepsut (18th dynasty) also speaks about the time when foreign rulers from Semitic origins ruled the land. [500]

Apart fromone King (Hian) there are no significant remains from the Hyksos Kings, and what remains for scholars to identify these kings are with the names that have been found on scarabs (seals).

Manetho gives the names of these kings, and a study of the names shows that this subject is more complicated than meets the eye, since the names that Manetho quotes are not like the accepted names of the kings of Hyksos, but more like the names of Kings from the 5th-6th dynasties: **Pepi**, **Uni**, **Isesi**, which are called by Manetho: **Apophi, Ianna, Assi**.

Apparently Manetho's explanation of the story about Hyksos is as follows: The period during which the God was angry with Egypt occurred at the end of the 4th dynasty.

In the eyes of later generations, with the fall of the 4th dynasty legitimate Egyptian rule ceased, and was not restored until the period of the Middle Kingdom, while the kings of the 5th-6th dynasties are accused of seizing the kingship. [501]

---

[500] J. H. Breasted, A History of Egypt, New York 1951, p. 215.
[501] Lambadin, Biblical Encyclopedia, Vol. 5. p. 253. (Hebrew)

This was also the later period in which the Asiatics ruled Egypt, and Manetho mixed the two periods.

The story of the Hyksos is therefore a mixture of suffering during the end of the 4th dynasty (the Exodus from Egypt), the names of the rulers who governed after the fall of the 4th dynasty, and a description of the foreign rule of Egypt which, according to the leftover remains, was much shorter than the time given by research.

Appendix 10: When was Arad destroyed?

In Chapter 3 we identified the destruction of Arad in the Early Bronze Age with its destruction during the time of Joshua, along with the destruction of other cities like Jericho, Ai, etc.

Here arises a problem: the destruction of Arad precedes the destruction of the rest of the Land by hundreds of years; while the other cities were destroyed during the period Early Bronze Age **III**, Arad was destroyed already during Early Bronze Age **II**.

How can we say that Arad was destroyed during Early Bronze Age II at the same time as the destruction of the other cities, during Early Bronze Age III?

It turns out that there is no real evidence for dating the destruction of Arad in Early Bronze Age II. This claim is based on the Abydos vessels that were found in the destroyed stratum. According to Professor Ben-tor, an expert in this field, the type of vessel found in Arad "is symptomatic of the Early Bronze Age II and maybe Early Bronze Age III." [502]

He goes on to say that in Syria these vessels are found in the layer of the Early Bronze Age III. [503] So we see that there is no real evidence that Arad was destroyed during Early Bronze Age II.

On the other hand, the jugs that were found in Arad are of the type attributed to Early Bronze Age III. [504] Accordingly, we can date the destruction of Arad to the Early Bronze age III.

Furthermore, Arad Ceramics were found in the settlements of the Negev which are customarily dated to the Early Bronze Age II, together with vessels from the Intermediate Bronze Age (Middle Bronze I). [505] Early Bronze Age III separates

---

[502] A. Ben-Tor, Problems in the Early Bronze Age II-III in Palestine, Thesis submitted for the Degree Dr of Philosophy, Jerusalem 1968, p. 147-148. (Hebrew)
[503] Ibid, p. 83.
[504] A. Ofer, The Highland of Judah during the Biblical Period, Doctorate, Tel Aviv 1993, p. 16. (Hebrew)
[505] Excavations and Surveys in Israel 1982 – Vol. 1, pp. 81, 84.

these two periods so how can vessels be used at the same time from periods that are hundreds of years apart?

This means that the Arad ceramics which are dated to Early Bronze Age II really existed at the end of Early Bronze Age III.

According to the scholar whose findings doubt the accuracy of the accepted dating: "half the sites belonging to the period Early Bronze Age II, continue also into the Middle Bronze Age I. It seems that there is room to question whether we should divide this period into two with a third period between them, or maybe see a chronological continuity from Early Bronze Age II to Middle Bronze Age I." [506]

The chronological continuation to Middle Bronze Age I can of course take place only from Early Bronze Age III, and not from Early Bronze Age II, which is earlier by hundreds of years. That is to say the accepted dating of the Arad Ceramics – Early Bronze Age II – is mistaken, and we should change it to the Early Bronze Age III.

Summary: the destruction of Arad from the Early Bronze Age has been dated to Early Bronze Age II. The findings do not clearly support a correct dating, and ignore other pieces of information.

Therefore the destruction of Arad and every other place where we find Arad Ceramics should be dated to the period Early Bronze Age III, the same period when other cities in the Land of Israel were also destroyed.

Appendix 11: Why the name Madon was not preserved?

In Chapter 4 we indicated that the biblical city 'Madon' is the site 'Tel Beth Yerah'. If so, why hasn't the name Madon been preserved?

The reasoning appears as follows. Tel Beth Yerah was abandoned at the end of the Early Bronze Age, and resettled again until the time of the Second Temple. The place was abandoned over a very long period of time and the name of Madon was forgotten.

With resettlement at the time of the Second Temple, it was named Beth Yerah (House of the Moon). Maybe it is the fact that the closest settlement is called Beth Shemesh (House of the Sun) (Joshua 19, 22), that is identified with the ruins of Hirbet Shamsin.

---

[506] E. Oren, The Valley of Uvda, Sites from the Early Bronze and Middle Bronze Age I, The Ninth Archaeological Congress of Israel 1982, p. 13. (Hebrew)

Appendix 12: Saul's Palace

David and Solomon lived during the Middle Bronze Age IIb. David succeeded his father-in-law, King Saul.

According to the Scriptures Saul chose to live on a hill named until his reign 'Benjamin's Hill' (Judges 19:14) and later 'Saul's Hill' (Isaiah 10,29).

Its location known from the Book of Josephus Flavius 'The Jewish Wars' which describes the destruction of the Second Temple.

Josephus tells that Titus reached Jerusalem from the north and set up camp "close to a village called 'Saul's Hill', some thirty Estadias from Jerusalem" (Book 5, 2: 1) some 30 Estadia about 5.5 km (one Estadia is 185 m).

Meanwhile, in addition to Josephus's testimony we found archaeological support for the Roman camp at the extremities of the neighbourhood Pisgat Ze'ev, north of Jerusalem, some 5.5 km from today's Old City of Jerusalem where the remains of a road were found littered with shards of Roman vessels from the Early Roman period. [507]

It is mistaken customary to identify Saul's Hill with the higer *tel* in the area – 'Tel el-Ful' which rises up above Pisgat Ze'ev to the west, one km from the Roman camp, while another site – Hirbet Hadasah – is only 200 meters away from the Roman camp, where many earthenware pieces were found from the time of the Second Temple. [508]

So, according to Jospeheus Hirbet Hadassah is Saul's Hill.

Could this Saul's Hill be the place where King Saul lived? The answer is negative, because no pottery from the period of the Middle Bronze Age was found in Hirbet Hadasah. That is to say this is a later settlement, named after the original settlement, which was somewhere nearby.

Archaeological surveys found only one site from the Middle Bronze Age in the entire area. This was a settlement above Zimri valley [509] (in the present-day neighborhood of East Pisgat Ze'ev, 'Tagar' and 'Kiseh Rachamim' streets.)

This being the only settlement in the area during the same period indicates that this was the site of Saul's city. Excavations at the site revealed the remains of a

---

[507] A. Kloner, Survey of Jerusalem - The Northeastern Sector, Jerusalem 2001, p. 23. (Hebrew)

[508] A. Kloner, Survey of Jerusalem - The Northeastern Sector, Jerusalem 2001, p. 24. (Hebrew); H. Khalaily, Excavations and Surveys in Israel, Volume 16 (1997), p. 95-97.

[509] S. Gibson, Hadashot Arkheologiyot 78-79, 1982, p. 65. (Hebrew)

wide building, in the middle enclosing a courtyard paved with stone panels, [510] which was very rare for those times.

The very high quality of building indicates the high prosperity of the elite inhabitants of the area and, it is reasonable, that this was part of the Royal palace of King Saul. The site is located at the beginning of Kiseh Rachamim street and is open to the public.

Summary: it follows that the place that was revealed above Zimri valley is the original Saul's Hill from the Scriptures, and the wide building that has been revealed is the Palace of King Saul.

Appendix 13: During which dynasty was the period 'Middle Bronze Age IIb'?

In the Chapter 'David and Solomon' we wrote that during the Middle Bronze Age IIb in the Land of Israel, the 12th dynasty ruled in Egypt. These facts do not fit the accepted dating which is this:

Intermediate Bronze Age	5th-11th dynasties
Middle Bronze Age **IIa**	12th dynasty
Middle Bronze Age **IIb**	13th -17th dynasties

Accordingly, the **12th dynasty** occurred much earlier in the period MB **IIa** and not in the period MB IIb. However, there are proofs that the accepted dating is not correct, and the **12th dynasty** was during the Middle Bronze Age **IIb**, as the following evidence shows:

"Until now all important Egyptian findings from the Middle Kingdom (12th dynasty) have been found in later levels." [511] and unconvincing excuses have been given to make the findings fit accepted dating concepts:

One excuse is: "It has been claimed that we should see in them objects that were traded during a later period." But "trading in antiquities is not persuasive", and so investigators prefer to give a different answer:

---

[510] A. Kloner, Survey of Jerusalem - The Northeastern Sector, Jerusalem 2001, p. 38; I. Meitlis, Excavations and Surveys in Israel, Volume 10 (1992), p. 125.
[511] N. Na'aman, The History of the Land of Israel – vol.1, Jerusalem 1982, p. 144. (Hebrew)

"Later on, since these were considered valuable objects, they were stored and passed from generation to generation, and in this way they survived in the later layers." [512]

However, this explanation is not convincing, since they include small objects as well as large ones, which makes it hard to distinguish their importance. They were all found in the later layers, at Tel el-Ajul (south of Gaza):

"A bead and scarabs of Eagyptian officials, as well as statuette, all point to this period (12th Dynasty), although it seems that none of the buildings in the area can be dated so early." [513]

The phenomenon of scarabs (seals) from the time of the 12th dynasty found in later layers repeats itself in other places: "the general archaeological findings in which they were unearthed means that most of them belong to the period MBA IIb".[514] Furthermore, not only were they found in a later period but their style is also a later style. [515]

The only place in which the findings of the 12th dynasty revealed in the stratum of MBA IIa is Byblos, on which the entire chronology of the whole Land of Israel is built. Though, actually, even there we are talking about a layer later than the MBA IIa.

This is how the vessels found are defined: "the earthenware vessels that still retain the style of the later period from the period of MBA IIa". [516]

It is clear from this wording that these vessels already belong to the period MBA IIb. (We should point out that in Byblos the MBA IIb is missing because this layer has mistakenly been called the MBA IIa.)

Additional evidence against the accepted dating is that the findings indicate that in the period of MBA IIb the Land of Israel was under the strong cultural influence of Egypt.

According to this dating something very strange happens and Egypt, which was poor, changed into a model for imitation. Kampinsky notes:

"It is interesting that the main (Egyptian) influence falls specifically in the mideterne period, not from the period of the Middle Kingdom." [517]

---

[512] N. Na'aman, ibid.

[513] O. Tufnel, The New Encyclopedia of Archeological Excavations in the Holy Land, p. 50.

[514] R. Giveon, the Footsteps of Pharaoh in Canaan, p. 25-27. (Hebrew)

[515] Ibid.

[516] A. Kampinsky, The Archaeology of Ancient Israel in the Biblical Period, Unit 6-7, p. 38. (Hebrew)

[517] A. Kampinsky, the Land of Israel and Syria during the late period of the Middle Bronze Age IIb, Doctorate, Jerusalem 1974, p. 5. (Hebrew)

Another problem with the accepted dating is the long period of the Intermediate Bronze Age. From this period (the Intermediate Bronze Age) where there are hardly any remains of buildings. According to this dating no land settlements were made for hundreds of years, even though people lived there with an unbelievably high technological standard of living:

"The relative abundance of metal utensils and the advanced technology with which they were created, stick out much more against the background of a miserable image of most of the settlements of that period." [518]

Therefore, we should make the dating like this:

The Intermediate Bronze Age	the middle of the 5th dynasty
The Middle Bronze Age IIa	the 5th -11th dynasties
The Middle Bronze Age IIb	the 12th -17th dynasties

Using this dating, all the problems that we have raised disappear.

To conclude: The Middle Bronze Age IIb was the period of the 12th-17th dynasties in Egypt.

Appendix 14: Who are the Shutu?

In the chapter 'David and Solomon' we identified the 'Shutu' of the Egyptian inscriptions with the Israelites. On the other hand, in archaeological literature we find that the term 'Shutu' refers to the Moabites who lived on the eastern side of the Jordan.

Albright, who identified the land of Shet with the land of Moab based on the verse from the prophecy of Balaam:

"I shall see him, but not now: I shall behold him, but not nigh: there shall come a Star out of Jacob, and a Sceptre shall rise out of Israel, and shall smite the corners of Moab, and 'Karkar' all the children of Shet". (Numbers 24:17)

He and other commentators concluded from this verse that Shet is a moniker for Moab, and therefore the 'Shutu' of the Egyptian inscriptions are the Moabites.

---

[518] R. Gufna, The Archaeology of Ancient Israel in the Biblical Period, Unit 3, p. 114. (Hebrew) In general we should mention that the time set aside for it is based on the assumption that it took place in parallel with the Intermediate period 1 in Egypt and for this assumption there are no proofs (Gufna, The History of the Land of Israel, vol. 1, Jerusalem 1982, p. 121).

However, this explanation is incorrect, because the first part of the verse speaks about two matters:

1. A star – raised above everyone else.

2. A scepter – that will strike his enemies.

We can expect the second part of the verse to parallel the first part: the scepter will kill the multitudes of Moab, and the star 'Karkar' all the children of Shet.

What do the words 'Karkar all the children of Shet' mean?

The word 'Karkar' is a harsh word, though in this context (star), it can mean that he will be merciful to his people, who are called the sons of Shet, that is to say the people of Israel.

It is customary to explain this as referring to King David and the Egyptians images showing the deep respect which the sons of Shet merited from the Egyptians of that generation.

The notion that Shet are the Children of Israel is strengthened by the fact that the members of the Shutu race appear in the Egyptian images similar to the mages of the Children of Israel who are pictured in the black obelisk of the Assyrian King Shalmaneser.

To summarize: The Children of Shet are the Children of Israel and not the Children of Moab, and they are also the Shutu in the Egyptian records.

Appendix 15: Is there a contradiction between the Sennacherib inscription and the Book of Kings?

Sennacherib says in his inscription that King Hezekiah sent him a considerable sum in silver and gold, as it is written in the Book of Kings. (Kings II, 18:14-16)

However, the Scriptures record that Hezekiah sent the silver and gold before the siege of Jerusalem happened, whereas Sennacherib says this after he tell about the siege of Jerusalem.

One can understand from the Scriptures that Sennacherib wanted to conquer Jerusalem despite the recent shipment from Hezekiah, and was forced to retreat because of the plague that killed his soldiers. According to Sennacherib's inscription he made do with Hezekiah's respectful present and returned to his country.

There is an apparent contradiction here and scholars prefer Sennacherib's version, according to which he did not retreat from Jerusalem in shame, as told in the Scriptures, but left after he had obtained Hezekiah's complete surrender.

It should be borne in mind that in the ancient world you won't find in the chronicles of kings admissions of defeat, only successes, unlike the Bible which tells of mostly of many failures, including that of Hezekiah. Consequently, the credibility of Sennacherib's inscription is likely to be lower than that of the Bible.

Actually, if we analyze in detail Sennacherib's inscription, which comprises a number of tablets, it seems that it can also be concluded that Sennacherib did not leave Jerusalem because of the taxes.

The story of the siege appears on one tablet which finishes with Hezekiah a prisoner in his own city, whereas the story about the tax appears in another tablet, without mentioning a connection between the tax and lifting of the siege.

If Sennacherib had left Jerusalem only on the merit of the taxes, why was the inscription silent about this? That is to say the inscription on the Assyrian tablet presents the positive aspects from Sennacherib's point of view, and does not mention the blow that he received. Nor does it go so far as to say explicitly that Sennacherib left the City because of the tax he received.

So, there is no contradiction between the inscription of Sennacherib and what is told in the Book of Kings.

Appendix 16: How many Kings comprised the Ethiopian dynasty?

In the Chapter 'When did Sennacherib besiege Jerusalem' we conclude that the siege of Samaria occurred in 696 BCE and remained in place until its conquest in the year 694 BCE.

Our dating raises the question in connection with the 25th dynasty – the Ethiopian dynasty – in Egypt. According to what we have shown in the chapter 'The Savior at the time of Jehoahaz', the Libyan dynasty which preceded the Ethiopian dynasty ruled until 696 BCE, with the siege of Samaria.

The Ethiopian dynasty comprised four kings: The founder, Piankhy, who began as the King of Ethiopia and then conquered Egypt; his son Taharaqa who began to reign in the year 688 BCE, and two additional kings: Shabaka and Shabataka who each reigned twelve years. So, where is there room for the Kings Shabaka and Shabataka?

Before answer worthy of note that Piankhy and Taharaka are both heavily documented but there are scarce records on Shabaka and Shabataka. One rare document records that Shabaka appointed Amenirdis to be a priestess of Thebes, while another records that it was actually Piankhy who appointed her. [519]

---

[519] J. H. Breasted, A History of Egypt, New York 1952, p. 546, ibid, p. 553.

The conclusion is that the Ethiopian dynasty actually comprised only two kings: Piankhy and his son Taharaka. Shabaka and Shabataka were nick names attributed to Piankhy.

Appendix 17: List of the Kings of Judah and Israel

In the Chapter 'When did Sennacherib lay siege to Jerusalem' we said that a number of the Kings of Judah and Israel observed a short year of six months. The following are the approximate years BCE in which the Kings of Judah and Israel began to reign.

Kings of Israel	Kings of Judah
	David – 968 Solomon– 928 Rehoboam – 888 Aviyam –871 Asa – 869
Jeroboam I – 888	
Nadav –867	
Baasha – 866	
Elah– 843	
Omri – 842	
Ahab – 831	Jehosafat – 828 Jehoram – 805
Ahaziyahu – 810	
Jehoram – 809	Ahaziyahu – 798 Athalyah – 798 Jehoash – 792 Amaziah – 753
Jehu – 798	
Jehoahaz – 770	
Jehoash – 754	
Jeroboam II - 739	Uziyahu – 737 in his father's lifetime By himself – 726
Zecharyah, Shalum, Menachem– 718	
Pekahiyah – 713	Yotam – 711 Ahaz – 707 in his father's lifetime
Pekach – 712	
Hoshea – 702	By himself – 703 Hezekiah – 699 Menashe – 670 Amon– 642 Josiah – 641 Jehoahaz, Jehoyakim – 609 Jehoyachin, Tzidkiyahu – 597 Destruction of the Temple – 586
Destruction of Samaria – 693	

These are the approximate years BCE in which the Kings of Judah and Israel reigned. The list raises the question at what age Hezekiah became king. His father

Ahaz was 20 years old when he became king and he reigned for 16 years. Afterwards Hezekiah was 25 when he began to reign.

According to plain arithmetic Ahaz died at the age of 36 when his son was only 25. This means that he gave birth to Hezekiah when he was eleven years old which seems far-fetched.

However, according to our explanation Ahaz reigned only eight years and died at the age of 28 when Hezekiah his son was 25 according to which he gave birth to Hezekiah when he was only three years old!

We have to say that "he was 25 years old when he reigned" means he was 12.5 years old, and that Ahaz gave birth to Hezekiah when he was 13.

Appendix 18: List of Assyrian Kings

In the Chapter 'When did Sennacherib lay Siege to Jerusalem' we showed that a number of Assyrian kings after Tiglat Pileser counted short years of six months which condenses the list of Assyrian Kings by some 27 years.

An analysis of ancient Assyrian inscriptions teaches that the period preceding Tiglat Pileser should also be shortened by an additional 14 years:

The inscriptions of King Shalmaneser III about Ahab and Jehu also imply the need to shorten the list some more.

Messengers of Jehu bring taxes to Shalmaneser III

The dating of Shalmaneser's inscriptions to the time of Jehu is possible only if we remove from the list of Kings those who reigned after Shalmaneser some 14 years. If so, the list of Assyrian Kings did not begin in 910 BCE but in 869 BCE as the amended list indicates:

Adad-Nirari II – 869-848

Tukulti-Enurta II – 848-841

Ashurnasirpal II – 841-816

Shalmaneser III – 816-781(During his 6th year he made war on Ahab, in his 18th year he received taxes from Jehu)

Shamshi-Adad V – 781-768

Adad-Nirari I – 768-740 (Received taxes from Jehoash King of Israel)

Shalmaneser IV – 740-735 (or 730)

Ashur-Dan III – 735 (or 730)-726 (or 721)

Ashur-Nirari V – 726 (or 721)-716

Tiglat Pileser III – 716-699 [In his inscriptions he mentions Azariah (Uziyahu), Menachem and Ahaz.]

Shalmaneser – 699-696

The Assyrian chronology from the time of the First Temple is based on solar eclipses which occurred in the month of Sivan during the time of King Ashur-dan.

Astronomical calculations show that in the year 763 BCE this hypothesis apparently contradicted the proposed change, though it should be remembered that in Hezekiah's time a disruption in the orderly movement of the planet occurred (Kings II, 20:11) so it is impossible to calculate the prior solar eclipses that took place.

Appendix 19: Who were the Habiru?

In the Chapter about the Habiru we reached the conclusion that Habiru-SA.GAZ are the Hittites, among the people of Canaan, (Genesis 10:15).

On the other hand, in the Chapter: 'When were the El-Amarna Letters written' we said that SA.GAZ are Ashkenaz, who are a completely different people descended from Gomer, the son of Japhet (ibid, 3).

How can we reconcile these two opposing identities? To answer this question let us present the generations of Asia Minor (Turkey) during antiquity:

At the time of the First Temple Asia Minor was inhabited by a people called Phrygian, while the Hittite people dwelt in Northern Syria and spread out to a number of states, among them one named Alalach.

Toward the end of the First Temple period the state of Phrygia and the Hittite states disappeared from the world. The Assyrian King Sargon conquered and destroyed the Hittite kingdoms, and the sons of Gomer (Gimiriah in the Assyrian records, Kimerean in the Greek books) destroyed the Kingdom of Phrygia, and replaced it with their own states.

According to the historian Herodotus, the Scythians arrived in Asia Minor, pushed out the sons of Gomer and settled in their place (Herodotus 4:11). That is to say the Phrygian were the original inhabitants, followed by the sons of Gomer and afterwards the Scythians.

In the chapter about Habiru we identified the Scythians with the Hittites. Accordingly, the Ashkenazies, sons of Gomer, (the Kimereans) arrived in Asia Minor and pushed out the Phrygian. Then came the Hittites (the Scythians) the inhabitants of Allalach and they took over the Ashkenazies.

The new kingdom was composed of both peoples: The Ashkenazies and the Hittites and from here on the names of SA.GAZ and Het are used interchangeably.

This is why the seers of the Hittite Kingdom swore both by the gods of SA.GAZ and of Allalach, and also explains the things Herodotus quoted about the Scythian claim to be the youngest of nations.

Accepted research dates the Hittites to the 14th and 13th centuries BCE, and does not connect them with the Hittite Kingdoms of the 8th century BCE (the Neo-Hittites) because of their different language. However, they also cannot ignore similaritities in writing and given names.

"The use of the Hittite script by the Neo Hittites is one of the connecting links to the ancient Hittites. Another link is to the clear preference of their rulers to be called by the names of historical Hittites. We should know however that the neo-Hittites are not descendants of the ancient Hittites." [520]

According to our research, the ancient Hittites are apparently the predecessors of the neo-Hittites, and the difference in language comes from their assimilation with the SA.GAZ.

This description explains a difficult verse in the Book of Joshua: "Every place where the sole of your feet shall tread I have given to you. From the desert and this Lebanon, until the great river of Euphrates, all the land of the Hittites until the great sea in the west these will be your borders". (Joshua 1:4)

This verse seems to imply that most of Turkey will be included in the Land of Israel, since this is the land of the Hittites, and that of course cannot be.

---

[520] B. Mazar, Biblical Encyclopedia, Vol 3, p. 337. (Hebrew)

However according to what we have said the matter is understood. It is only at the end of the days of the First Temple that the Hittites arrived to take over Turkey, and their original land was North West Syria.

Thus writes Shalmaneser the King of Assyria at the time: "From the mountain of Amana until the Mount of the Lebanon I took control of the land of Het entirely."

'Mount Amana' is 'Toros Amanos' at the extreme western edge of the latter day Turkish–Syrian border, and from here south until the Lebanon is the land of Het, which is discussed in this verse in the Book of Joshua.

Summary: The 'Habiru-SA.GAZ' are the assimilated Hittites and Ashkenazis.

Appendix 20: The Crumbling of the Kingdom of Judah

To understand the situation during the time of Jehoyakim let us quote two verses from the Book of Kings:

"Pharaoh Necho, the King of Egypt, came up and he gave a punishment to the land, a hundred bars of **silver** and a bar of **gold**" (Kings II, 23:33).

"**Silver and gold** Jehoyakim gave to Pharaoh.

However, valued the land to give the **silver** according to Pharaoh.

Each man according to his value took forth **silver and gold** from the people to give to Pharaoh Necho." (Ibid, 35)

These verses raise a number of questions:

1. In other places in the Scriptures, the ratio between silver and gold was 1 to 10 (Kings II 18:14; Chronicles 22:14) whereas here the ratio between them is one to a hundred. Why?

2. The last verse starts out with *silver and gold* and finishes up *silver and gold*, whereas in the middle it mentions only *silver*, what does this change mean?

3. What is the explanation for "however valued the land to give the silver according to Pharaoh"?

The answers to these questions are as follows:

Jehoyakim inherited a large kingdom from his father. Pharaoh, for understandable reasons, was interested in reducing Jehoyakim's power and so he plotted to isolate Jehoyakim by bringing the heads of the different districts directly under his authority.

He set up two different types of taxes: a heavy silver tax (one hundred bars) and a token gold tax (one bar) when pharaoh himself fixed how the silver tax should be divided between the different districts and left Jehoyakim to fix only the posting of the gold tax. The rulers of the different districts understood from that Jehoyakim was King only in name without any real authority, and that they don't need to consider his opinion.

As a result of Jehoyakim's loss of authority to tax his subjects, rulers of the different districts appointed to collect the tax brought it straight to Pharaoh Necho, including the gold which meant that Jehoyakim ceased to be King over them.

One mystery is now clarified. A second mystery involves excavations which revealed that in the period El-Amarna there was more gold than silver in the Land of Israel. In Megiddo, for example, "the vast amount of gold in the El-Amarna period was prominent; on the other hand it contrasted with the extremely small amount of silver... The opinion – built on many other areas from the time of the Egyptian Empire – is that silver was very rare as opposed to gold."[521]

Silver is usually less rare than gold, but because the tax on silver was a hundred times more than the tax on gold the silver was taken to Egypt and the gold remained behind.

Pharaoh Necho's method was one of divide and rule, and we find a clear expression of this process also in the El-Amarna letters. The Kings of the cities in the Land accused each other of treason, each one vying to show that he is truly faithful to the King and this was the situation when Jehoyakim was under Pharaoh Necho's authority.

Appendix 21: Where was the Seal 'Gemaryahu, Son of Shafan' found?

In the Chapter 21 we mentioned that in the great palace in the City of David, an impression was found of Gemariah, the son of Shafan, one of Jehoyakim's ministers. This matches our suggested identification of this site as the palace of Jehoyakim.

On the other hand, according to the excavator – Y. Shilo – Gemariah's seal was found on a floor built above the ruins of the palace, in the strata from the end of the Iron Age (Locus 967), which is a latest stratum from the El-Amarna period.

Actually this finding does not contradict our dating because the diagram accompanying Shilo's article indicates that the seal-impressions were not found

---

[521] D. Amir, The Galilee in the Bronze Age, Dan 1997, p. 168.

on that floor (Locus 967), but on the level beneath it (Locus 1110) in a much earlier period. [522]

Why did he write about the impressions found in Locus 967 and not in Locus 1110? Apparently the contradiction between the date of the destruction of the First Temple according to the accepted timeline (end of the Iron Age) and the date of Locus 1110 in which these impressions were found forced the excavator to ascribe these impressions to Locus 967.

It seems, therefore, that he should add this sentence: "The floors of the impressions had a sub-level in addition to what was presented as Locus 1110" [523], and since we are talking about a sub-level he allowed himself to mark Locus 1110 in which he found the impressions only as a sub-level (of locus 967). And therefore he was able to resolve the contradictions between the position where the seal was found and the place in which it *should* have been found.

However, according to what we saw in section 5, the destruction of the First Temple did not occur at the end of the Iron Age, but during an earlier period, so there is no problem in finding the impressions in layer 1110.

In conclusion, the impression from the seal of Gemariyahu, the son of Shafan, was found in the ruins of the Palace in the City David, built during the period Late Bronze Age /Iron Age 1, and not on the floor that was built above it.

Appendix 22: Who destroyed the Temple at Shilo?

In Chapter 21 we showed remains in Jerusalem dated from the time of El-Amarna. Excavations at Tel Shilo, north of Jerusalem, reveal that a Temple stood here in the generation before the El-Amarna period. [524]

Huge jugs were found in the storerooms together with a large amount of animal bones, ritual vessels and the symbol of the Hittite divinity: "There was apparently

---

[522] Y. Shilo, A Hoard of Hebrew Bullae from the City of David, Eretz Israel 18 (1985), p. 75, (Hebrew) in the illustration. (Look at the lower arrow there!)
[523] Ibid.
[524]The earthenware vessels that were found on this site are from the Middle Bronze Age IIb together with earthenware from the Iron Age I.
According to the accepted dating 350 years separate between these two periods, and therefore the investigators decreed that on this site stood a temple in the period of MB. Immediately afterwards a similar temple was set up in the Iron Age.
The fact that these findings from the two periods were uncovered together is explained by the common excuse that they were storage pits from the Iron Age dug down into the strata of the Middle Bronze Age (I. Finkelstein, the Archaeology of the Israelite Settlement, Jerusalem 1988, p. 226-227).

an isolated cultic place, to which offering were brought by people from various locales in the region." [525]

"Shilo was destroyed... Traces of burning were found in the row of rooms, and mudbricks from the collapsing upper parts of the walls buried these chambers before the fleeing inhabitants could remove their contents... Collapsed burnt bricks accumulated on these floors to a height of over a meter. Some of the bricks had been baked by the blaze that raged here." [526]

According to the dating system that we suggested, these findings are from a period before the destruction of the First Temple.

What explanation is given for the presence of a Temple at Shilo when Jerusalem's Temple already stood? Who destroyed it with such anger, without trying to save its contents?

The answer is: The Book of Kings tells us that even after the First Temple was built, the people continued to offer sacrifices outside the Temple, and not only to the Lord alone.

The Temple at Shilo which contained a pagan god's emblem, belonged to one of those cult center's to divinities that were to be found in the same generation: "on every high hill and under every green tree" (Jeremiah 2:20), and particularly in places like Shilo, which had links to an ancient holiness.

The person who abolished this was Jehoyakim's father, Josiah, the King of Judah, who led a holy war against idol worshipping Temples. He did not stop with the destruction of pagan gods in the land of Judah and continued to areas controlled by the Kingdom of Israel: "also the altar which is in Bethel he burnt into fine dust... And also all the platforms in the cities of Samaria, and did the same as he did to the ones in Bethel". (Kings II, 23:16-19)

The harsh destruction found in Shilo and the mighty fire, which cleansed the Land of Israel of idol worship are traces of the actions taken by Josiah.

Appendix 23: What did Ezekiel mean by the words "in the 27th year"?

According to the dating we suggested, in 584 BCE Egypt was conquered by Nebuchadnezzar. In the Book of Ezekiel there is a verse which apparently contradicts this date.

---

[525] I. Finkelstein, the Archaeology of the Israelite Settlement, Jerusalem 1988, p. 219.
[526] Ibid, pp. 217, 225-226.

"And it came to pass in the seven and twentieth year, in the first month, in the first day of the month, the word of the Lord came unto me, saying... I will give the land of Egypt unto Nebuchadrezzar king of Babylon".

The number of years in the Book of Ezekiel is counted from the exile of Jehoyachin in 597 BCE, 11 years before the destruction of the Temple.

The prophecy was given in 570 BCE, according to which the conquest by Nebuchadnezzar should have taken place afterwards. Instead, contrary to what we said Nebuchadnezzar's conquest had already taken place in 584 BCE.

Actually, this prophecy was given, not in the 27th year (570 BCE) but already in the 11th year (586 BCE) as the order of the prophecy shows.

In the Book of Ezekiel there are five prophecies about Egypt (chapters 29-32) that were given on these dates:

year 10, the 12th of Tevet (the 10th month)

year 27, the 1st of Nisan (the 1st month)

year 11, the 7th of Nisan (the 1st month)

year 11, the 1st of Sivan (the 3rd month)

Year 12, the 1st of Adar (the 12th month)

From the order of the prophecies it is clear that the second prophecy was in the 11th year, which was 586 BCE, and this matches with the dating of Nebuchadnezzar Conquest in the year 584 BCE. Then why is it called the 27th year?

A possible explanation is that the first Babylonian conquest was in 612 BCE, when Nineveh was conquered, which marked the start of the Babylonian Empire. Ezekiel, who prophesied here for the first time the Babylonian conquest of Egypt counts years from the founding of the Babylonian Empire, and therefore the 11th year of the Exile of Jehoyachin is referred to as the 27th year.

Nevertheless, this year is year 11, in the order of the prophecies, and the conquest of Nebuchadnezzar took place two years later.

Appendix 24: Why 'Sai' is not mentioned in Ezekiel's prophecies?

The city of 'Sai' is known as the capital of the 26th dynasty which is named 'The Saitic dynasty'.

The prophet Ezekiel who lived at the time of the 26th dynasty prophesied the disaster that was about to befall Egypt. In this prophecy he listed the Egyptian cities of that time that would be affected (see chapter 30). Surprisingly, Sai is not one of them.

Why didn't the prophet mention the capital city? To answer this question we must first clear up: where Sai is located?

Today there are two places with a name approximating Sai: 'Sa el-Hagar' west of the Delta – the biblical city of **Tzoan**, and 'San el-Hagar' in the east.

Nothing has been found in either place to indicate that it was the capital of the 26th dynasty, though Sai's accepted location is thought to be in the west. Why?

The reason is because nothing significant has been found in the western site even from other periods which may be due to its bad preservation. On the other hand, many findings from earlier periods have been found on the eastern site, so that the same explanation cannot hold water.

However according to the Egyptian historian Manetho we can prove that Sai was indeed in the east, since it is mentioned as one of the cities "in the Saitic borough east of the Bobastis River." [527]

This description of the district of Sai matches Tzoan, which is in the east and not Sa-Al-Hagar which was in the west, because the Bobastis River flows in eastern Egypt and Tzoan is even further east.

Also the Roman geographer Strabo called Tzoan 'Sai',[528] and should therefore be identified with Sai which was the capital of the 26th dynasty.

So, why don't we find any remnants there? We can actually find the remnants of the historic Sai if we follow the proofs that the 26th dynasty was actually the end of the 18th dynasty and the 19th dynasty:

Rameses II from the 19th dynasty decreed that Tzoan should be the capital, and he built a grand city close to it named after him – "Per-Rameses" where numerous impressive findings were excavated. This is Sai, the capital of the 26th dynasty.

Tzoan, then, is Sai the capital of Egypt during the 26th dynasty. Ezekiel mentions it in his prophecy "I will set fire in Tzoan". (Ezekiel 30:14)

Appendix 25: Which Script was in use in Judah during the days of the Restoration?

---

[527] Josephus Flavius, Against Apion, 1, 14.
[528] The Geography of Strabo, Book 17, 1, 20.

We dated the LMLK seals to the Restoration, which raises this question:

The LMLK seals are in the ancient Hebrew script which dates to First Temple times. With the Restoration after the Babylonian exile the ancient Hebrew script fell into disuse and was gradually replaced by the Aramean script which is used to this very day.

How, then, can the LMLK seals be dated to the time of the Restoration?

However the truth is that this assumption, that during the time of the Restoration the ancient Hebrew script was in disuse is based on a mistaken foundation.

We can prove this from the collection of seals immortalizing the Restoration, which were written in the ancient Hebrew script:

The collection of seals includes, among other things, the stamp of 'Slomit amat Elnathan Pahva' (Slomit the wife of Elnathan the governor of Judah), who is considered to be the daughter of Zerubbabel, the first governor since the Restoration, mentioned in the Book of Chronicles. (Chronicles I, 3:19)

In his comment about the seals written in the ancient Hebrew script, N. Avigad writes:

"The amazement remains about the special ancient script that is peculiar to them. For example the seal of Shlomit, according to its script alone, should be related without any suspicion to the 7th century BCE (the days of the First Temple), but the title 'Pahva' specifies clearly that it should be related to the Persian period... Similarly, it is possible to say about the seals that, according to the form of the script only they would not be related to the same person from the Persian period; but from the archaeological assemblage it specifies they must be related to that period." [529]

The archaeological findings teach us, therefore, that during the time of the Restoration the ancient Hebrew script in which the LMLK seals were made remained in use.

Appendix 26: The Inscription of Achish the son of Pady

An inscription dedicated to Achish the son of Pady, the King of Ekron, was found in the Philistine city of Ekron. Our dating to the period 'Late Iron Age II' (the days of the Restoration) answers on the amazement that this inscription raised. Who was Achish the son of Pady?

---

[529] N. Avigad, Stamps and Seals from the Royal Archives from the Period of the Return to Zion, Kedem 4 (1976), p. 14. (Hebrew)

The Assyrian inscription states that during the time of Hezekiah a King named **Pady** ruled in Ekron. He was faithful to Sennacherib, the King of Assyria and he did not join the rebellion of Hezekiah. In the following generation his son **Achish** ruled, who was faithful to Essarhedon, the son of Sennacherib. (7th century BCE)

In the excavations of Ekron a Temple to the goddess Ptagia was unearthed with a decorated inscription from the same King which read: "This house was built by Achish the son of Pady... for Ptagia his Lord."

The wording of this inscription is similar to the Phoenician inscriptions, while the other Philistine inscriptions from the period ending Iron Age II (the period of the Rosette), are similar to the inscriptions in Judah and not to the Phoenician.

The scholars were astonished: "The similar wording of the inscription in Phoenician surprised us because we knew the script that was widely used in Palestine in the 7th century BCE was influenced by Hebrew and not by Phoenician writing... It is amazing how similar the wording of the inscription and the words used in Phoenicia... It is amazing that this Epigraphal find from Palestine from the 7th century BCE points to a similarity with Phoenecian wording." [530]

However, after we've concluded that the period at the end of Iron Age II is not the 7th century BCE but the Persian period, their astonishment disappears, because Achish did not live during the 'Late Iron Age II', but during an earlier period.

So we cannot automatically compare the inscription of Achish to the inscriptions from the period at the 'Late Iron Age II', but to an earlier period where Phoenician sources were an imitation.

(Vessels from the end of the Iron Age were found in the temple. However this only teaches us about the date when the building was destroyed and not about the date when it was built.)

Appendix 27: Why were the Emblems of the Persian Kingdom found particularly in Judah?

In the chapter: 'Who was LMLK' we showed that the emblems of the Wings and the Rosette found in Judah were in fact emblems of the Kings of Persia. This recognition raises the question: why are these emblems so much more common in Judah than in other states over which the Kings of Persia ruled?

An answer may be found in a saying from the Talmud, which refers to the shape of the 'Susa the Capital' above the eastern gate to the Temple Mount in Jerusalem. Two explanations are offered:

---

[530] S. Gitin et all, A Royal Dedication Inscription from Tel Miqneh/Ekron, Qadmoniot 113 (1997), p. 43. (Hebrew)

1. That people should remember from where they came.

2. That they stand in fear of the government (Babylonian Talmud Menachot 98a).

The combined explanation meant that Judah was not a normal state of a people dwelling on its land, but of a people who remained faithful to their land even when exiled from it and who also managed to return to it.

The messianic faith (which gave the Jews strength to return to their land) tells us that in the future a savior will arise from their midst to rule over all the nations, and the memory of the great Kings from the time of the First Temple helped to preserve this faith in their hearts.

This unusual people aroused the suspicions of the authorities, as seen from the letter the King received from the enemies of Judah and from the reply that was sent to them.

The enemies wrote: "The King should know that the Jews who came from you to Jerusalem, are building the city to rebel" (Ezra 5:12).

The King answered thus: "I ordered an investigation, and it was found that this city from antiquity always held itself up above the Kings and was frequently rebellious... Therefore you were command to stop these people and the city should not be built until I command it.". (ibid, 19-22)

Consequently, because of the problematic nature of Judah, the rulers decided to strengthen the signs of their acceptance of the authority of the Persian Crown.

On the other hand, the Jews also had reason to show their loyalty, to remove all suspicion from them. (Similar to what happened in the Exile, when Jews tried very hard to be more patriotic than the locals).

This is why the emblem 'Susa the Capital' was engraved over the entrance to the Temple Mount. This was to remind the Jews to be obedient to the regime, which granted them permission to go up and build the Second Temple.

[It is not explained how this emblem of Susa appeared over the gate. However, knowing the government emblem engraved in the palaces of the Kings of Persia, it appears that the rosette was the shape of the capital.]

This is why the emblems of the Persian wings and the Rosette are very often found in Judah more than in other places because Judah had to work especially hard to show its loyalty to the King.

Appendix 28: Why was Jerusalem so Small?

In the chapter 'The Books of Ezra and Nehemiah' we concluded that the expansion of Jerusalem to the Western Hill occurred in the time of Ezra. And Jerusalem during the First Temple extended only to the Eastern Hill.

According to one opinion Jerusalem covered 50 dunams,[531] and according to another 40 dunams [532], an area smaller than other cities in the Land of Israel during the same period. Why was the capital of the Kingdom so small?

A lack of water sources in the area seems to have been the reason for the city's smallness. So writes H. Geva: "There are only a few small springs around the city ... the only source of water in was the Gihon spring, which reduced the possibility of increasing the population of the city." [533]

Gihon spring

Only at the time of the Second Temple water ducts were built to channel water from the springs in the south to the city, and with them the possibility of increasing the city's population.

Summary: Jerusalem, the capital city during First Temple times was small due to the lack of water sources.

---

[531] H. Geva, Estimating Jerusalem's Population in Antiquity, Eretz Israel 28 (2008), p. 55. (Hebrew)
[532] E. Mazar, Jerusalem - 4000 year-old Capital, ibid, p. 125. (Hebrew)
[533] H. Geva, Estimating Jerusalem's Population in Antiquity, ibid, p. 55-56. (Hebrew)

Appendix 29: The Ivories of Samaria

It is said of Ahab the King of Israel that he built 'an ivory house': "the Ivory house that Ahab built". (Kings I:22-39)

The commentators explain that we are speaking about a house made from ivory. This seemed weird, since ivory is too weak to be used as a building material until the excavations in Samaria revealed a treasure of decorations made from ivory. From this we understand the Scriptural description 'a house of ivory' to mean a house decorated with ivory.

The discovery of these ivory decorations in the palace closely matches what is written in the Scriptures and apparently proves that the palace in Samaria is indeed the palace of Ahab, and contradicts what we wrote in the chapter 'Which was the Capital City?' that this was a building from the Persian period.

However, were these ivories really found in Palace from the Iron Age period?

The answer is negative. As N. Avigad writes: "These ivories were found in the stratigraphic layer that has been completely disturbed and they have been moved from their place more than once, the last time during the Hellenistic period." [534]

If so these Samarian ivories have no connection to the Second Temple period building that mistaken called 'the Palace of Ahab'.

Appendix 30: Is the Altar revealed on Mount Ebal Joshua's Altar?

One of the best-known discoveries in biblical archaeology is the altar found on Mount Ebal which dates to the end of the Late Bronze Age / beginning of the Iron Age. This is the recognized date when the Children of Israel began to settle the Land of Israel. According to Zeral who excavated the site and many others, this is the altar built by Joshua. (Joshua 8:30-34)

According to the date that we have given, this altar is from the end of the First Temple era a much later period when this area was inhabited by the remains of the Kingdom of Israel and other peoples who had been exiled to it by the Cuthites.

Even if we try to adhere to the accepted date, it is hard to see this altar as Joshua's Altar.

---

[534] N. Avigad, The Ivory House which Ahab Built, in: J. Aviram (ed.) Eretz Shomron, Jerusalem 1973, p. 75. (Hebrew)

Excavations showed that the site on Mount Ebal was set up in two stages: in the first stage the area was demarcated, and a floor composed of ashes and animal bones was raised in the center, and in the second stage an altar was built above this ancient holy area. [535]

The use of the holy place did not begin with the building of the altar, but was preceded as a site of worship without an altar, and not according to what was written in the Book of Joshua.

Some want to explain that these two stages on Mount Ebal do match Joshua's Altar, according to the opinion presented in the Jerusalem's Talmud "Stones have been immediately set up on it, the Blessings and Curses were said after 14 years". (Sota 7:3)

The explanation according to this opinion is that with the early beginnings of settlement, 12 stones were set up on Mount Ebal, and after fourteen years the altar was built.[536]

Actually, this opinion comes later only the ceremony of blessings and curses, that are written in the Torah separate from the brought Stones which to the site, but does not postpone the building of the altar to a later time.

Summary: according to our dating above, the altar that was discovered on Mount Ebal is not Joshua's Altar, but an altar from the end of the First Temple period.

Even according to the accepted dating, it is hard to see this altar as Joshua's Altar because we are speaking about an altar that was existed as a site of worship where sacrifices were brought before the altar was built.

---

[535] A. Zertal, Eight Seasons of Excavations at Mount Ebal, Qadmoniot 89-90 (1990), p. 43-46. (Hebrew)
[536] Z. Koren, About the Altar of Mount Ebal, in: Haim Beyehuda, 2004, p. 107-108. (Hebrew)

Index

Names

Places